BERMUDA SHORTS

The hidden side of the richest place on earth

T. C. SOBEY

BARRICADE BOOKS INC.
New York

Published by Barricade Books Inc.
150 Fifth Avenue
New York, NY 10011

Printed in the United States of America.

Library of Congress Cataloging-in-Publication Data

Sobey, T.C. (Timothy C.)
    Bermuda shorts / T.C. Sobey.
        p.   cm.
    ISBN 1-56980-060-X (pbk.)
        1. Bermuda—Anecdotes. 2. Bermuda—Humor. I. Title.
F1631.S63 1995
972.99—dc20   95-705
                                               CIP

First printing

FOR C.J.
Incidentally

I AM indebted to Mr. David L. White OBE, and *The Royal Gazette* for permission to reprint hundreds of articles, letters to the editor, and other miscellaneous material.

Thanks also to the incomparable Peter Woolcock for so graciously allowing me to include a selection of his sharp-witted and often insightful cartoons. Fridays wouldn't be the same in Bermuda without opening up *The Royal Gazette* and turning to the editorial page for his latest.

Appreciation is extended to the staff of the Bermuda library in Hamilton, especially Mr. Patrick Burgess, who promptly came to my rescue whenever a microfilm machine or photocopier broke down, as they did frequently. During my final week of research, which took place intermittently over a three-year period beginning in 1992, all four microfilm machines and the photocopier broke down at the same time remaining out of action for several days and leaving me virtually helpless.

I must have been intoxicated on the gallons of Pepto-Bismol I was consuming because, with my deadline looming ever nearer, I rashly promised Patrick a new microfilm machine so advanced it would put the technology at NASA to shame if: a) he would only get one machine up and running, and b) this book earns enough revenue to warrant such a lavish, and I might add, noble, gesture on the part of such a humble writer as I. Naturally the decision as to what constitutes "enough revenue" will be a completely subjective one on my part.

Lastly, I wish to thank Lyle and Carole Stuart of Barricade Books for this opportunity. If it weren't for you both, I doubt I would have completed another book, and I shudder to think how the literary world would cope with such a profound loss.

AUTHOR'S NOTE

MORE THAN three hundred newspaper articles and letters to the editor are contained in this book, and each one is reproduced exactly as it appeared on the day of its publication, with real names, dates, events, British spelling, as well as reporter's original headlines and sometimes inconsistent punctuation. About 10 percent of the articles have been shortened by omitting repetitive and/or irrelevant sentences, and occasionally a word has been added in brackets to explain terminology readers may be unfamiliar with. None of the articles have been taken out of context or manipulated in any way. What you read is precisely what was reported.

In the case of the letters to the editor, no editing was performed whatsoever. In some instances, however, their author has chosen to sign with a pen name rather than using their own.

It is interesting to note that although the articles span a thirteen-year period, from 1982 to 1995, most of the politicians named are still active in government or public life today.

CONTENTS

IF ALL daily newspapers in the world were as readable and as unintentionally funny as Bermuda's *Royal Gazette*, I suspect everyone on this planet of ours would be much more relaxed.

I know I am. And that's saying something. Although I moved to this terribly civilized colony of Great Britain several years ago and awake each day to the most inspiring beauty—sapphire waters, fluttering palm trees, the distant sound of ferryboats chugging along their routes in the harbor below (not to mention an abundance of the most delectable dark rum found anywhere)—my Scottish psychiatrist still admonishes me regularly for taking life and its day-to-day problems with more seriousness than they deserve.

My mother is to blame. She has passed along a gene programmed for worry that both myself and my sister have inherited.

Decisions can be absolute hell. White wine or red? Steak or lobster? Receptive or intrusive?

But let's be honest, we live in a very serious world. Begin to feel too complacent and *wham!*—somewhere nearby there is a bank clerk working in the overdraft department simply aching to bring you back to earth.

No matter how determined you are to put a smile on your face and avoid antagonism, irritants are lurking around every bend. High on my personal list is the media: television, radio, and those eternal crypts of misery themselves, our newspapers, capable of instilling fear and anxiety into an otherwise cheery day. I don't know about you, but ten minutes with a weekday edition of the *New York Times* and I gravitate towards a blue-labeled bottle of Smirnoff and those Percodan tablets leftover from Nana's hip operation, still reposing tantalizingly in the medicine cabinet.

And therein lies the reason for writing this book: to share my own natural antidepressant with the rest of the worn-out worried masses. It is a remedy which needs no prescription, rather a *subscription* to the one and only *Royal Gazette*.

Here under one rooftop is a sprinkling of some of my favorite stories that have had me smiling and shaking my head in disbelief most mornings over coffee ever since I picked up my very first copy.

If you ask me, there is too much anxiety and apprehension in this world. Why must progress go hand in hand with hourly bulletins of bad news? Was early man bombarded throughout the day with urgent news flashes: "This afternoon's top story . . . Three clansmen seriously injured by falling rocks whilst skinning bison...Two surviving toddlers ask the disturbing question, 'When will the bloodbath end?' Could *you* be next . . . ?"

Our primitive ancestors may not have had much in the way of material comforts, no goose-down duvets or Brown Jordan patio furniture for the summer cave, but I cannot believe they worried half as much as we do in these so-called modern times. What with Bosnia and Rwanda, shootings, gang warfare, car-jackings, infanticide, poverty, disease, torture, government deficits, corporate greed, marital violence, all manner of misery and destruction— not to mention the latest bulletin on O.J. Simpson's bloody socks—enough is enough!

Imagine how much more positive we would feel if we began each morning with a message of hope rather than one from Bryant Gumbel of imminent doom, which is how I am frequently left feeling after listening to the 'news.'

I have a suggestion: "Today's top story...Leading newspapers and all three major networks ban bad news for a one-year trial period."

Naturally this isn't going to happen overnight. Until then, we'll have to persevere and unearth some humor from the news we have at our disposal. After reading a few of my favorite *shorts* from the local paper, I think you'll agree there's no better place to find it than the Bermuda Isles.

Not exactly the "friends and family" calling circle

BEFORE WE come to our first *shorts*, I should provide you with some background on the individuals you are about to meet.

Bermudians are a rare breed. The fact that they number less than sixty thousand sets them apart in the world right away.

For the most part, the island's population is a fairly uptight group made up of a multitude of nationalities: Bermudians, British, Portuguese, Americans, Canadians, Aussies, New Zealanders, and countless others. Together they form a broad spectrum of cultures all thrown together onto one tiny patch of earth barely big enough for a game of hopscotch, named for the Spanish explorer Juan de Bermudez, who first spotted the islands in 1503. The islands have been known by a number of different names, most notably *the Bermudas*, *the Isle of Devils*, and *the Somers Isles*, the latter in honor of Sir George Somers, founder of record, whose sighting of Bermuda in 1609 was responsible for the first settlers arriving three years later. Lamentably, Somers did not witness this historic event because he died in 1610 during his second visit. His body returned to England, but his heart was buried—literally—in St. George's.

This trend continues. Many residents' hearts belong to Bermuda, but every three months, they wish their bodies were a million miles away. You see, paradise has its price. At least, this one most assuredly does. Living on a remote tiny island twenty-two miles long and barely two wide can do strange things to your head. Some blame the sun. Some say it's the humidity. Others will tell you it's just, well, Bermudians themselves. They're peculiar. A little bit of the British stiff upper lip, a touch of Caribbean apathy, and an average per-capita income consistently ranked amongst the highest in the world and you've got the perfect recipe for a country that is (how shall I describe it politely?) *eccentric* to say the least.

Ask anyone outside this tropical aberration about their perceptions of Bermuda, and several impressions will likely pop to mind. Beautiful beaches, balmy climate, a center for international banking and insurance, a tax haven. Guaranteed you will hear "Very British, isn't it, my dear?" at least once during your investigations. These views may come from people who have never set foot on Bermudian soil yet have definite ideas on what the place must be like.

For the most part, they're right. Life here is unlike anywhere else on earth; a country where the less fortunate have a net worth of three to four hundred thousand dollars, usually the value of a typical Bermudian-owned home. Due to strict property ownership laws, foreigners cannot contemplate buying houses that cost less than a million unless it's a condominium facing the parking lot for around $500,000. Real estate is definitely not cheap.

This tiny, otherwise insignificant group of islands only a few hundred miles off the coast of North Carolina, is arguably the richest and luckiest place on earth. A walk along opulent Front Street in the capital city of Hamilton with its candy-colored shops overlooking a turquoise harbor makes you feel as though you have clicked your heels and landed in something a lot better than the Emerald City. Mark Twain, once a regular visitor to these shores, wrote that the color of the water was an almost "hysterical blue." I do wish people wouldn't quote Mark Twain so much. Was there nothing on which the man didn't have an opinion?

The other side of Bermuda, though, the side which most vacationers never stay long enough to see, is what transpires in everyday life. Nothing is ever as it seems on the surface, and Bermuda is no exception. Glitzy magazine and television advertisements create a picture that is so far from the truth, it's positively laughable. What do Bermudians themselves get up to, living and working in this extraordinary land?

As you will discover, quite a lot.

Bermuda is not perfect. Life here has its ups and downs like everywhere else. Bermudian families may be more fortunate materially than most but occasionally, just occasionally, even the mildest, most loving husband is driven to pick up a cricket bat and bring it down with the force of Hercules upon the head of his beloved mate. A Bermudian's problems are different from those of the average mortal eking out a living in, say, Great Falls, Montana, for innumerable reasons.

They are burdened with very few day-to-day worries. Per-capita incomes are considerable; there are no personal or corporate income taxes; thanks to the Gulf Stream there are no oil bills to worry about; expansive wardrobes are not required; automobiles are not an absolute necessity (thousands make do with scooters only); liquor is cheap and plentiful; politically, the country is stable with well-established foreign connections; there is virtually no unemployment; disease and hunger do not exist; and until very recently there was no national debt.

Assuming that Lindsay Wagner is yours, what more in life could you possibly want?

But paradisiacal as it may sound, you cannot spend your whole life at the beach. Even the most ardent of sun worshippers soon admits the novelty wears off, unless you are particularly vacuous—for instance, a male hairdresser on contract from England.

Nor can you hop in the car and "get away" for the weekend when all you have at your disposal is a measly twenty-two-mile strip of land. Setting out for a Sunday drive entails one question and one question alone: "Shall we go right or left today, darling?" "Might as well go left, sweetheart . . . We went right last weekend, remember?"

Demented as it sounds, you will begin to crave snow and ice, possibly even a blizzard. Hell, at least then you can strap on a pair of skis and actually *go* somewhere! Anywhere. Just get me off this island!

Island fever. That's what it does to you.

Take these locals for instance. Something tells me they've been on the island a tad too long. And remember, these are actual newspaper articles, complete with their original headlines.

WOMAN IS BOUND OVER

An angry woman who went at her ex-boyfriend's curtains with a knife was yesterday bound over to keep the peace for a year.

Regina F. Francis, 25, of Crawl Hill, Hamilton Parish, pleaded guilty in Magistrates Court to a charge of Breach of the peace.

Sgt. Earl Kirby, prosecuting, said police responded to a domestic complaint at Friswell's Hill on Monday. When they arrived at the scene, they found Francis outside the residence she had been asked to leave.

Francis picked up a knife and began to tear curtains adorning the complainant's front door and threatened to kill anyone who touched her.

When she was arrested, Francis told police she would still go in to "get" her former boyfriend.

Francis told the court she was angry when she said she would still "get" her ex-boyfriend. And under questioning from Senior Magistrate the Wor. Granville Cox, Francis said she still loves him.

Mr. Cox said: "I have been warned by women against violence against women not to use the word and not to say the word love or marriage. I am not saying those words ever again. As far as I am concerned those words have gone out of fashion.

"Is there an association for violence against men?"

Mr. Cox bound Francis over in the sum of $200.

CHRONIC WINDOW BREAKER

A chronic window-smasher, who says he does it to be "removed from society," was yesterday committed to Supreme Court for sentencing after admitting he smashed a storefront window at the Music Box for the fourth time since 1986.

Irving Winston Butterfield of no fixed abode was arrested on Sunday after store owner Eddie DeMello reported the smashing of a 12x16 foot Music Box window, valued at $1,000.

Police Insp. Peter Duffy, prosecuting, said the incident was Butterfield's eighth conviction for window breaking.

His record included hits at Bermuda Island Cruises head-quarters, the Donald Smith Travel Agency, John W. Swan Ltd. in 1985 and 1986 and DeMello's Music Box in 1986, 1987, 1988 and on Sunday.

He was jailed one year each for his last two window-smashing convictions at the Music Box.

Insp. Duffy said DeMello was completely frustrated by Butterfield and did not know how to defend his property.

When Acting Senior Magistrate the Wor. John Judge committed Butterfield to Supreme Court for sentencing, the 58 year old window smasher said:

"Good, that's lovely. That's what I want. Actually, I should have been up here for murder, not you sir, just some of the people I hang out with."

DeMello, who was in the court room, said he was the one who was ready to commit murder.

FOUR YEARS FOR AN 'UNPROVOKED' ATTACK

A Devonshire man who pleaded guilty to severely beating a man for touching him in the upper body was sentenced in Supreme Court yesterday to four years in prison.

Reginald Chesterfield Wilson, of Northcliff Lane, struck the victim several times with a cedar stick and his fists after he took exception to the man touching him with an open hand in the chest/shoulder area during an introduction February 9 this year at the St. George's Cricket Club.

A summary of the offence by Crown Counsel Mr. Brian Calhoun noted that Wilson, 34, continued to beat the man while he was on his back on the ground.

The victim suffered a fractured vertebra, a cut to the forehead that required 14 stitches to close and numerous contusions. He required two days treatment in hospital.

In the summary, Mr. Calhoun said Wilson's largely unprovoked attack was apparently caused by his medically diagnosed paranoid personality compounded by the use of alcohol and "herb."

Mr. Paul King, defending, told the court that Wilson requested help to deal with his problems.

"Mr. Wilson needs assistance to work through his feelings of anxiety and perceived threats," said King.

Wilson said he was very sorry for what he did, adding that it was the result of "an act of provocation and misunderstanding."

Chief Justice the Hon. Sir James Astwood told Wilson he was fortunate he wasn't facing more serious charges.

"You could have killed this man," said Sir James. "You're a big man. You have to learn to control your temper."

CARPENTER STRUCK COLLEAGUE ON HEAD

A playful exchange of insults resulted in a carpenter hitting a co-worker several times with a hammer, Magistrates Court heard yesterday.

Robert Saunders, 47, of Mount Hill, Pembroke, pleaded guilty to causing grievous bodily harm to Daniel Johnson on January 28.

Police prosecutor, Insp. Peter Duffy, told Magistrate the Wor. Kenneth Brown, the two carpenters were working at Cumberland House on Victoria Street in Hamilton when the incident occurred.

Johnson and Saunders were involved in what at first appeared to be an exchange of playful verbal insults but it deteriorated into a slanging match involving insults about their parents, he said.

"The defendant then lost his temper and struck the complainant with a hammer on his forehead, shoulder and both legs."

Johnson went to King Edward VII Memorial Hospital, where he was treated for slight cuts and bruises.

Saunders was taken to the police station where he admitted the offence.

DISCHARGE FOR MAN WHO BEAT WIFE

A jealous husband who beat his wife with a metal comb was yesterday given a conditional discharge for a year.

Wesley Mallory admitted assaulting his wife on Thursday.

Insp. Peter Duffy, prosecuting, told Magistrates Court that Mallory, of Smiths' Parish, and his wife were walking on Hermitage Road with their three children when an argument broke out because Mallory was jealous of a man who gave his wife a ride to work.

The argument continued in their bedroom at home. Mallory, 39, became violent, punching and hitting his wife about the head, Insp. Duffy said.

Mallory's wife suffered bruises on her face and a cut on her wrist, after Mallory hit her with the metal comb.

Acting Senior Magistrate the Wor. John Judge told Mallory: "I strongly disapprove of men assaulting women, but I am not sure imposing a penalty will improve the situation between you and your wife."

Mr. Judge gave Mallory one year's conditional discharge.

MAN 'HIT WIFE WITH CRICKET BAT'

Alcoholism drove a man to hit his wife with a cricket bat, a court heard on Tuesday.

William Weldon, 31, of My Lord's Bay, Hamilton, admitted he beat his wife and threatened to kill her earlier this month. Senior Magistrate the Wor. Granville Cox ordered a social inquiry report and adjourned the case until July 5.

P.c. Earl Kirby, prosecuting, said Weldon's wife returned to her home on the morning of June 7 after spending the night at her sister's house.

"The defendant was furious and told his wife he would kill her," the prosecutor said. "He pushed her into a chair, held a knife to her leg though he drew no blood.

"He then kicked her left leg and she staggered backwards. She ran to the door but he caught her, making more threats. Weldon then took a cricket bat to her left knee and hit her on the thigh."

Weldon told his wife he loved her so much he wanted to kill her, P.c. Kirby continued. After the attack she was taken to the King Edward VII Memorial Hospital for treatment and released.

Weldon told Senior Magistrate the Wor. Granville Cox he was confused when he committed the crime.

"She had been drawing away from me for a couple of months. When she didn't come home that night she didn't leave a note or phone as usual. It made me think she was out messing around."

Weldon said he had a problem with alcoholism.

HE WAS DRIVEN TO DESPAIR...

A jealous husband will be digging into his bank account to pay for a classic case of mistaken identity that prompted him to bash in the car of a man he suspected was having an affair with his wife.

The 'Well I Never'—names are being withheld to protect the humiliated—began on Monday evening at a road in Riviera

Estates, Southampton, when a man looked out of his window, and saw that the tires of his car had been slashed.

Upon further investigation the man also discovered that the back of his car had been bashed in.

Just as he turned to go back into his house, the man spied a car speeding away from the scene—backwards.

A friend followed the car and was able to jot down the license plate number before losing sight of it.

But just when the man thought he would have to bring police into the matter, the man with the penchant for slashing tires and bashing cars returned to the scene in a bashful mood.

The story he told was of a jealous husband, a wife he suspected of being unfaithful, her suspected lover—and the poor, unsuspecting man who lives on Riviera Estates.

It seems the man had seen the car in question parked outside the home of his wife, and suspecting that it belonged to a man he thought was having an affair with his wife, he slashed its tires—and then drove his car into the back of the vehicle, damaging both cars extensively.

But, just as he was speeding away from the scene—backwards—he saw his wife's suspected lover. Only the man wasn't leaving his wife's house—he was leaving the house next door.

And he didn't get into the car the man had just finished slashing and bashing.

The jealous husband has agreed to pay for the damages he wrought on the vehicle in question.

MAN PUNCHED TWO BYSTANDERS

Psychiatric and social inquiry reports were ordered yesterday for a 37 year old Hamilton Parish man who said he punched two bystanders in the face after suffering a stroke.

Derrick Simmons of My Lord's Bay, admitted two counts of assault on August 17 in St. George's.

Prosecutor Sgt. Cyril Plant said for no apparent reason Simmons first hit a woman standing at a bus stop near Mullet Bay at 9:30 a.m.

Fifteen minutes later, he punched a man standing at a bus stop on the Duke of York Street in the face and jaw, causing him to fall against a wall.

Simmons yesterday told Magistrate the Wor. Granville Cox he committed the offences because he was suffering from a stroke at the time.

"I was just having a stroke, an attack, a sickness, like," he said.

Mr. Cox remanded the defendant in custody until September 2, when both reports will be submitted.

FIGHT ERUPTS AS WOMEN GO FOR SAME MOVIE SEAT

Big trouble erupted at the Little Theatre when two women went for the same seat, a court heard yesterday.

The fur flew and while none of the injuries lived up to the movie title, 'Marked for Death,' a few scratches were enough to warrant prosecution.

Yesterday, Sheena Ann Smith pleaded guilty to assaulting Jean Marie Saltus and causing actual bodily harm. But she insisted she was provoked.

Insp. Peter Duffy, prosecuting, told Senior Magistrate the Wor. Will Francis, that Saltus contacted police on November 23 and complained about the incident of the previous night.

He explained that Saltus was asked by the manager to leave her seat at the back of the Theater because it was reserved.

But as she left she clashed with Smith, and suffered scratches to her face in the fight which followed.

Insp. Duffy said Saltus was nine months pregnant at the time of the incident, but Smith disagreed and said her opponent was "as skinny as could be."

Smith, a 23 year old hospital worker of Glebe Road, said it was she who was pregnant and she claimed that Saltus got the idea from reading police statements.

She added: "She didn't like the idea of having to move so both of us passed words and we ended up getting into a heated argument."

Imposing a six month conditional discharge Mr. Francis said: "I hope you will in the future try to do your best to keep out of a fight because it could have unfortunate and serious results. Try and walk away from trouble."

MAN HIT CLERK WITH TRASH CAN

A 36 year old man admitted in Magistrates Court yesterday that he hit a bank clerk over the head with a trash can when he was asked to show his identification.

Truck driver Robert Leroy Wilson, of Southampton, pleaded guilty to unlawful assault causing grievous bodily harm.

Insp. Peter Duffy, prosecuting, said Wilson went to the Bank of Butterfield just after 10 a.m. on August 23 to collect his deeds.

The bank clerk filled out the necessary paperwork and asked Wilson for his identification.

Wilson, who said he was "a little bit hyper" at the time, hit the complainant with a plastic trash can.

Insp. Duffy said the complainant received minor abrasions on the left side of his head and had to be treated at King Edward VII Memorial Hospital.

Wilson said: "He (the bank clerk) didn't know what he was doing. He gave me my deeds and then took them away again.

"I was asking him what the problem was. He was trying to get the deeds back from me and was going to tear them up."

Senior Magistrate the Wor. Will Francis fined Wilson $400.

MACHETE MAN IS JAILED

A man who punched his wife in the face and waved a machete at the man trying to protect her was sent to jail for three months yesterday.

Coolridge Taylor, 40, of My Lord's Bay Lane, in Hamilton Parish, pleaded guilty to possession of an offensive weapon and assault when he appeared in Magistrates Court.

Taylor told the court he only attacked his wife to "shut her mouth."

Insp. Peter Duffy, prosecuting, told the court that at 12:45 a.m. yesterday one of Taylor's four children called the police after they "became terrified of their father's actions."

Taylor then turned on a male friend of his wife, who was trying to protect her. He ran from the house after Taylor threatened him with a machete.

"No one's supposed to interfere when a man argues with his wife," Taylor said. "The best thing to do in that sort of situation is to leave. I told him if he didn't leave I would go upside his head with a machete. He left right away."

Senior Magistrate the Wor. Will Francis sentenced Taylor to three months in prison for having the machete and another two months for assault. The sentences are to run concurrently.

MAN WHO SET FIRE 'HAD LONG-TERM DRINK PROBLEM'

A man with more than 25 previous convictions who admitted starting a fire in his wife's three-storey home on Spring Hill, Warwick, walked out of Supreme Court yesterday after being given a suspended jail sentence.

William Boorman, 41, pleaded guilty to a reduced charge of unlawfully setting fire to a pile of clothing so that a building was likely to catch fire. He was sentenced to one year, suspended for two years.

Mr. Trevor Moniz, for Boorman, told Puisne Judge the Hon. Mr. Justice Ward, his client suffered from a drinking problem.

Sgt. Alistair Brown of the police CID confirmed: "I would say over the last five years alcoholism has been the main cause for Mr. Boorman getting into trouble."

Mr. Moniz said: "At the time of the incident Boorman was living separately from his wife at the Harbour Light Facility of the Salvation Army. The ordeal of separation was too much for him and caused him to start drinking."

By the time he arrived at his wife's home he was under the influence of alcohol and was difficult to deal with.

Boorman said in a statement he wanted to start a business in the basement of the house, but his mother-in-law was filling the basement with clothes for the Seventh-Day Adventists.

"I wanted to burn the clothes brought by my mother-in-law so they would be damaged and they would have to be thrown out," Boorman had said.

Said Mr. Moniz: "Quite clearly the intention was only to damage the clothing."

Mr. Robin McMillan, prosecuting, said: "The Crown accepts the position that he did not intend to burn the house."

Mr. Justice Ward told Boorman: "The sentence must be one that will help you with your alcoholism and will also reflect the gravity of the offence in the eyes of the law.

"The purpose of the suspended sentence is to enable you to get treatment for your addiction."

SMACKED WITH WET SHEETS

A Sandys Parish man who resented having dirty linen thrown in his face, avenged himself by punching his aggressor in the face thereby loosening three of his teeth.

Lance Murray Crockwell, 26, of Cook's Hill Road, pleaded guilty to the grievous bodily harm charge when he appeared in Magistrates Court yesterday.

P.c. Earl Kirby, prosecuting, said the incident took place last month in the Southampton Princess' laundry room where Crockell was a supervisor. When Crockwell was arrested he told police the complainant had knocked his glasses off and made fun of him.

But yesterday, Crockwell stood in his own defence, reading from a written statement he had prepared earlier.

"I was bending over to get a third load of work when all of a sudden, as I came back up, a bundle of wet sheets hit me dead in the face, knocking my glasses off. No one should ever have those dirty sheets in their face, there are lots of germs transmitted through them-—urine, and sometimes blood can be found in the linen.

"I know two wrongs do not make a right but I have asked for forgiveness from the complainant, his mother, and from God himself. I know God has forgiven me and in my heart I know that I am no criminal. Thank you."

Magistrate the Wor. Ephraim Georges said it appeared Crockwell was under stress, but said it was quite possible he had overreacted to the degree of provocation.

Mr. Georges ordered a social inquiry report, and allowed Crockwell free on $300 bail. He is due to return to court for sentencing on August 31.

FEUD BETWEEN SHOP WOMEN ERUPTED INTO BRAWL

A feud between two female Washington Mall shopkeepers erupted into a heated fight after the women swapped accusations about their respective husbands, Magistrates Court was told yesterday.

The confrontation took place last June 23 when Veronica Fubler, who runs Veronica's Footwear, went into La Petite Boutique to talk with manager Sabrina Minors about unfairly competing with her.

"I went into La Petite Boutique and I said to Sabrina I wanted to speak with her about accusing my sister of calling her shop to price a pair of shoes," said Fubler.

"I said that people like her would not prosper in business. She likes to sell everything that the next person is selling. I reminded her that she was the first person to complain about Busy Body moving into the Mall and selling what the Hosiery Hut was selling."

"I said: 'You are keeping your husband'," said Fubler.

Fubler explained at the time of the fight Minors' husband was unemployed.

"She told me to get the so-and-so out of her shop and she told me that again a few times," said Fubler.

"I was walking to the door when she said: 'When you are away you don't even know where your husband is'."

"I was pushing open the door to leave when she kicked me. And that's when the fight began, after she kicked me."

Fubler appeared in court charged with assaulting Minors after they argued about unfair competition.

Minors told the court Fubler's mother and uncle joined the fight.

"Veronica's mother came in and started to attack me from behind, hitting me on my head, and the fight just went on with Veronica on the front of me and her mother on the back," said Minors.

"Veronica's uncle came in as well. Then afterwards they left the shop and the dress rack was wrecked and a few other things got pulled apart."

Fubler's mother, Lorir Neverson, said she and her brother had only gone into La Petite Boutique to break up the fight.

"They were both fighting and I said to them: 'Break it up! Just stop!'. I couldn't separate them because I am smaller than they," said Mrs. Neverson. "It's not that I grabbed Sabrina by the head and beat her. Miss Minors is a bigger woman than me. Now could I really grab her and beat her?"

After the fight three police officers turned up at the Washington Mall. Two officers were interviewing Fubler in her shop when Minors' husband and brother arrived at the store.

"The husband pointed his finger at me and said he was going to get me for what I did to his wife," said Fubler. "The brother said nobody did that to his sister."

"In doing so he started to push open my shop door and it took both officers to restrain him."

Defence lawyer Mrs. Ann Cartwright DeCouto told the court that the charge against her client was a serious one.

"But prior to the incident there had obviously been a concerted effort by the complainant to lure trade away from the defendant's shoe store by prominently displaying shoes in the window of her clothing store," said Mrs. DeCouto.

The defence lawyer said the complainant's behaviour had been provocative. "Her conduct went far beyond acceptable commercial rivalry and bounded the malicious."

Senior Magistrate the Wor. Granville Cox said he had serious qualms about the prosecution's case, and had to find Fubler innocent.

"I have doubts about who was the aggressor," he said. "The only story I believe here is Mrs. Neverson's. On that basis I have to dismiss the information."

WOMAN BREAKS LEG IN FREAK ACCIDENT

A 52 year old woman is in hospital with a broken leg after being involved in a freak accident yesterday morning in which she got caught up in a truck door, dragged along the road and run over.

The truck was being driven by the victim's ex-husband, Mr. Charles Grant, 62, of Claytown in Hamilton Parish, said police spokesman Sgt. John Instone.

Sgt. Instone said Mrs. Phyllis Grant apparently tried to open the truck door from outside as the vehicle was moving, without her ex-husband knowing, and wound up falling down and being run over by the truck.

A bystander told a reporter the woman was dragged along the road some distance, before her left leg went under the wheel and the truck stopped.

The accident happened just before 9 a.m. on Parson's Lane just south of Palmetto Road.

Police are still investigating, said Sgt. Instone.

WOMAN: I SHOULD HAVE SLAPPED HIM

A woman yesterday said she should have slapped a man in his face for provoking her into "ranting and raving" at the Heron Bay MarketPlace, a court heard yesterday.

Janet Doreen DeSilva admitted using offensive behaviour at the Southampton grocery store, but said she would never have bothered anybody if the man had left her alone.

"If I had slapped him in his face he would have left me alone," she told Acting Senior Magistrate the Wor. John Judge. "I was just looking around the place. I don't bother nobody. They just pick on me."

The 29 year old DeSilva, of North Shore Road in Hamilton Parish, was arrested a few minutes before 5 p.m. on Monday when officers found her yelling and waving a stick at MarketPlace employees in the car park.

Sgt. Earl Kirby, prosecuting, said officers warned her about her behaviour but "she refused to stop ranting and raving."

Mr. Judge ordered a social inquiry report and told DeSilva to return to court in two weeks for sentencing. She was released on $500 bail.

MAN WHO BEAT HIS NEPHEW FINED $800

A Hamilton Parish man who admitted beating his teenage nephew, opening up a cut above his eye which required several stitches, was fined $800 in Magistrates Court on Thursday.

Clinton Egbert Simpson, 38, said the 17 year old deserved the beating because he was a "rude little boy."

"He's got no manners. He needed a few cracks," Simpson told Senior Magistrate the Wor. Will Francis.

Prosecutor Sgt. Kenrick James said Simpson hit the boy on March 30 in retaliation over an incident the day before. The teenager had struck him with a cricket bat in an attempt to break up a fight between Simpson and his younger brother, Sgt. James said.

The next day when the boy was alone in the upper apartment eating potato chips, Simpson approached him, Sgt. James said. He "rammed the Pringles can into the left side of his face and slapped him," Sgt. James said.

Before imposing the fine, Mr. Francis reprimanded Simpson, telling him it was "no way for a fully grown man to behave."

POLICE TOLD ACCUSED RAPIST FELT HE 'NEEDED A WOMAN THAT NIGHT'

"I just felt like I needed a woman that night," is the explanation a 22-year-old was yesterday said to have given police, when asked why he allegedly raped a Warwick woman at knifepoint in her home last summer.

The accused rapist also faces 11 other charges, including three of indecent assault and two of intended rape, as well as burglary and housebreaking charges.

The Supreme Court heard how after being arrested for a simple burglary, the defendant took police on a car tour of the places he allegedly committed the rape and other sexual crimes, before he was even suspected of those crimes.

REPORTER'S NOTEBOOK

A sign of just how quickly times have changed in the world of electronic music technology was driven home recently.

A family man in his mid-30s, he was being harassed by his seven-year-old daughter about something she wanted to do.

On and on the youngster went until he snapped, "oh stop it! You sound like a cracked record."

Swiftly came the child's response.

"Daddy," she said, "what's a record?"

JURORS LAUGH AT ACCUSED IN RAPE CASE

Several members of a Supreme Court jury yesterday burst out laughing as the defendant in a rape trial gave his version of the incident.

The 29-year-old Devonshire man has pleaded not guilty to repeatedly raping a 16-year-old school girl at his home on January 12.

He took the stand yesterday to give his version of what transpired after the girl appeared at his doorway shortly after 4.15 p.m. asking for money for gas.

Under questioning from Crown Counsel Mr. Stephen Harrison, the man said he told the girl he did not want her in his house because she was "trouble."

However, he agreed to go looking for money and, as he did so, put a shirt on to hide his naked upper body out of a sense of modesty, he said.

He eventually made his way into his bedroom in search of money, he said.

He then left the bedroom for a few moments, and when he came back the girl was lying naked on the bed reading a magazine and masturbating, he said.

Mr. Harrison questioned whether the girl had enough time in those few moments to remove her cycle gear, clothes, boots with zips and laces, underpants and socks, and then settle on the bed with the open magazine.

The man replied that was exactly what happened, and he had been very surprised by the sudden turn of events.

"Would you say you were horrified?" asked Mr. Harrison.

"Well, horrified might be too strong a word I think, more surprised and stunned," he replied.

The man shouted at the girl to put her clothes on and leave his house, he said.

She replied the magazine was "making her hot," and managed to topple him off balance so he fell onto the bed with her.

She shouted at him to have sex with her in the same way he had sex with her aunt (the man has a relationship with the girl's aunt).

Mr. Harrison suggested the incident might have been a fantasy of the man's, but he replied: "No, it really happened."

Some members of the jury, who had been stifling giggles, then began to laugh outright.

The man said he had intercourse with the girl for a short time, but then "came to his sentences" and stopped.

Puisne Judge the Hon. Mr. Justice (Martyn) Ward, said he did not understand why the girl so willingly let the man go after trying so hard to engage him in love making.

The man said the girl had become relaxed, and it was only then he managed to push himself away.

Mr. Harrison asked if it was true the girl pushed the man's head into her breasts so hard that he almost suffocated. He replied it was true.

After the man disengaged from sex, the girl became angry with him, and suggested she was a better person to have sex with than her aunt, he said. After several more angry and largely incoherent comments, the girl left the house.

The man then set about re-arranging the furniture in his bedroom, a task he had been meaning to do before the girl arrived on his doorstep.

Mr. Harrison suggested the man moved furniture to conceal evidence of the incident, but he denied this.

The case resumes this morning.

JUROR IS ADMONISHED FOR OVERSLEEPING

The Supreme Court trial of accused crack dealer Kenneth Leroy Minks was delayed by 1 hour and 30 minutes yesterday because a male juror overslept.

The case which was set to reconvene at 9.30 yesterday morning started at 11 a.m. after the juror showed up and nonchalantly apologised to Puisne Judge the Hon. Justice Ward for his tardiness.

"If I should fine you, the money you are getting will be paid back to Government. What you need is an alarm clock," Justice Ward said.

"I suggest you use the money that Government pays you to buy yourself an alarm clock, because Government is paying you to come here on time. You must buy an alarm clock."

Before adjourning the case Mr. Ward warned the jury: "Be in your places and no one will oversleep this time."

The case continues this morning at 10.30.

MAN KICKS WOMAN WITH BABY IN LAP

A man who kicked his ex-girlfriend in the forehead while she was sitting in a hospital ward with her baby in her lap was sent to prison for six months yesterday.

"I can't believe you attacked a woman with a child in her lap!" said Senior Magistrate the Wor. Will Francis, noting that attacks in the hospital were becoming a serious problem.

Gamiel Dennis Richardson, 22, of Serpentine Road, admitted unlawful assault causing bodily harm.

Prosecutor Sgt. Donald Grant said that last November 27, Richardson accompanied by his new girlfriend, visited his ex-girlfriend Natasha Hudson at the hospital.

When Richardson left the room, a heated argument took place between the two women. And when Richardson returned, he lashed out at Hudson, who was sitting in a chair with her baby in her lap.

Richardson kicked Hudson in the forehead, causing the back of her head to strike the wall.

"I was provoked," Richardson said in his defence. "She kicked me in my privates several times."

LAWYER: PUNCHING WOMEN IS NORMAL

A Devonshire youth yesterday admitted pushing a young woman to the ground and punching her in the face because she failed to respond to his sexual advances.

Raymond Perott, 23, was standing outside a Court Street pool room at 3.30 a.m. on February 20 when the woman walked by.

P.c. Earl Kirby, prosecuting, said Perott started talking and making advances to the woman, who continued walking toward a nearby telephone booth.

The irritated Palmetto Road, Devonshire, man followed her and as she was about to pick up the receiver, grabbed her, threw her to the ground and punched her in the face, P.c. Kirby said.

Duty counsel Mr. Tim Marshall told the court the action was "a normal occurrence" for someone his age.

"He was just interested in finding out a little more about the girl," he said. "He did it because he says she was quite good looking."

Magistrate the Wor. Granville Cox said: "You mean it could have ended in marriage—something like that?"

Mr. Cox ordered a social inquiry report and released Perott on $500 bail to return for sentencing in two weeks.

GOSSIP 'PROVOKED ASSAULT'

A 31-year-old Pembroke woman was fined $300 in Magistrates Court yesterday after pleading guilty to assaulting another woman.

Patricia Bullard of Cedar Avenue admitted hitting Alfreda Robinson on the head three times on Parliament Street last November 26 for remarks the woman had made about her family.

Bullard maintained she did not punch Robinson as reported by Det. Sgt. John Eve, prosecuting, but used an open hand slap.

"My intention was not to harm this girl," Robinson said. "I don't feel she should have spread idle gossip. She has a vendetta. My home is worth protecting."

PICK ON SOMEONE YOUR OWN SIZE

A Warwick man who admitted assault causing actual bodily harm told a Magistrate yesterday he did pick on someone his own size when he threw a woman out of his house on April 23.

"When will you men learn to respect women?" Acting Senior Magistrate the Wor. Ephraim Georges asked chef Larry Charles Burgess, whom he noted was a "big guy."

"If you feel like roughing up someone, pick on someone your weight, your height, your size."

"She is, your honour," Burgess replied.

Burgess, 27, of Glenwood Park, was arrested after a woman complained he hurt her when he forced her to leave the house Burgess shares with his sister. The woman had been visiting the sister, but had an argument with Burgess, who told her to leave.

When she wouldn't, he grabbed her by the neck and arm and forced her out, causing bruising, Insp. David Chew, prosecuting, told the court.

Mr. Georges fined Burgess $250.

CHOSEN POET

Mrs. Judy-Ann Bean has been chosen to represent Bermuda at the 2nd Annual Poetry Convention in New Orleans. The convention, which is held from July 5-8, features potential poets who will present their best poem. The winner will receive $10,000 and a chance to publish a book, while the runners-up will each get $1,000. Mrs. Bean will be presenting her poem titled, "Hey Nigger."

GOLFBALL WAS AN UNWELCOME MOURNER

Mourners had to duck a flying golf ball as it sped through a graveside ceremony just as the body was being lowered into its final resting place.

The ball came from nowhere, shocking people grieving the death of Mr. David Smith, PLP MP, Mr. Nelson Bascome said yesterday.

"Everyone was surprised," said Mr. Bascome who had been at Monday's funeral. "It didn't hit anyone but no one knew where it had come from as we didn't see the golfer at the time.

"The Minister was just saying a few words and the ball appeared to come from nowhere."

Mr. Smith was buried at the Seventh-Day Adventist Cemetery next to the tenth fairway at St. George's Golf Club. Works Minister the Hon. Clarence Terceira has already promised to examine ways of moving the hole because it lies so close to a private house.

Mr. Bascome related the story in the House of Assembly yesterday after Dr. Terceira had claimed only Mr. Addison Tucker who lives in the house had had any problems.

"The residents in the cemetery have not complained," said Dr. Terceira, who said the changes would have to wait till after the summer.

ALLOWANCE CUT FOR TEEN DRINKER

A mother's scolding was the biggest punishment teenage drinker Sergio Burgess could get.

She was so annoyed he had been caught with a beer bottle, she has now also withdrawn his weekly allowance, a court heard.

Burgess, 16, of Broome Street, Somerset, admitted drinking in a public place when he appeared before Acting Senior Magistrate the Wor. Ephraim Georges yesterday.

But defence lawyer, Ms. Charlene Scott said: "His mother has severely reprimanded him and taken away his allowance, so it shouldn't happen again."

Burgess, a pupil at Devonshire Academy, was spotted buying the drink from Arnold's Supermarket in Somerset and drinking it as he spoke to a friend.

Mr. Georges told him: "You knew you were doing wrong, if you persist in this kind of behaviour, you will be pulled up time and time again." He gave Burgess a six month conditional discharge.

JUDGE FOR THE WEDDING

A man who was fined $250 for assaulting his girlfriend promised to send the Senior Magistrate the Wor. Granville Cox an invitation to his wedding.

John Inchcup of Somersall Road, Smith's Parish, told the Magistrate he still loved his girlfriend and she still loved him.

"Why don't you do something about it?" Mr. Cox said.

Inchcup's girlfriend, Betty Jean O'Brien, told the Magistrate that Inchcup beat her last December after she asked him to put up the Christmas tree. She said he was drinking with a few of his friends at the time and after they left he told her she had embarrassed him in front of his friends.

"He pulled my hair and pulled me down on the couch," she said. "Then he slapped me over my head and he was punching me in my head and he started pulling my breasts."

She said she didn't realize she had punched him in the mouth until he started spitting blood on her.

The fight broke up when Inchcup's sister and niece arrived at the house and took her away. The next day she reported the incident to the police whereupon she was taken to the hospital.

Inchcup, acting in his own defence, said O'Brien asked him to put up the Christmas tree in an unpleasant manner and after his friends left she started to argue with him.

He said he grabbed her arm and pulled her down on the couch where she ripped his shirt. She also kicked him in the mouth and broke his tooth.

"What upset me, I did slap her up the side of her head," he said. "We just had the fight, that's all."

O'Brien admitted he had a couple of drinks with his friends, but he denied it had anything to do with the fight. "The reason it started was the Christmas tree."

Mr. Cox said he had to accept the prosecution's case.

MAN BEAT UP HIS EX-WIFE FOR BEING LATE, FINED $200

A man who beat up his ex-wife and kicked in the door of her car was given a conditional discharge in Magistrates Court yesterday.

Senior Magistrate the Wor. Will Francis ordered 31-year-old Stacey Simpson of Hamilton Parish to pay his former wife $200 for the damage he did to her car and said he was free to go.

The court heard a social inquiry report on Simpson revealed that he had never been in trouble before.

The inquiry was ordered earlier this month when Simpson pleaded guilty to assaulting his ex-wife and to damaging her car because she was 20 minutes late to pick up their son.

The court heard that when the woman arrived at Simpson's house he began shouting at her and struck her in the face with his hand.

He also kicked her in the leg and punched her in the mouth causing a split lip. And while she was trying to get away in her car, he jammed her arm in the door, prosecutor Sgt. Peter Giles said.

She and her son were only able to leave after neighbours restrained Simpson, Sgt. Giles said. The woman was then taken to hospital where she was treated for her injuries.

Simpson was later arrested at his house and admitted the offence saying he had been angry with his son's mother for being late.

"If we all lost our tempers because we were kept waiting by ladies, it would be a very rough world," Magistrate the Wor. John Judge told Simpson after hearing the facts earlier this month.

WAIT, WAIT, WAIT

If you are calling the bank for an appointment for a loan, you'd better be patient.

If you need a driver's license, get out the calendar.

When was the last time you had to call the dentist? How far ahead did his receptionist suggest for the appointment? We are a population of some 56,000 people [1987]. If you deduct those babies who do not yet have teeth, the toddlers whose gums are just showing their pearlies, the oldies who sport store boughten chewers, those whom you couldn't drag into the dental chair and those who insist on going away to have their teeth done, surely one should not have to wait a week, two weeks, a month for an appointment.

Your bike, (car, truck, van) breaks down. You take it for repairs and if you are real lucky, you can get it in three or four days! Either there are not enough mechanics or there are too many bikes (cars, trucks, vans).

You wake up with a great gutzer (bellyache to the uninitiated) and when it doesn't go away, you decide maybe it's the old appendix acting up, and perhaps Doc had better have a look at you— today or at least before three o'clock tomorrow morning. Scribbler wishes you the best of luck for an immediate appointment.

It's even worse if you need your MD to set up a consultation with a specialist. And at this point, it simply isn't funny!

The copier goest puffft. The typewriter is making a funny noise. The fridge won't freeze; the washer won't spin; the dryer won't heat.

SOLUTION: Use more carbon paper; get out the old quill and ink; gorge yourself on the rapidly defrosting food from the freezer; and blinking well wash by hand and hang it out! And get on line for service.

Thank goodness there are still plumbers who make house-calls . . . next week!

And yet we are only 56,000 people! These things do not get better all by themselves. And people simply get madder!

Now . . . and now . . . *Dallas* has gone off the air just before the bitter end! What to do? Give the tv two aspirin and call ZBM [TV] in the morning.

DISHWASHER WANTED TO BE A STAR

A dishwasher who wanted to be a star was ordered to be detained in St. Brendan's [psychiatric] Hospital for pestering a television newsreader who twice had to call police to remove Michael Phipps, who claimed she was supposed to coach him to be a singer.

Phipps, 22, of Valley View Lane, Spanish Point, pleaded guilty to two charges of invading the woman's privacy when he appeared in court last month. The case was adjourned until yesterday for psychiatric and social inquiry reports.

At the previous hearing, Sgt. Peter Giles, prosecuting, said Phipps had knocked at the woman's door shortly before midnight on July 17.

"He had been pestering her for about two months," he said. "She told him to leave or she would call police, but he attempted to open the door, but found it locked. Police were summoned and he was arrested."

Sgt. Giles said Phipps made a statement "which didn't make very much sense, but said she was supposed to coach him to be a singing star, and that they were to be married. The complainant says she knows nothing of this.

"She is very distressed by the attention of the accused."

Two weeks later, Phipps wrote to the woman apologising for his behaviour and "making statements of an amorous nature," said Sgt. Giles. And on August 13, she saw him at the ZBM [TV] complex at Fort Hill.

"She was frightened and went into the studios and told the receptionist not to let him in. He was persistent, but was persuaded to leave."

Sgt. Giles said Phipps had a history of mental problems and had previously been treated at St. Brendan's, but he had been certified as fit to plead to the offences.

"He has made promises he will stay away from her, but always breaks them and goes back," he added.

MAN SHOUTS AT MAGISTRATE

Two policemen escorted a homeless man who shouted at Magistrate the Wor. Ephraim Georges out of court yesterday.

Angelo Wolfe admitted wandering abroad and was jailed for 28 days.

Sgt. Peter Giles, prosecuting, said two policemen were on patrol on Front Street, Hamilton, when they approached Wolfe.

After asking him if he had any money or a place to stay, Wolfe made no reply and was arrested and taken to the Hamilton Police Station.

Wolfe, 27, said: "I had a dollar that they had taken from me. I went into town to get some cigarettes. You're going to lock me up?"

After Mr. Georges passed sentence, Wolfe shouted "no, no" and was led out of the courtroom.

DRUNK WHO HIT BACK AT STONE-THROWER IN COURT

A homeless man who assaulted a boy after being peppered by stones while asleep on a park bench was given a six months conditional discharge in Magistrates Court yesterday.

Llewellyn Simmons, 49, escaped a heavier sentence because of the provocation, said Senior Magistrate the Wor. Will Francis.

"I hope, however, in future you will think more clearly before you act," added Mr. Francis.

Simmons pleaded guilty to assaulting Karim Clarke, causing slight facial bruising.

Sgt. Earl Kirby, prosecuting, said Simmons was intoxicated when he slapped Clarke on Saturday.

Simmons told the court he had got drunk and fallen asleep on a bench at Par-La-Ville Park.

He was awoken after three boys, aged between 12 and 13, began throwing stones at him for no apparent reason.

"One rock struck my leg, one the shoulder, and another the side of my head."

Simmons, who is unemployed, said he did not intend to hurt the boy.

INCEST CASE

Paul de la Chevotiere made light of allegations that he had sex with his daughter when she and her husband confronted him, a court heard yesterday.

"What are you complaining about?" he asked her. "I didn't tie you up," Attorney General Mr. Saul Froomkin told a Supreme Court jury.

REPORTER'S NOTEBOOK

There is no doubt great concern in the community about the apparent breakdown of the family unit and the values it stands for.

But News and Views host Mr. Rick Richardson may have been slightly misled last Monday when telephone callers jammed ZBM TV lines during a show on the breakdown of the family.

"We're going to have to have another show," Mr. Richardson told viewers when he saw his lines jammed with calls. It was obviously a hot topic, he said, with people having lots to say about it.

But unbeknownst to him, the lines were jammed by dozens of calls from people who had thought they'd won TV Bingo, a new and very popular contest launched by ZBM and the MarketPlace [supermarket].

To ease the jam, programmers were forced to flash the message "Please stop calling" about TV Bingo. But they didn't seem to pass the message onto Mr. Richardson.

LETTERS TO THE EDITOR

OUT OF ORDER

Dear Sir,

May I please sincerely express my experience at a local bus stop. While waiting for passengers to exit the bus, a well-known elderly couple began to step off the bus, at the same time the female bus driver stood up and told the woman of the couple that she didn't have a bath today. The woman replied, I did too bath this morning. To my surprise, the bus driver then told the woman in a loud and unkind voice how badly she smelled, and she was turning her stomach and her passengers' stomachs. The bus driver also told the passengers who were generally tourists that she didn't have to accept her on the bus, and that she really wasn't supposed to let her on board smelling like that. I believe the bus driver's behaviour was totally uncalled for and disrespectfully out of character for the public worker.

N. SHAKIR

CIVIL STIFFS

Dear Sir,

I am told that this is a true copy of a memo now being circulated in a certain Ministry:

"NOTICE: EFFECTIVE FROM 1st APRIL, 1986

"The Minister regrets that it has come to his attention that Civil Servants dying on the job are failing to fall down.

"This practice must stop as it is impossible to distinguish between death and the natural movement of Civil Servants.

"Any Civil Servant found dead in an upright position will be the subject of a Commission of Inquiry and will also be dropped from the payroll." (Signed) "The Minister"

Your investigative reporter might be interested.

I.C. Cunningham
City of Hamilton

PREMIER'S MOTION

Dear Sir,

While watching ZBM's excellent TV series Bleak House on Friday, the following news flash came across the screen: "Premier's Motion Passes."

All viewers, I am sure, hope that now he is more comfortable.

At your convenience.

IVAN M.T. BOWEL
SOUTHAMPTON

FOR THE RECORD

Errors appearing in The Royal Gazette can be brought to the attention of the News Editor between 10 a.m.-4 p.m. Monday-Friday at 295-5881. Ext. 260

We reported yesterday Senator Lynda Milligan-Whyte as saying politicians should be careful to criticise all civil servants and all Government departments. Sen. Milligan-Whyte actually said politicians should be careful *not* to criticise all civil servants and departments.

QUOTE OF THE DAY

"We now live in a Bermuda where one, two or three marriages are common, a Bermuda where, when someone comes back from abroad and says 'Hello, John, how's Mary?' the answer is 'Who's Mary?'"

Mrs. Lois Browne Evans on the need to update the law on wills in our complicated society.

"...AND ON THE RIGHT YOU CAN SEE GOVERNMENT'S FIRS~
AS BERMUDIANS ARE VERY CONSERVATIVE AND WANT

My God man
. . . have you no decency!

CHAPTER TWO

IN BERMUDA, little things mean a lot.

Behavior that in other places wouldn't warrant a turn of the head is often considered a crime here. For example, Bermuda is the only country I know of where it is against the law to be homeless, and offenders are routinely sent to prison for months at a time. Police officers have been known to stop citizens and threaten them with arrest for not wearing underwear.

The origin of Bermuda's laws go way back to those early settlers in 1612 (all sixty of them) and their first governor, Sir Richard Moore, who was empowered by the laws of England to enforce rule single-handedly in the new land. By all accounts, he did a marvelous job of keeping law and order until his departure in 1615. His replacement, Governor Daniel Tucker, was a somewhat different story, a man who would have inspired the Marquis de Sade such was his cruelty and heavy-handedness.

Powers of punishment were clearly outlined in Dale's Code, the version of the Laws of England administered by him. They read as follows: "According to the power of His Majesty's [James I] Letters Patent granted to you, we give you authority, with such and so many of the Council as we shall hereafter appoint, to punish and correct their misdemeanors according to the form and manner of the Laws of England as near as may be, and in cases of rebellion to use martial law."

More than twenty offences were punishable by death. Serious crimes, not necessarily carrying a death sentence, included adultery, alcoholic drinks sold without license, blasphemy and profanity, neglect of conjugal duties, drunkenness, scandalous living, the acting out of stage plays (if only this applied to local amateur productions today), swearing, vagrancy, wife beating, and, oddly enough, incontinency.

Inequities existed in domestic disputes. Wives who scolded, nagged or quarrelled with their husbands were faced with the ducking stool. "William Robinson and his wife were censured" at the Assizes of June 1639, "he to be bound to the good behaviour and shee to be ducked 4 tymes in the sea."

Lord knows what Governor Tucker would think of the situation today, almost four hundred years after his arrival. How I'd love to be around when he attempted to "duck" a certain clerk at The Irish Linen Shop on Front Street. It is unlikely he would survive to carry out the punishment if he selected the particular one I am thinking of. Man, is she mean.

For a democracy which possesses the world's oldest parliamentary system outside of Britain, present-day laws are curiously harsh, rivalling those of Moslem nations. In contrast to the United States where there are more murders per week than the size of an average paycheck, Bermudian courts are busy prosecuting citizens for such heinous acts as stealing glasses of milk and riding bicycles on sidewalks, or they are disciplining some poor bugger because a policeman considered his shorts too short for shopping in town.

Yes, crime on this island is rampant. For some unbeknownst reason, Bermudians are terrified of the naked body. Not even the naked body really, just the sight of a male torso in public, on the street or perched on a scooter, is enough to send otherwise level-headed residents scurrying off to the action line to call the police, and sometimes, fortunately for me, the newspaper.

When the sun goes down, real pandemonium breaks out. I've often wondered if it has anything to do with those tropical night-time breezes from the south, but there is something in the air that makes islanders restless and frisky, beckoning them to strip off their clothes, hop on a scooter, and whiz off for a late-night drive along Oleander Road. Call me old fashioned but personally I prefer a hot bath before retiring; Bermudians revel in taking bike rides naked.

What can I say? It's that simple.

Hotel elevators have the same draw. Ditto the urge to stop by a visiting cruise ship and flash passengers. Well, that shouldn't come as too much of a surprise. Didn't the cruise literature mention something about Bermudians being a friendly lot?

If you're under the impression Bermuda is a sleepy little island, you are dead wrong. Be prepared for the unexpected. A stranger off the street bursts into your home while you are sitting down to dinner and makes himself comfortable in your favorite armchair, or you are abruptly awakened in the wee hours of the morning by a pair of buttocks in your face, and they do not belong to your mate. Most inconvenient after a night out is the obstacle course of human bodies lying on the road *sans* Bermuda shorts, *sans* anything at times. Oh yes, it happens, I tell you. The things you have to put up with in the tropics.

Then there is sex. Don't believe that old joke about the only people coming here are the "newlywed and nearly dead." Entirely misleading. Bermudians are a frisky lot, as are the half a million tourists who come here each year.

Like the British, Bermudians may give the impression they have neither sex nor bowel movements, but don't be fooled. Homosexuality may have only been legalized in 1994 (until then, consenting adults caught in the act could be sent to prison for up to ten years), but if every bisexual and homosexual Bermudian male was imprisoned, vacancy rates in the housing market would skyrocket. Cabinet ministers and members of Parliament would be tossed in the paddy wagon first, not that there'd be much room left in the island's only prison because their sons would already occupy most of the vacant cells. ("It only happened once at boarding school, Father . . . never again . . .")

Not everyone is aware that Bermudians are such marvelous storytellers. They sort of remind me of Meryl Streep in *Out of Africa*. Come see if you don't agree. Remember, dress code is optional.

TALES OF A MONSTER

A 24 year old Devonshire man told two young girls to help him masturbate or a monster that lived in his cellar would be mad, Magistrates Court heard yesterday.

The man pleaded guilty to wilfully committing an indecent act between May 1 and 15 in the presence of a child, intending it to be seen by the child. He said he was guilty of the same charge between May 16 and 31 and on August 23.

He also said he was guilty of inducing a child to commit an indecent act between May 1 and 15 and between May 16 and 31.

Acting Senior Magistrate the Wor. Ephraim Georges asked for a psychiatric report and a social inquiry report on the man and committed the case to Supreme Court for sentencing. The man was remanded in custody.

Crown Counsel Mr. Doug Schofield said that during the first two weeks of May a seven and eight year old girl were near the man's residence and heard his television set. They saw him watching pornographic shows, Mr. Schofield said.

The man told the girls a monster lived in the cellar and if they didn't help him, the monster would be mad, court was told.

He then had the girls help him masturbate, Mr. Schofield said.

On another occasion, the man invited the girls into his house and he was wearing a robe at the time, Mr. Schofield said. The girls were shown pornographic magazines, he said. The man took off his robe and sat naked on the couch.

The man masturbated in front of the girls.

A member of the girls' family overheard some discussion about the incident. Fearing reprisals, the man asked to be taken into custody, he told court.

The man admitted he had a problem and said similar events had occurred other times over the past three months, Mr. Schofield said.

The man is single and lives with his girlfriend, court was told.

He has a previous conviction for committing an indecent act, Mr. Schofield said. He was given a sentence of three months which was suspended for a year, the Crown Counsel said.

IMPAIRED

A man wearing pyjamas and barely able to balance on his livery cycle was fined $400 and taken off the road for a year when he admitted impaired driving.

David Gaskin, who arrived in Bermuda aboard a Royal Navy submarine, claimed he was at a pyjama party before getting on his livery cycle shortly after 1 a.m. yesterday.

"What a party," Acting Senior Magistrate the Wor. Ephraim Georges said. "I was looking at you thinking how fast fashions change these days. It must have been some pyjama party."

The 20 year old was stopped along The Lane after nearly striking the round-a-bout at Crow Lane in Paget.

Insp. Peter Duffy, prosecuting, said officers signalled to Gaskin to stop when he continued swerving from side to side. He almost fell off his cycle after pulling over to the side of the road, Insp. Duffy said, adding he smelled strongly of alcohol and had glazed eyes.

Gaskin was arrested and taken to Hamilton Police Station where a breathalyser test showed he had 183 milligrams of alcohol in 100 milliliters of blood.

OLD MAN GRABBED WOMEN'S SKIRTS

A man who sat outside Washington Mall grabbing at the skirts of passing women and swearing was fined $75 in Magistrates Court on Friday.

Raymond Saints, 57, of Paget, was cautioned by police about his behaviour but swore at them as well, and declared he would shoot them all if he had a gun.

Insp. Peter Duffy, prosecuting, said Saints was sitting on flower pots outside Washington Mall on the afternoon of October 12 causing the disturbance.

When approached by police he told them to leave him alone as he was an old man, and that he would shoot them all if he had a gun.

He was arrested and taken to Hamilton Police Station where he apologised for his behaviour, Insp. Duffy said.

Senior Magistrate the Wor. Will Francis said he believed the matter could be settled by the small fine.

BIZARRE CASE IN COURT

In a bizarre sex case now before the Supreme Court, a Canadian man, who lived in Bermuda, testified he woke up to find another man in a single bed with him and a woman.

A Paget man is on trial for breaking and entering with intent to rape, indecent assault and trespassing on May 5.

Donald James Bourne, formerly a chef at Sonesta Beach Hotel, said he and the woman returned to her Warwick apartment at roughly 3 a.m., after spending the evening in a discotheque.

They fell asleep naked, covered by a sheet, Bourne told the court.

At about 5 a.m., he said, "I was knocked into the wall, and I awoke."

He said that when he reached for the woman: "...I came into contact with a large mass. I wasn't sure what it was. I immediately hit the light switch. The first thing I saw was a man's buttocks in my face," Bourne testified. "The sheets were pulled off."

Bourne said he and the woman pushed the man off the bed, then he sat up and put on his glasses.

"What is going on?" Bourne demanded. To which the alleged intruder replied: "What are you doing in my home?"

The woman pushed the man back out through a door which led from the bedroom, into a storeroom, through a laundry room and out into the back yard.

"There was no struggle," said Bourne. "After he went out, (she) closed the door and locked it. Then she broke down."

The woman was not in court. Statements she made during a preliminary hearing earlier were read to the court by Court Clerk Mrs. Julie-Anne Rocha.

She said it was during the moments between wakefulness and sleep she became aware of someone else but until the lights came on assumed it was Bourne.

"I was surprised and shocked to see three people in the room instead of two," she stated. "I saw a man's bottom sitting almost on my face...He was even wearing shoes on the bed."

The police were not called immediately, testified Bourne, because the woman thought the intruder might be related to her landlady.

In her statement, however, the woman said she was now sure this was not so.

Bourne identified the accused man from mug shots shown to him by police and later picked him out of an identification parade at Hamilton Police Station. However, the woman was unable to identify her assailant from the same lineup.

Under cross examination by Mr. Brian Smedley Q.C., for the accused, Bourne said the woman had perfect eyesight and admitted she was much closer to the man, touching him even, than he was.

"You mean you were just sitting there on the edge of the bed, thinking, 'I must memorize the face in case I have to identify him in an identification parade'?" asked Mr. Smedley. "Why didn't you leap out of bed and go for him?"

"I wonder that sometimes myself," answered Bourne. He said he stared at the man for as long as a minute while the woman yelled and pushed him out of the room.

Mr. Smedley suggested Bourne had wrongly identified his client as the culprit.

Also on the stand yesterday was the landlady. She said nothing disturbed her sleep that night.

The case is being tried by Crown attorney Mr. Barry Meade before Puisne Judge the Hon. Justice Ward. It continues this morning.

JAILED FOR INDECENCY

A six month prison sentence was last week imposed on a 35 year old Somerset man after he admitted a charge of indecency.

Calvin John Burrows of Woodlands Road, Sandys Parish was arrested on October 15 after the incident on Par-La-Ville Park.

Burrows, who represented himself, chose not to give evidence in his defence.

In a statement to police Burrows said: "This morning I was in the park playing with myself. I'm not sorry I did it. I did not upset anybody and I had all my clothes on."

P.c. Peter Giles, prosecuting, told the court that Burrows has had several similar previous convictions.

Said Magistrate the Wor. John Judge: "You have confessed to masturbating in a public place and seem unrepentant.

"They (the public) have the right to go to the park without having their eyes affronted by this filth."

After receiving his sentence Burrows laughed.

EXPOSURE CHARGE DISMISSED

A Paget Parish man was acquitted on Friday on a charge of indecent exposure after a magistrate ruled that it was the police officer's word against the defendant's that the man exposed himself in public.

Clifton Nathaniel Williams, 31, of Dudley Hill, was convicted, however, of maintaining a radar detector in his car without a license and fined $800.

Williams pleaded not guilty to both charges.

The charges were laid on September 10 this year after Williams was stopped by police in his car on South Shore Road on suspicion of carrying drugs. Police officers told Williams that both he and his car would be searched.

D.c. Kimberley Vickers testified that she found a radar detector on a shelf under the steering wheel in Williams' car. She said the device was plugged into the car's cigarette lighter on the dashboard.

D.c. Kenneth Bourne said he informed Williams he would be reported for having the radar detector.

"At that time, the defendant walked to the rear of (his) vehicle and said 'search me I don't have anything' and in doing so pulled down his shorts revealing his penis and buttocks."

D.c. Bourne said that during the incident a bus had pulled up to a stop sign nearby. Williams was arrested and charged with indecent exposure.

But when he took the stand, Williams, a self employed tractor operator, denied pulling his pants down explaining that he had pulled the waistband of his shorts outward to reveal to D.c. Bourne that he was not wearing underwear and therefore could not be hiding anything. He was also wearing a white T shirt.

"I asked D.c. Bourne 'Why are you searching me? There's nothing I can hide in these clothes.' He said I might have something tucked inside my under shorts," Williams said.

"I told him I didn't have under shorts on at the time and he said, 'I don't believe you.' I showed him that I didn't have any under shorts on and he said he was going to book me because I didn't have any under shorts on and it was indecent for me not to be wearing them."

Williams testified that since he bought a Volkswagen Scirocco, he had been stopped and searched by police eight times in 19 months.

TIME TO ZIP UP

A Sandys Parish man—who told police he exposed himself to a woman on Mangrove Bay Road because he liked her—was sent to prison for six months.

Jomo Trew, 23, admitted indecent exposure when he appeared in Magistrates Court yesterday.

Trew, of Bridge View Lane, was following the girl with his pants undone exposing himself. When officers arrested him he said he did it because he liked her, P.c. Earl Kirby prosecuting said.

ALABAMA'S BUBBLES

A St. George's man who admitted wandering along Somers Wharf with his pants down and urinating in public early yesterday told the arresting officers he "had bubbles."

Alvin (Alabama) Anderson, 46, was fined $100 for using offensive behaviour in a public place when he appeared in Magistrates Court yesterday.

P.c. Earl Kirby, prosecuting, told the court Anderson was seen at about 1:30 a.m. walking along the St. George's wharf with his pants at his knees.

After he saw police he continued walking, began to urinate, and then started shouting at someone, P.c. Kirby said.

Mr. Richard Hector, defending, said Anderson was trying to "get away from public scrutiny so he could relieve himself."

But Acting Senior Magistrate the Wor. Ephraim Georges asked: "Yes, but with his pants at half mast?"

Anderson told the court it wouldn't happen again. "Next time I'll go to the station," he said. "I just couldn't reach the station at the time."

COSTLY HISTORY LESSON

A homeless man who was arrested for being "disgusting" in the Bermuda library told the court he went in because he liked to read about the Island's history.

But Mr. Georges said he could find those history books in Casemates [Prison].

John Fox, 44, was sent to prison for two months after he confessed to wandering abroad and to being drunk and incapable on Tuesday shortly after 5:30 p.m.

INDECENT EXPOSURE

Urinating in a public place cost a Bob's Valley Lane, Somerset, man $200 when he admitted openly exposing himself.

Marvin Smith, 34, was arrested close to 4 p.m. last Thursday when police on patrol saw him standing on the edge of the Royal Navy Field with his zipper undone.

Smith told the court he was "totally drunk" and needed to relieve himself.

"It was just a matter of urinating," he said. "It's not in my nature to expose myself. I can't believe this—$200 for urinating? Thank you."

Sgt. Peter Giles, prosecuting, said Smith was facing Main Road when police noticed him. Sgt Giles said traffic was heavy at the time and school children were in the area.

When he saw officers, Smith ran off but was caught and arrested a short time later.

GOING UP...ONE NAKED MAN

Club Med guests were faced with an unexpected surprise when a naked man rode up and down the resort's elevator, Magistrates Court heard yesterday.

Maurice Burrows, 24, admitted trespassing, wandering abroad, and exposing himself in the early morning of September 18.

Acting Senior Magistrate the Wor. Ephraim Georges sent the homeless Burrows to Casemates for six months on each charge to run concurrently.

P.c. Earl Kirby, prosecuting, said when police arrived hotel security had custody of Burrows who was wrapped in towels.

Later, Police found his clothes and traces of marijuana at the beach club facility.

Burrows told Mr. Georges he had no excuses.

SEX IN THE PARK CASE THROWN OUT OF COURT

A bizarre case of false identity wound up with one woman being ordered out of Magistrates Court and the man she accused of beating her with a rum bottle being set free yesterday.

Charles Williams was acquitted from a charge of wounding Helen Fox during an episode in broad daylight at Bernard Park on September 16 last year.

Fox, of Sousa Estate in Devonshire, accused Williams, of Brooklyn Lane in Pembroke, of hitting her with a rum bottle and cutting her eye.

She said: "He is a maniac. He tried to get smart with me. I was trying to get away from him. He made a pass at me."

At the end of her statement she said: "I forgot. He also took my dress off and threw it in the trees. It was covered in blood."

Williams, who was unrepresented, asked why she had waited eight months before reporting the incident, which was alleged to have happened in Bernard Park in Hamilton on September 16 last year.

Fox then swore at Williams and Magistrate the Wor. Kenneth Brown, who ordered her to be escorted from the court room.

Williams, who knew Fox from frequenting Bernard Park, said he was "walking through the footpath (in the park) to go have a drink and to play some cards with my mates."

He said that he came across Fox having sex with a man.

"They always have sex in the park, everybody knows," he said.

He said he asked if he could get by and she picked up one of the bottles lying around and swung it at him, cutting his thumb.

Williams said: "She kicked up because I interrupted her sex act."

One of Williams' witnesses, Margaret Minks, of Somerset, said she and another man known as "Muscles", took Williams to King Edward VII Memorial Hospital with her shirt wrapped around his hand.

Minks said that the man who Fox was having sex with probably was the one who "roughed her up."

Minks said she believed the same man, who Fox was having sex with, assaulted her about a year ago—broke her arm and threw her overboard.

Williams' second witness, John DeRosa, of Prospect, said that Fox was mad with Williams.

"At one time, she decided on Mr. Williams and she confronted him but he refused her offer," he said.

Then Williams said: "The woman don't appeal to me."

Mr. Brown acquitted Williams.

NAKED INTRUDER STRIKES AGAIN

A man who breaks into homes naked struck for the 11th time since late July on Tuesday morning when the occupant of a Pembroke house discovered him and forced him to flee.

Police put out a warning directed particularly at women living alone to secure their homes following the rash of prowlings and break-ins.

Community relations officer Insp. Roger Sherratt, said on Monday about 10 women had reported incidents involving a nude man, and a semi-nude man. It is possible it is not the same man in all the cases.

Insp. Sherratt said a number of the break-ins and prowlings took place in Warwick, and several were in Paget and Pembroke. Anyone with any information should call the police emergency number at 5-2222.

SANDYS MAN CAUGHT NAKED

A 26 year old Sandys man who was completely naked except for a lady's brassiere and a black hood over his head was arrested by police yesterday after he was seen by a woman in the Warwick area.

The incident occurred around 11:15 yesterday morning, when the woman, who was walking near the railway tracks in Warwick, saw a nude white man standing behind some bushes.

The police were called and after a search of the surrounding area, the man was arrested and charged with indecent exposure.

Police said that this was the second report of a flasher in the area. The man is expected to appear in court over the next few days.

ENGAGED, MAN SAYS FLASHING JUST A PRANK

A soon-to-be-married 25 year-old Somerset man received a $500 fine in Magistrates Court last week after pleading guilty to exposing himself in public.

John Stephen Siggins, of Ferry Lane, told the court that he was only pulling a prank when he dressed up in Hallowe'en clothing on November 22 last year, and exposed his private parts to a group of tourists on a Spicelands horse riding tour of the Railway Trail in Warwick.

But the court heard that Siggins repeated the act in the same place on January 2 before another group on the Spicelands tour.

This time he wore female underwear and a blond wig, and was caught by police.

Insp. Peter Duffy, prosecuting, said police chased after Siggins and found him with a paper bag full of female clothing.

"It was just a prank," Siggins said. "It will never happen again. I plan to get married. I'm very sorry for what I did. I guarantee it will not happen again."

However, before sentencing him, Mr. Francis said: "You seem to have gone to some length to try and offend these guides. Can I take it that if you did not get caught, you would have done it again?"

"No your honour," Siggins said. "I was going to give it up because I have too much to lose and I'm not prepared to gamble on it. I promise not to be here again."

MAN STOLE MINI-SKIRT

A 28 year old man yesterday pleaded guilty to stealing a black mini-skirt and was fined $75.

Kenneth Joel DeSilva, a single man who until recently had been living at a Salvation Army housing shelter, admitted he stole the $26 mini-skirt from the clothing line of an apartment on Spanish Point Road.

In what he described as a "rather unusual" incident, police prosecutor Insp. Peter Duffy said DeSilva showed up at the apartment on the afternoon of October 23 with no clothes on, looking for a woman he knew who lived there.

"The complainant, who knows the defendant," Insp. Duffy said, "told him to go away."

DeSilva was later found partially clothed on Arlington Lane in possession of the woman's black mini-skirt that he had apparently taken from her outside clothing line.

"It was fairly obvious to police at the time," Insp. Duffy said, "that the defendant was under the influence of drink or drugs."

In a rambling statement, DeSilva—who has been previously convicted of minor drink-related offenses—told Magistrate the Wor. John Judge that he had fallen in the water off Spanish Point and was looking for some dry clothes.

Mr. Judge fined him $75.

FLASHERS TARGET CRUISE SHIP VISITORS

Two female cruise ship passengers reported that two men exposed their private parts to them in broad daylight on Monday in the middle of Hamilton.

The two women, both off the Horizon [cruise ship], were walking past the Par-La-Ville Park entrance on Queen Street when the two men indecently exposed themselves to them. The incident happened at about 3 p.m. and the two women immediately reported it to police.

MASKED FLASHER SHOCKS WOMAN

Police are looking for a man who jumped out of the bushes late on Thursday afternoon on Horseshoe Bay Road wearing a black ski mask and nothing else.

A 26 year old Paget woman was walking along the road at the time and reported the incident to police.

The man was described as white, roughly 5ft. 10 in. and between 25 and 30 years old.

MAN WHO LOST HIS TROUSERS FINED

Police found Vincent E. Outerbridge asleep on a road without his trousers on, Magistrates Court heard yesterday.

Officers saw the 47 year old Hamilton Parish man lying on his back, and could not wake him for several minutes.

When he eventually came round, his speech was so slurred they could not discover his name or address.

Outerbridge, of Redkiln Road, admitted being drunk and incapable on Barkers Hill, Devonshire, just after midnight on Tuesday. He was fined $150.

WARNING OVER RUDE T-SHIRTS

T-shirts and other clothing with obscene messages written on them are against the law in Bermuda.

This was the warning from police yesterday after they received a recent slew of complaints from members of the public about people wearing clothing, mainly T-shirts, displaying obscene messages, including four-letter swear words—correctly and incorrectly spelled, and cartoon animals in sexual positions.

"We would like to point out that it is an offence to wear or sell clothing displaying such obscene messages that may be offensive to others," Police spokesman P.c. Gary Venning said.

"This is so, whether the obscenity is written or in the form of a picture. While it may be fashionable, it is not permitted by law and we would strongly urge those responsible not to wear them in public."

COMMISSIONER DECRIES NEW TREND

The Police Commissioner yesterday wagged a figurative finger at Bermuda's women, saying some had sunk to "a new low" in moral behaviour.

It seems the Island's women have been fighting in public more often lately, and that has Commissioner Frederick (Penny) Bean hot under the collar.

Worse still, "several" of these scraps have taken place at night, and in bars.

And "at least one or two" of the fights ended with one woman hitting another woman over the head with a bottle.

But the incident to which yesterday's daily Press release was devoted occurred Wednesday in "broad daylight."

"Police are today investigating a bizarre case of assault which has led to the Commissioner of Police expressing his disappointment at the behaviour of some of the Island's female population," it said.

Two local girls, 16 and 17, were riding an auxiliary cycle along Angle Street on Wednesday afternoon when they were "narrowly missed" by a car being driven by a woman.

The driver allegedly cursed the girls loudly and both vehicles stopped "whereupon a violent fight broke out in the middle of the street," the statement said.

The girls "managed to escape on their cycle" but were chased onto Glebe Road and allegedly pushed off the bike by the car. The woman driver then sped off leaving the two girls injured. They were treated for cuts and abrasions.

"The matter is under investigation but the Commissioner, Mr. Bean today described this apparent trend of violence by women against women as a new low in moral behaviour," concluded the release.

SHIRTLESS MAN IS FINED

A Club Med staff member who admitted running through the streets of St. George's with no shirt on was fined $100 in Magistrates Court yesterday.

John Maechling, 24, was stopped by police at 5 p.m. on July 14 as he was running westwards on Water Street in St. George's.

Sgt. Cyril Plant, prosecuting, told the court the young man had been seen twice the previous week and warned about his state of undress.

This time they arrested him, explaining once again that he was improperly dressed.

Maechling apologised to the court, and said he had been training for an upcoming race in St. George's.

Senior Magistrate the Wor. Granville Cox fined the young man $100.

SMASH AND STRIP WOMAN IS JAILED

A woman who smashed the front window of a restaurant was sent to prison for six months yesterday.

Janet DeSilva, 26, of Crawl Hill in Hamilton Parish, admitted kicking in the window of the front door to Crockwell's King Fried Chicken on March 1.

The 6 ft 10 in. by 3 ft. 8 in. window was worth $250, prosecutor, P.c. Peter Giles, told Magistrates Court.

After hearing that DeSilva had a number of previous similar convictions since 1982, Senior Magistrate the Wor. Granville Cox sentenced her to six months and ordered her to pay for the window.

DeSilva also admitted a further charge of acting in a manner likely to cause a breach of the peace on March 2 in Sandys Parish. P.c. Giles said police found DeSilva outside Casemates Prison pulling off her clothes.

Mr. Cox bound her over in the sum of $200 for one year for this offence.

MAN LIVING IN FEAR OF STALKER

Bermudian Mr. Kenneth Robinson says he's living in fear—of a woman who has stalked him for two years.

He says the obsessed woman follows him around, lurks near his home at night and steals his clothes from the washing line.

Paint has been thrown on his walls and doors. And this week the headlights of his car were smashed and a tyre gashed with a weapon like an icepick.

"There's no telling when she's going to strike," he told the Royal Gazette.

"She wants something she can't have—me. She wants me and she can't have me because I don't want her."

Mr. Robinson, 40, lives with his girlfriend. He says he has never had a romance with the 41 year old stalker.

He says he met her on the street while doing his job as a Hamilton Corporation roadsweeper, but was only a "close friend."

"She caused me to move from my residence on Parsons Road. Since then I've moved to Smith's, but on Monday night she was up my house. She threw a whole bunch of loquats down in my yard.

"In the morning I parked my car down BAA field and I found she'd smashed both my headlights and a front tyre was flat.

"She wants to own me and control me. This is the worst thing she's done so far."

Mr. Robinson said repairing the car will cost him more than $500.

"I'm tired. The police say there's nothing they can do unless she admits she did it. They say I have to see her and catch her.

"Me and my girlfriend have a registered letter for her to stay away from my residence, but she still comes around.

"She hangs around two or three nights a week. It's frightening. You can't sleep, you can't put your clothes on the line. You can't lie down and watch tv like you want to. You can't even take a bath because you're on the run in and out. If I hear the dog bark once or twice I have to go to the yard because she unties the dog." The woman is a part-time housekeeper who lives in Devonshire, said Mr. Robinson.

He believes this is not the first time she has stalked a man. And he feels the problem could be a wider one in Bermuda.

"There's a man divorced from his wife for two years, and his wife is still stalking him. There should be a law against women stalking men." Police declined to comment.

PROWLER JAILED

A 56 year old man who said he was prowling in Fairylands to see a "naked woman" was sentenced to three years in prison.

Edward Hamilton (Doc) Richardson pleaded guilty to prowling outside a Fairylands home on February 24.

Crown counsel Mr. Stephen Harrison told the court that the house where Richardson was prowling had been under observation after being the subject of several prowlings and break-ins.

"At 8:50 a.m. police arrested Richardson after watching him walk around the house," Mr. Harrison said.

When asked by police why he was circling the house Richardson said: "I was prowling. I ain't doing nothing wrong. I was prowling to see a naked woman."

Investigating officer Sgt. Andrew Boyce informed the court of Richardson's lengthy record involving charges such as break and entry, indecent assault, indecent exposure, prowling, and possession of an offensive weapon.

Sgt. Boyce added that Richardson's first charge began in 1957.

Chief Justice the Hon. Justice Ward asked Richardson if he had anything to say and he replied: "At the time I was depressed. My father and my brother suffered from cancer and I needed someone to talk to.

"I asked a probation officer to come see me at Casemates and no one came, so I had no one to talk to. I'm sorry for what I've done."

The Chief Justice said: "You have a long list of previous convictions. People should be able to feel safe in their homes.

"We can't help you anymore than you help yourself."

REMANDED

Running around on Front Street in a pair of tattered underwear led to a man being remanded in custody pending a psychiatric report.

In Magistrates Court, Calvin Burrows, 25, of West Side Road, Sandys Parish, pleaded guilty to wearing improper dress.

When the Wor. Granville Cox asked the man why he was wearing only a pair of underwear outside the Rendezvous Restaurant on Sunday morning, Burrows said he did not know.

When Mr. Cox asked if it was because he lacked clothing, Burrows said yes.

Sgt. George Rushe, prosecuting, told the court Burrows had spent quite some time in prison for similar offences.

Mr. Cox asked Burrows, "Do you like it up there (prison)?" Burrows nodded his head and smiled.

Mr. Cox ordered the psychiatric report and set sentencing for July 25.

WRONG BED

A Long Bay Lane resident was stunned last Sunday to find a strange man sleeping in his bed when he returned to his home.

Police said yesterday the man entered his home about 12.30 p.m. to find the strange man sleeping in the bed. The man escaped from the house when he was disturbed.

RELAXED INTRUDER DISTURBS WOMAN

A Pembroke woman called the police on Thursday afternoon when a strange man entered her home, locked the door and proceeded to make himself comfortable.

Police report that the woman was relaxing at her Langton Lane apartment around 3 p.m. when the man, holding his chest, walked through the front door and sat down near her.

The woman ran out screaming and the man escaped over the balcony.

FATHER FURIOUS AT 'SKINNY DIPPING' SAILOR

A furious father has blasted a sailor's saucy antics in swimming naked off Albuoy Point.

Mr. Michael Benevides witnessed the sailor's naked leap into Hamilton Harbour—and so did his eight-year-old daughter Melissa.

Mr. Benevides was angry at the way the sailor and his friends did not seem to care that other people were in the area when the stripshow started.

He reported the incident to the police and the sailor was arrested but not before a chase along Front Street.

Vacationing from his job as a fire-fighter in Connecticut, Bermudian Mr. Benevides said: "I found it a very nasty incident. He just stripped down to the raw in front of everyone.

"There were lots of people on Albuoy Point sitting on the benches. I was sitting with my daughter and her friends enjoying some food when this happened.

"I called the police and told them someone was 'skinny dipping' in the harbour."

But before the police arrived the sailor had dressed himself and had set off running along Front Street. Mr. Benevides gave chase and pushed the man to the ground enabling police to seize him.

He said: "The guy was telling the cops that they do it all the time in England. I lived in England for three years and I know it is against the law there.

"They told me that they did not want to do any harm but they should respect the laws of Bermuda. There were a lot of people about and most of them seemed upset."

Mr. Benevides added that he believed the sailors were drunk. He said he hoped the exhibitionist had been punished by his superiors.

In fact, the man was handed over to his ship, HMS Broadsword and is expected to be disciplined on board ship.

DISCHARGE FOR WEARING NAUGHTY T

An 18-year-old Pembroke man who did not realise the T-shirt he was wearing was against the law ended up in Magistrates Court on Friday.

Nikia J. Burchall of Middletown, Pembroke pleaded guilty to being indecently dressed on March 24.

Prosecuting Sgt. Kenrick James told the court that Burchall was seen at 7.25 p.m. on Beacon Hill Road in Somerset by police wearing a T-shirt that said "F--- What you Heard."

"The officers told Burchall that he would be arrested for wearing such a shirt," Sgt. Kenrick James said.

Burchall's lawyer Opposition Leader Mr. Frederick Wade said: "The words that were on the T-shirt were probably obscene but not indecent.

"Mr. Burchall bought the shirt from a store in Hamilton and was unaware that wearing it was illegal.

"He was arrested and taken to the police station. I think that has been sufficient punishment already."

The Wor. Edward King said it was highly unlikely Burchall would wear another indecent T-shirt, and he gave him an absolute discharge.

OBSCENE CALLER WAITS FOR REPORTS

A man who called up the secretary of the New Testament Church of God saying, "I want you, I want you, I want you," pleaded not guilty to making an obscene phone call.

Kevin Daniels, 29, of Flatts Hill, Smith's Parish, telephoned the church's secretary five times on the afternoon of June 19.

Insp. Duffy said that on the first call Daniels said he wanted the woman but did not identify himself.

He then made four other calls during which there was only silence and breathing.

Later that same day, between 8.30 and 9.30 p.m. the Reverend Goodwin Smith, pastor of the New Testament Church, also received eight silent phone calls at his home on St. Anne's Road.

Daniels, who also pleaded guilty to making a harassing phone call, admitted making the calls after he was arrested by police, and said he had phoned the operator early on June 19, in order to learn the church's number and the pastor's number.

He could not explain why he made the calls.

REPORTER'S NOTEBOOK

Foul language and cleavage on a Sunday afternoon did not go down well with one local resident seeking wholesome family entertainment when he turned on his tv set.

Apparently the operators of ZBM Channel 9 agreed.

But we wonder how many cable-corrupted residents didn't.

"I thought I heard a few words I don't normally hear," Southampton viewer Mr. Randall Bassett called up to say. "Then I heard another 'f' and I thought: 'This kind of entertainment on a Sunday afternoon!' It had to be an 'R' rating."

The last straw for Mr. Bassett was "a lady's breast" and a few explicit utterances. It was off with the TV and onto the daily news-paper to register a complaint.

ZBM must have had the same idea because at exactly that point it cut off the broadcast of "Hostage," the matinee movie about an airplane hijacking.

An apologetic message flashed across screens telling viewers the explicit language content of the film had forced ZBM to take the film off the air immediately.

In its place, came a "wholesome" movie featuring near-naked African tribal men ripping apart African animals. There was no swearing (though maybe in an African language), but close-ups of freshly killed game didn't help the digestion of Sunday dinner.

A ZBM programmer said the person on duty decided to take the original movie off the air entirely on his own initiative because of "explicit language."

However, the programmer subsequently viewed it and found "not one iota of nudity" in the film.

"I must refute the nudity charge," she said, adding perhaps the film's leading lady, the buxom Karen Black, had given the impres-sion of nakedness.

Things don't look good for the hit series NYPD Blue.

ALL THIS AND A MOON TOO

Plumber Milton Trott was fined $200 yesterday by Senior Magistrate the Wor. Granville Cox after he pulled down his trousers and thrust his naked bottom towards policemen waiting to search him.

The 34-year-old from Bailey's Bay swore at policemen when they warned he would be searched after he was arrested on Mullett Bay Road, St. George's, on Sunday, December 30, last year.

Insp. David Chew told the court the man was taken to the police station cells but an hour later it was discovered that he had smashed a glass cover of an electric light.

Trott pleaded guilty to using insulting words, damaging police property, as well as to speeding at 54 k.p.h. and to failing to obey a stop sign.

He was fined a total $505, ordered to pay $60 compensation and banned from driving for three months.

DANCE SCHOOL OGLER CAUGHT IN STAKE-OUT

A 22-year-old man was ordered to behave himself after he pleaded guilty in Magistrates Court yesterday to a breach of peace charge in which he repeatedly stared at women exercising at a Hamilton dance school.

Police Sgt. John Eaves said Albert Simons of Boaz Island had visited the Jackson School of Dance on Burnaby Street repeatedly since late March to watch women exercise. He said some of the dancers were frightened by Simons' attitude and demeanour.

After the school's staff failed to get a satisfactory answer from Simons for his presence there on March 30, they called police. A cat and mouse game ensued as Simons disappeared each time the police showed up throughout the day. Finally they took positions in the school and apprehended Simons when he appeared.

Simons, whose wife was in the United States at the time, said he went to the school to meet women.

"I was just trying to pick up a nice lady friend," he told Senior Magistrate the Wor. Granville Cox. "You know what I mean. I meant no trouble. I won't go around there no more. I will maintain pure, good behaviour."

GOVERNMENT SENDS SKINNY DIPPING BHC BOSS PACKING

Bermuda Housing Corporation chairman Mr. Ward Young yesterday lamented Government's decision to throw his general manager, Mr. John Gardner, off the island after he'd been caught skinny-dipping.

Mr. Young described father-of-three Mr. Gardner as a "first class" manager who had done a great job during his four years with the corporation.

Although Mr. Gardner's second two-year contract was up a few months ago, it was extended for six months while applicants for his job were interviewed.

No suitable applicant was found and the corporation requested Mr. Gardner's contract be extended for another two years.

But after the 51-year-old Scotsman's appearance in Magistrates Court last Friday for being caught skinny-dipping at Chaplin Bay in Warwick by an off-duty police officer, the Immigration Dept. said it would not grant the extension.

Mr. Gardner was given a year's conditional discharge after pleading guilty to indecent exposure, which occurred on June 25.

Labour and Immigration Minister the Hon. Sir John Sharpe yesterday refused to confirm or deny that the nude swimming incident was a reason for not extending Mr. Gardner's contract.

Police prosecutor Insp. Peter Duffy said while the incident may have been out of character for Gardner, it was still frowned on by society.

INDECENT EXPOSURE PROBED

Police are investigating a complaint by a woman that a man emerged from bushes wearing nothing but a balaclava when she was walking along an access road to Horseshoe Beach at about 1.30 p.m. on Monday.

MAN INTRUDES ON WOMAN'S PRIVACY

Karen Richardson's trip to the supermarket ended in fright as she was followed round the store by a man with a mental age of 10, a Magistrates Court heard yesterday.

And it ended when she felt warm air on her leg as she reached to the top shelf for an item.

When she looked down she found David Tucker, 34, lying on the floor looking up her dress.

Yesterday Tucker, of Bushy Park Drive, Somerset pleaded guilty to intruding on Richardson's privacy. He was remanded on bail for four weeks for probation and psychiatric reports.

Crown Counsel, Mrs. Cheryl-Ann Mapp told Magistrate the Wor. Kenneth Brown that Richardson had twice moved to different aisles in the Somerset MarketPlace because Tucker was following her round.

"She went to an aisle where there were other people because he was making her feel uncomfortable," said Mrs. Mapp.

Tucker has a record going back 14 years and in August was put on two years probation for indecent behaviour, said Mrs. Mapp.

Mr. Peter Farge, defending, said Tucker has a mental age of only 10.

LETTERS TO THE EDITOR

SANTA SCARES DAUGHTER

Dear Sir,

I'm writing in regards to an encounter that my 2 and a half year old daughter and I had with Santa on Friday, November 25, in a Hamilton store.

We went to the store to have a picture taken, (she had met him several times before with no problem or negative reaction) and without warning she was taken from me and "PLOPPED" on his lap, not so much as a "HELLO" or have you been a good girl. With loud music playing behind him and all the chaos, she started to cry, and the first and only words out of his mouth was, "She'll be fine mummy," and he turned to the cameraman to say "CLICK CLICK" just take the picture. Needless to say she is now afraid of him!

It is ok to include Santa in your promotional activities but as Santa is an important role model for "children" please ensure that he and the people working around him know the significance of this.

DISILLUSIONED CHILD

SLIGHTLY KINKY

Dear Sir,

I see in this weekend's Mid Ocean [newspaper] that Government wants to straighten another piece of road. Go do it in another country—personally I like Bermuda the way it is: slightly kinky!

TOM BUTTERFIELD
HAMILTON

RED NOSE

Dear Sir,

On Good Friday afternoon while discharging family members at the Airport who were enroute to the USA, we heard Rudolph The Red-Nosed Reindeer blaring loudly all through the building!

Can you imagine what our incoming Easter visitors must have thought?

RUTH CONYERS
PAGET

HASTY WEATHER REPORT

Dear Sir,

Tonight, Wednesday, March 24th, I watched the ZBM Channel 10 evening news at 7 p.m. anxiously waiting the weather report. In my position, the weather can make or break my business day and, as the day had been windy and quite cold, I was hoping for a better forecast for tomorrow. Imagine my surprise when news-woman Janelle Ford told the audience that "Tomorrow will be partly cloudy, good-night!" Quite stunned at such a lack of a report, I immediately called the station to voice my concern.

The phone was answered by Mr. Dave Burchall who, with an arrogant and cavalier attitude, told me that if I wanted a weather report I should call 977!

Well, Mr. Burchall, I did just that. And as for your comment that weather does not constitute news, it would be quite helpful if you shared that view on air with your audience. For those of us whose livelihood is often affected by the weather, we depend on the news to provide the service of a weather report, just as newsrooms do all over the world. It's a small minded attitude like your reply that will encourage your audience to flock to cable when it finally does arrive.

    MISS K.J. LACEY

    WARWICK

SPELLING TEST FOR GIBBONS CO.

Dear Sir,

    The other day I went into Gibbons' store from Church Street. I looked at the department to the right as I entered and saw that according to the large sign it sold STATIONARY. I had to admit the goods were not moving.

    NIK

    SOUTHAMPTON

FOR THE RECORD

Mr. Arnett Joyiens of Dundonald Street, Hamilton, has asked us to point out that the Howard R. Joynes, 24, imprisoned for handbag snatching is not a part of his family.

(AS A RELIEF FROM ELECTION NEWS, IT'S COM

...NG TO LEARN THAT A HORSE IS NOT A VEHICLE.)

On the rocks

THERE'S AN old joke Bermudians willingly tell foreigners, and it goes something like this: What's the definition of Bermuda? Sixty thousand alcoholics clinging to a rock.

And that isn't too far from the truth.

By the time Bermuda's third governor, Nathaniel Butler, arrived on the island in 1619, there was a new dilemma to deal with. Captain Butler was most alarmed at what he determined was the main cause of crime in the colony—the enormous amount of alcohol being consumed. He was amazed that in a settlement of twelve hundred people, two thousand gallons of alcohol were being swilled every three months, even though approximately half of the inhabitants were women and children.

Drunkenness was probably the most common sin at the time; miscreants were routinely presented at every Assizes and placed in the stocks for many hours worth of penance.

Those drinking genes have stood the test of time. I know very few people living on the island who decline a good drink each evening and in some cases, each morning. Those who do decline attend Alcoholics Anonymous or have lost the use of their limbs. Half a day in the stocks, which still stand in the square at St. George's, might assist the tipplers with their rehabilitation.

Having done some "clinging" myself in the past as a resident of these sunny isles, I have a fair idea as to why people drink so much. It is quite scientific, terribly complex, and took me ages to discover:

There's bugger all to do. Everybody's so filthy rich—even the poor—that boredom is contagious.

I remember the time, one glorious June day in the mid-eighties, this dear middle-aged white lady from a local real-estate firm arranged to drive me to view a house in Somerset I was considering renting. She picked me up in Warwick around two in the afternoon, and we set out for that ever-so-quaint little town near old Casemates prison, about twenty-five minutes away. I was greatly anticipating the enjoyable drive along Harbour Road and the coast because at that stage I did not own a car and hadn't been in one in quite some time.

We settled into her compact British-made automobile, and off we went. At the time I thought she was awfully sweet and awfully giddy although not what I would call an awfully good driver. She couldn't seem to keep her car on the left-hand side of the road, but she was a good talker and genuinely friendly which is more than I can say about some other agents I have met.

It wasn't until we reached Somerset and began a tour of the house that I realized she was as drunk as a skunk. Several times she had to stop and hold a wall to maintain her balance. Discovering this made the return drive to Warwick a hair-raising one, let me tell you.

Everybody drinks. Lorry drivers pass you on the road taking swigs from brown paper wrappers; sales clerks disappear for quick nips in the back of shops; one recent Minister of Health, still a Member of Parliament today, has been publicly accused in the House of Assembly of being an addict herself, precipitating a hasty exit from the Parliament building for a much-needed glass of I don't know what.

Bermudians handle their booze differently than the residents of other countries I have spent extended periods of time in. They end up on roofs, in the middle of roads, destroying hospitals, taking craps in the harbor, and, most inexplicably of all, crying "RAPE!" when they fall off toilets.

Then there is Bermuda's drug problem, or I should say what they consider a problem. Everyone is against drugs. Government, police, antidrug groups, parents, teachers, television, radio, bumper stickers, and posters all proclaim the evils of marijuana. Indeed one quarter of all prisoners have been incarcerated for drug-related offenses, usually for supplying or for importation.

Totally ignoring the country's severe problem with liquor, which is available in pretty packages on every street corner from Somerset to St. George's at fabulously tempting prices, the powers that be have decided that marijuana is to blame for the downfall, or ultimate downfall, of Bermudian society. Knowing how paranoid everyone is about drugs—it's as if the whole country is smoking up they're so paranoid—those brave enough to buy the evil bud or bring it into the country, either for personal use or to sell take enormous risks. Why the government bothers is beyond me when all a fellow has to do is take a short walk to the Warwick Bowling Lanes on Middle Road and you will find several extremely friendly Rastafarians who are only too happy to oblige with some really good dope. Not that I have any personal experience with this practice . . . I mean, I've just heard it happens there, that's all.

So pour yourself a stiff drink, roll a joint, haul out the hash and crack pipe, fill up your syringes, and settle back in your favorite chair. These next articles all have to do with the consequences of sinning with substances.

If you've ever awakened on a Saturday or Sunday morning with a monstrous hangover, staggered into the bathroom for a tall glass of water and a couple of codeine tablets, and suddenly remembered your appalling behavior of the night before, you will sympathize with the experiences of the people to follow. If you haven't, then you should have been a judge.

PARTY GOER ENDS UP ON A ROOF

A night on the town turned into a night in jail for a Hamilton Parish man. Stephen Paul Collier, of Blue Hole Hill, left a Hamilton nightclub at 3:30 a.m. on May 29 and was arrested 90 minutes later when police found him lying in the roof gutter of a Bailey's Bay home.

The incident resulted in Collier pleading guilty to a charge of prowling and a confession that he does not remember how he got there. Police Insp. Peter Duffy, prosecuting, said Collier was so intoxicated when police brought him down from the roof that he was unable to stand up. The Inspector speculated that he got on the roof by using a step ladder.

Lawyer Mrs. Ewa Hancock said Collier left the nightclub with friends in a taxi. Homeward bound, the driver kicked all the passengers out of the cab because someone was smoking—an action that apparently left Collier adrift in the Bailey's Bay area.

Mrs. Hancock said Collier had no criminal intent in ending up on the private property. "He does not remember being on the roof and he apologises to the court," she said. "We are dealing with an isolated incident that is out of character."

Mr. Judge ordered a social inquiry report on Collier to be ready for June 20. Bail was set at $500.

JAILED FOR 'REVOLTING ACTION'

A 36 year old man who dumped a box of leaves and human excrement into Hamilton Harbour was jailed for six months. Franklyn Dennis Simmons, of no fixed abode, admitted being a public nuisance on October 17, when passersby saw him empty the box and its contents into the water off the flagpole.

He told police: "I had a bowel movement and got rid of it." "What you did was extremely revolting," Mr. Georges told the defendant, who has a psychological disorder.

"You are a young, able-bodied man and you could be earning a living being a productive member of society, but you seem to have a personality problem," Mr. Georges said.

Simmons said that he was upset that someone had stole a meal he bought and was drunk when he committed the offences, including wandering abroad, using offensive words and drinking in public.

Mr. Georges sentenced him to six months in prison, but said he may be transferred to St. Brendan's [psychiatric] Hospital after psychological evaluation.

TEEN GREW CANNABIS

A teenager sporting the green t-shirt of an Agriculture and Fisheries employee admitted cultivating cannabis when he appeared in court on Friday.

Kevin John Boys, 19, of Homestead Lane, Southampton, pleaded guilty to the Magistrates Court charge.

Sgt. Earl Kirby, prosecuting, said police attended Boys' Southampton home and noted a strong smell of cannabis. They searched the small private dwelling with his permission and in his presence.

When officers approached a closet door, Boys nervously told them there was nothing in it. The top half of the closet was found to contain clothes while three electric strip lights suspended over 19 flower pots were found in the lower half.

Boys told the officers the plants were cauliflower.

'GUILTY, JUST GUILTY'

An 18-year-old electrician who said he was "guilty, just guilty" of possessing cannabis, was told he was facing "jail, just jail" as a result.

Chan Kwame Durham told the Wor. Granville Cox that he was "guilty, just guilty" of possessing 0.36 grammes of cannabis which was found on him during a search at Hamilton Police Station on December 2 last year.

"He has cannabis, just cannabis, and I am going to give him jail, just jail," said Mr. Cox.

Mr. Cox then ordered a social inquiry to be conducted, but said: "If he can have cannabis, just cannabis, and if he doesn't care about the law, then he can have jail, just jail."

Durham was released on $350 bond and ordered to re-appear in Magistrates Court on July 11.

LIVING IT UP

When Alvin (Alabama) Anderson lay down at the road side after living it up at a weekend wedding he knew he was drunk.

"But if the police had left me alone and let me sleep, I would have been sober the next morning," he told Senior Magistrate the Wor. Granville Cox yesterday.

Anderson admitted being drunk and incapable, but said he had an explanation for his actions when he appeared in Magistrates Court.

Anderson told Mr. Cox he had been to "Cleavie's" wedding and was "feeling good. It was late when I left. I had helped clean up and they gave me a bottle. I know I was drunk when I went to sleep," he said.

Sgt. Peter Giles, prosecuting, said police patrolling South Shore Road saw Anderson laying on the ground. He appeared to be asleep and when they attempted to awaken him, they were unable to do so. He smelled of intoxicants and when he was eventually roused he made an unintelligible reply. He was detained by police.

Sgt. Giles said Anderson had a police record dating back to 1957, and this conviction marked his 24th for being drunk and incapable, but before he could go into particulars, Mr. Cox stopped him saying: "I know all about Alabama's convictions." Telling him he needed a wife and tender love and care Mr. Cox granted Anderson a year's conditional discharge.

ARRESTED DRUNK FOR THE FIFTIETH TIME

Rudolph Folder hit the half century mark yesterday—the 50th time he has been in court after over-indulging.

And he promised it would be his last as Senior Magistrate the Wor. Granville Cox gave him a one year conditional discharge, the condition being that he attends an addiction services course.

Folder started his court appearances 25 years ago when he was first fined for being drunk and incapable. Since then there have been an average of two appearances a year, all on the same charge.

Four times, Folder, of Victoria Park, Prospect, has been sent to jail, and Mr. Cox warned him yesterday he should go down "for a long period" before agreeing instead to the discharge.

Folder, 54, said he had once given up drink for six months. "I just stopped, that's all," he told Mr. Cox.

"I will do it this time. I promise I will stop drinking," he added, after pleading guilty.

Sgt. Peter Giles, prosecuting, said Folder's latest flirtation with the law came on Monday night, when he was discovered asleep in the doorway of Mount St. Agnes Academy in Dundonald Street, Hamilton.

Officers tried to wake him. "After several attempts they succeeded," he added. "He then had great difficulty getting to his feet."

WOMAN WARNED AGAINST DRINK

A woman who found herself in a "disgraceful plight" late Thursday was warned against having too much to drink when she admitted swearing at police.

Janine Oatley, 24, was given a conditional discharge for six months when she appeared in Magistrates Court yesterday.

P.c. Stuart Pybus, prosecuting, said the Coot Pond Road, St. George's woman called the St. George's police station several times on Thursday morning shouting offensive words into the telephone.

A short time before 10 p.m. the same night, she threw an unknown object through an eastern window of the police station and then ran to Water Street where she was arrested.

Oatley told the court she was "under the influence of alcohol" and apologised for her behaviour.

Acting Senior Magistrate the Wor. Ephraim Georges told her: "Stop drinking and pull yourself together. You don't want to find yourself in that disgraceful plight again."

EXPECTED HIS SON TO SMOKE

A Sandys man told a court on Tuesday he expected his young son to smoke marijuana when he reaches age 15.

And Lesley R. Simmons, 35, who admitted drugs possession, said he had "smoked weed" since he was 12.

Simmons, of Long Bay Lane, Sandys, was fined $100 for having .43 grams of cannabis in his possession.

Sgt. Earl Kirby, prosecuting, told the court the drug was found in Simmons' pocket when he was arrested on another matter.

Sgt. Kirby said Simmons admitted he had smoked marijuana since he was in junior high.

The Wor. Granville Cox asked Simmons when he expected his three-year-old son to start smoking the drug.

"I really could not say," Simmons replied. "I would guess about age 15."

But Mr. Cox said the courts existed to "stamp out drugs," and threatened to send Simmons to jail because of his attitude.

"I do not think your son will start because I will send you into captivity," Mr. Cox told Simmons.

"Your display of callousness shows me there is no reason not to sentence you to a prison term even if this is your first offence," Mr. Cox said.

But he decided to fine Simmons after he apologised, saying he was sorry for what he had said.

"I hope my son never does it," Simmons said.

THE COCAINE ROAD

A 20-year-old yesterday said he found a package of cocaine lying on St. Monica's Road as he bent over to pick up his hat on the street.

Steven Richardson admitted having 0.47 grams of the drug when he appeared in Magistrates Court, but he said he did not use the drug himself.

"I threw my hat down when I was singing a song, and when I bent over to pick it up, it was just lying there so I picked it up," Richardson said.

MAN 'HAS NO HOME'

A 34-year-old man who said he was an orphan and didn't have a home was given a six-month conditional discharge in Magistrates Court yesterday when he admitted shouting offensive words.

Richard Simmons, who reportedly lives at the Salvation Army shelter on Marsh Lane, Pembroke, said he was homeless and nobody would talk to him about it.

P.c. Earl Kirby, prosecuting, said police saw Simmons shouting offensive words at passers-by on Church Street, Hamilton, opposite the bus terminal and then outside the Imperial Building a few minutes later.

Acting Senior Magistrate the Wor. Ephraim Georges told Simmons he has to get some help.

But Simmons replied: "Don't oppress me anymore. I've got a lot of hurt in me cause I don't have a home."

Author's note: Obviously the *Deal-a-Meal* and *Sweatin' to the Oldies* royalties have run out for poor Mr. Simmons.

NO MORE BEER

A 55 year old man who's been picked up drunk by police 52 times over the past quarter century yesterday promised the top magistrate he'd swear off beer completely.

Rudolph Folder, of Mary Victoria Road, Devonshire, admitted being drunk and incapable, and was given a one year conditional discharge.

Prosecuting, Police Sgt. Earl Kirby said Folder's prior sentences ranged from 5 pounds to seven days in jail.

Folder told Senior Magistrate the Wor. Granville Cox he'd given up hard liquor and only drank beer.

Mr. Cox asked how many beers he would be drinking in the future, and when Folder didn't understand, the Magistrate dispatched duty counsel Mr. Peter Farge to investigate.

"Mr. Farge, how many beers is he going to drink?" asked Mr. Cox.

"I'll check it out, sir," replied Mr. Farge, then went into conference with Folder.

After a few moments, Mr. Farge reported: "He's not going to drink anymore."

HE LETS THE VODKA FLY

A 63 year-old retired man pleaded guilty in Magistrates Court yesterday to being drunk and incapable.

Insp. Peter Duffy said that Wayland Brian Smith was found in a hedge along Devonshire Bay Road near South Shore Road at 7:45 p.m. on September 14 after police were called to the site.

Insp. Duffy said Smith, whose breath "smelled badly of alcohol," was unable to get to his feet and had to be helped to the police car to be taken to Hamilton police station.

"Yeah, I had a 40 of vodka," Smith told the court. "I wish I had some vodka now. That stuff is good man. When I get money, I let her fly, man, on my vodka."

Senior Magistrate the Wor. Will Francis said: "Look, I don't want you to go out of here and come back in this condition again. Next time you appear in court you appear sober, you understand?"

Smith was remanded in custody for a social enquiry report due October 1.

MORNING AFTER

A heavy night's drinking left Malcolm Smith more than double the limit when he went driving the next morning, a court heard yesterday.

When he was tested at 9:30 a.m. he still had a reading of 228 mg. of alcohol for each 100 ml. of blood. The limit is 100 ml.

"It was from the night before," said Smith of Sylvan Dell Road, Paget.

"It must have been a good night. I can only admire your constitution," Magistrate the Wor. John Judge told him.

Mr. Judge banned Smith for 18 months and fined him $400.

FISH BONE TALE DOESN'T IMPRESS

A Roberts Avenue resident who has served several jail terms was fined $250 yesterday when he appeared in Magistrates Court.

Gary Leon Trimm, 30, admitted the drugs possession offence discovered when police stopped him in the St. Monica's Mission area after he hurried away from them.

Sgt. George Rushe, prosecuting, told the court Trimm tossed a hand-made cigarette from his mouth but claimed it was only a fish bone.

"You didn't see me with that," Trimm told police when they showed him the marijuana joint. "I just threw a fish bone from my mouth."

HURRY UP PLEASE MISTER, IT'S TIME

A man who asked police if he could finish smoking his marijuana cigarette after being arrested for possession of the drug was fined $300 in Magistrates Court yesterday.

Ralph Gibbons pleaded guilty to possession of cannabis.

Sgt. Peter Giles said the Abbots Cliff resident was seen by police narcotics officers on the night of October 19 driving on North Shore Road into the residential area.

Sgt. Giles said that when police stopped Gibbons he said: "Okay, I've got a spliff."

When he was arrested, he asked police for time "to finish my smoke."

A subsequent search of Gibbons turned up 2.91 grams of cannabis.

WOMAN CRIED 'RAPE' AFTER FALLING OFF TOILET

Bermuda's official rape figures for 1989 were reduced by one yesterday when a 37-year-old woman was sentenced for accusing a man wrongly.

Judy Johnson had been so drunk she had fallen off her toilet and received facial injuries which she told police the rapist had caused.

Yesterday, Magistrate the Wor. Kenneth Brown put Johnson on two years probation with a condition she attends Alcoholism Services.

Johnson admitted earlier this month making a false report and her case was adjourned until yesterday for a social inquiry report.

She described a man to police and then confirmed he had raped her in a face to face confrontation arranged by police, said Sgt. Peter Giles, prosecuting.

Sgt. Giles said police had found Johnson in a "dishevelled state" at her home in Tribe Lane, Devonshire, on December 15 last year.

At the earlier case it was stated the suspect had been arrested and detained for up to six hours. Mother of three Johnson had been at home with her youngest child and had injured herself in her drunken state.

But she had been afraid to tell her live-in boyfriend the truth and made up the rape story.

In his judgement Mr. Brown said he was taking into account Johnson's bid to combat her severe drinking problem in his sentence.

"I also accept that this particular offence came when she panicked. It wasn't activated by spite or malice towards the man—if it had been I would have had no alternative but to send her to prison.

"The potential seriousness of this action is that the complainant could have suffered appalling consequences because of her report."

After the case, police spokeswoman P.c. Rosanda Jones said Johnson's rape report was deleted from police figures on January 3.

It means Bermuda's official crime figures now show 14 rather than 15 rapes for last year.

LYING IN WAIT—FOR THE BUS

A Devonshire man found lying drunk in the street told police he was waiting for the bus, Magistrates Court heard yesterday.

Prosecutor Insp. Peter Duffy said police were called to the Halfway House Restaurant on the North Shore Road in Flatts with a report that a man was lying in the road.

Upon arrival, police found Dwayne Burgess in an intoxicated state, unable to stand without assistance, or answer their questions coherently. The 29-year-old painter was then taken into custody.

Burgess, of Dock Hill, was fined $100 by Senior Magistrate the Wor. Will Francis after pleading guilty to being drunk and incapable.

TRAFFIC HAZARD

Police found 54-year-old Urban Ned Fleming lying in the road and drinking while traffic backed up behind him Magistrates Court heard this week.

He was found resting on one arm in the middle of Khyber Pass, holding up the traffic and drinking from a bottle of vodka, Insp. Peter Duffy said.

When arrested he immediately got up and swore at the officers, smashing the bottle on a wall and violently breaking away.

Fleming, of Smiths Avenue, Warwick, admitted drinking in a public place, using offensive words and resisting arrest last Wednesday. He was placed on 18 months probation, concurrent with his current probation.

MAN FOUND ASLEEP ON FRONT STREET

A Sonesta Beach Hotel employee who told police he lived on board the cruise ship *Atlantic* after they found him sleeping under the porch of Front Street shop A.S. Cooper's was yesterday fined $200 in Magistrates Court for wandering abroad.

Patrick Brophy, 24, of the Sonesta Beach staff quarters, admitted the charge and said he had been very drunk and felt sleeping there was "the safest thing to do with my body."

Sgt. George Rushe, prosecuting, told the judge that Brophy was woken by police at 7:05 a.m. yesterday and told them he lived on board the *Atlantic*, which was docked alongside.

"He said, 'I'm on land as much as the ship is,' but then said he worked at Sonesta Beach.

"He later said: 'Everyone should live on a police boat,'" said Sgt. Rushe. "He has no previous convictions."

Said Brophy: "I was drunk and fell asleep as I thought that was the safest thing to do with my body at the time."

LYING IN FRONT OF TRAFFIC

A 31-year-old woman who said her mother and brother were trying to kill her with a hammer, pleaded guilty in Magistrates Court yesterday to offensive language.

Insp. Peter Giles, prosecuting, said Janet Doreen DeSilva, of North Shore Road, Hamilton Parish, was arrested at 8:40 p.m. on October 25th after she swore at police officers who were trying to stop her from lying on the road in front of traffic.

Insp. Giles said police were called to a Hamilton Parish address after they received reports that a woman was "smashing the contents of a house."

When police arrived, DeSilva's mother and son were attempting to restrain her but DeSilva was able to get out onto the road where she lay down in front of traffic, Insp. Giles said.

DeSilva, who was on probation for previous offences, said she was shouting and swearing because "my mother and brother were trying to kill me with a knife, I mean a hammer, and there was blood all over my shirt."

Acting Senior Magistrate, the Wor. John Judge ordered a social inquiry report and a psychiatric report due on November 16.

Bail was set at $250.

FINED $300 FOR PLANT

A 32-year-old Smith's Parish man who admitted owning a cannabis plant was fined $300 in Magistrates Court yesterday.

Inspector David Chew, prosecuting, told Senior Magistrate the Wor. Granville Cox, that police found a cannabis plant during a raid on Dennis Sousa's Flatts Hill house at 5.45 a.m. on May 29.

"The officers found a plant in a tin can outside the house," said Insp. Chew. "When they asked Sousa if he owned the plant, he said: 'Yes, that's my youth'."

ROLLED JOINTS

After being arrested at the Airport for possession of cannabis, an American woman asked Customs officials if she could have her drugs back.

Karen J. McKenna, 27, pleaded guilty yesterday when she appeared in Magistrates Court.

Sgt. Peter Giles, prosecuting, told the court on July 21, when McKenna arrived at the Airport, customs officers searched her belongings and found cigarette papers and rolled cigarette ends in her handbag. The contents of the rolled cigarettes proved to be 1.2 grammes of cannabis.

Acting Senior Magistrate the Wor. Ephraim Georges fined McKenna $100 for possession of cannabis and $75 for the cigarette papers.

PIPE PROVES COSTLY

A 35-year-old man who pleaded for leniency was fined $100 for having a pipe in his pocket when police searched him on March 4.

Phillip Woods, of Sunnyside Park, Southampton, admitted in Magistrates Court yesterday.

Woods asked the court for leniency and presented two character references.

The Wor. Granville Cox handed down the fine and warned Woods not to use the pipe again.

MAN ADMITS BEING DRUNK

A 36-year-old man said, "Leave me alone, I'm a Seventh-Day-Adventist" when police found him lying on his back on Front Street after a drinking bout, Senior Magistrate the Wor. Granville Cox was told yesterday.

Mr. Cox threatened Vernon Smith, of Reid Street, with jail, but fined him $100 after telling him: "I might have to try something else in the future."

ARM LOCK WAS GOOD FOR HIS SHOULDER

Arrest brought immediate relief for a drunken carpet layer with a dislocated shoulder.

John Robert Holmes told Magistrates Court yesterday he was so drunk that he had forgotten all the abuse he hurled at a police officer in the early hours of last Sunday.

But his lasting memory was of his shoulder, which popped back into place when the officer placed him in an arm lock before charging him with offensive behavior.

Holmes, 22, of Boss's Cove Road, Hamilton, pleaded guilty to the charge and heard Insp. Peter Duffy outline the incident which happened at about 1 a.m. in Front Street.

Insp. Duffy told Senior Magistrate the Wor. Will Francis that Holmes was clearly drunk and was involved in a dispute with another man. He refused to calm down and gradually turned his attention to the police officer.

Holmes became abusive towards the officer and continued to swear after he was warned that such behavior could land him in trouble. He was arrested and swore all the way to the police station.

Holmes told the court he was very drunk and was on his way home when he was approached by a man with whom he had an argument the previous week.

He said: "I don't even remember any of this except that we were arguing. I don't remember the police or anything. I would not start cussing at the cops. The next thing I remember is that I had a dislocated shoulder and they put my arm behind my back and it popped back in."

Fining Holmes $200, Mr. Francis said, "This was a very public place and it sounds like you were very abusive. If you are going to get that drunk you had better get drunk where you are not likely to get yourself into trouble."

'ONE TOO LITTLE'

A social inquiry report was ordered on a 23-year-old man in Magistrates Court who went berserk at the Spinning Wheel [bar] after having "one much too little to drink."

Ondrey P. Ascento of Town Hill, Flatts, pleaded guilty to using offensive words, assaulting a police officer and causing $350 damage to the bar's cedar door.

The offences occurred about 3 a.m. Saturday when Ascento began verbally abusing patrons at the Court Street bar.

Police Sgt. George Rushe, prosecuting, said Spinning Wheel management called police who asked Ascento to leave. He began swearing at the officers and, while leaving the premises, smashed his crash helmet against the cedar door.

On the street, Ascento continued to verbally abuse police and, after being warned of possible arrest, he struck one of them. He was restrained, then arrested, but continued swearing at them at the Hamilton police station.

Ascento told Senior Magistrate the Wor. Granville Cox that he was sorry for the trouble caused.

"I had one much too little to drink that night."

"You mean you had one much too much," Mr. Cox said.

"Yeah."

Mr. Cox ordered the social inquiry report for February 6.

US NAVY MAN IS FINED FOR DAMAGE

The American serviceman who went on a $5,500 spree of destruction that ended with him smashing an ambulance into a tree, received fines totalling $1,250 in Magistrates Court yesterday.

James Douglas Allgeier, 19, pleaded guilty to the five charges against him.

On August 16 at about 2:56 a.m., Allgeier's drunken rampage began. Police received a report that someone was smashing windows of a building in the Crow Lane area, police prosecutor Sgt. Earl Kirby said.

"When they arrived they saw Allgeier walking in the area with cuts to his hands. He was taken to hospital for treatment and no charges were made because the building was derelict," Sgt. Kirby said.

The court heard that after Allgeier was released from King Edward VII Memorial Hospital at around 4:15 a.m., a hospital employee called a taxi for him and he went outside to wait.

Shortly afterward, Sgt. Kirby said breaking glass was heard from the hospital grounds where the Ministry of Health has its pest control office.

Allgeier smashed the office windows causing $1,900 of damage.

He then headed back to the hospital where he caused further damage. Windows of the gift shop, dialysis unit, nuclear medicine department, physiotherapy section and the emergency room were smashed causing $3,691.95 damage.

While in the hospital Allgeier also turned on a fire hose and flooded the entrance to the Ministry of Health.

Next, he took a hospital ambulance that had keys in it, and drove off. Allgeier got to South Shore Road, Paget, before crashing into a tree.

Police ended Allgeier's destructive trail when they arrested him in the Botanical Gardens and took him in for questioning.

Sgt. Kirby said: Allgeier told police he had been drinking at pubs in Hamilton and couldn't remember anything that had happened since around 10 p.m.

"He said he had gotten upset before leaving the pub because he had been ignored by a lady and threatened by a man who said he'd been interested in his girlfriend."

Mr. Cox said the US Navy would pay the damage bill of $5,591.95 now and added that the bill for damage to the ambulance, once known, should also be paid by them.

Allgeier said: "I apologise to the community and I'm extremely ashamed of myself."

RESTING WITH NIGHT TRAIN

A man who was "resting" on a bench until it was time to go to work was told if he came back to Magistrates Court he'd be sorry.

Milton Eve was given a six month conditional discharge when he admitted wandering abroad.

Sgt. Peter Giles, prosecuting, said police found Eve, 37, sleeping on a bench on the playing field at Harrington Sound Primary School at 2:30 yesterday morning.

Eve, who works as a caddie at Mid Ocean Golf Club, said: "I was resting there until I was to go to my job. I was drinking my Night Train (red wine) to make my skin brown."

Acting Senior Magistrate the Wor. Ephraim Georges warned him: "If you come back here before Christmas you'll be sorry."

GOING HOME TO HIDE

A Devonshire man yesterday told a court he would make sure he went directly home and hide inside after finishing work so he would not "get pulled apart" by police.

Stephen Perinchief admitted having 26 milligrams of cannabis, and obstructing police when he appeared in Magistrates Court.

Thirty-nine-year-old Perinchief was approached by police on Court Street shortly after 3.30 p.m. on December 4 last year.

He jumped into the car and tried to lock his car, Insp. Peter Duffy, prosecuting, said.

Perinchief admitted having the drug, but said he was already in the car and made no attempt to lock the doors.

He said police had been "harassing" him for the past six months.

"They've taken my shoes off in the rain," he said. "They've taken my pants off at street corners.

"I want to get this over with and then I'll go home and hide after I knock off so I don't get pulled apart anymore."

The Wor. Will Francis fined him $75 for having the drug, and $100 for obstructing officers.

HIS WIFE WAS THE JUDGE

A St. George's man who said a "sudden change of atmosphere" was responsible for his drunkenness, was given a six month conditional discharge when he appeared in Magistrates Court yesterday.

Percival Pearman, 53, was found lying face down on the sidewalk on Water Street in St. George's at 8.55 p.m. Monday. His speech was unintelligible and he was unable to stand.

"I quite agree with the sentence, but I wasn't drunk when I left the bar," Pearman said.

"It was all the fault of certain elements. This sort of thing can happen when you go from the relaxed atmosphere of a bar into the outside air.

"I'm paying the price," he said, pointing to his cast. "When I fell I broke my arm. You don't really need to sentence me—my wife's done that job for you."

"You'd better not let people know where this 'bad air' is," Magistrate the Wor. Granville Cox told him. "They might go there and get drunk cheap."

LETTERS TO THE EDITOR

HOLDING HIS OWN

Dear Sir,

One must surely feel sorry for the rookie MP who in the House of Commons remained totally silent during lengthy debates on Agriculture and Finance but when the topic was changed to the Water Supply, rose to his feet and announced to all and sundry (over the BBC!): "I know nothing about Agriculture or Finance but when it comes to water, I can hold my own.

Moya Boyd
Somerset

ON THE FERRY

Dear Sir,

One morning, a week or ten days ago, I was waiting at the dock across from Hamilton for the ferry. As I waited I noticed a motorbike parked by the steps and thought what a splendid way to go to work!

When the ferry came, one of the crew on-loaded the motorbike.

I was enjoying the trip when the ferry slowed down out in the harbour. Two of the crew opened the gates and, with no further ado, ran the motorbike overboard, closed the gates and we proceeded on the run to Hamilton.

I sat there with my mouth open, too amazed to say a word. Is there an explanation?"

Jane Grimason
Bedford, New York

THAT'S BAROQUE, NOT ROCK

Dear Sir,

May I, on behalf of the Bermuda Festival, thank you for the full account of its 1989 programme published in The Royal Gazette. But may I also correct one inaccuracy.

Your account quoted me as saying that John Wallace "...normally plays rock type music with well known British symphony orchestras..." My tongue may have slipped, or I may have spoken indistinctly. In any case, what he normally plays is 'baroque' music; and I should not want your readers to be misled into expecting otherwise.

Peter Lloyd

FAST TIMES AT TCD

Dear Sir,

Through the medium of your paper I would like to point out to Mr. T.W. Richardson one small mistake that was made at the end of his letter regarding the ladies of the TCD [Bermuda's Motor Vehicle Department] that was published today.

In his last paragraph, Mr. Richardson states that if the ladies were in the TCD building when it caught fire, the fire would be extinguished and damages repaired before they reached the exit doors.

Obviously, Mr. Richardson has never been at the TCD at 5 p.m. to witness the miracle of resurrection. When one is "fortunate" enough to witness the daily track meet at this hour, I am sure that numerous bets are placed on our TCD "athletes" in their quest for Olympic gold.

NEXT!

City of Hamilton

FOR THE RECORD

A photo caption in yesterday's newspaper incorrectly reported Government received a $50,000 grant from the Menuhin Foundation Trustees. The money was in fact given by Government to the Foundation.

QUOTE OF THE DAY

Mr. Austin Thomas on the Hon. Ann Cartwright DeCouto, Minister of Health and Social Services:

"Last Friday she took an hour and a quarter to lay out the recommendations of the report. As she got down at the end of her speech, I observed her hands were shaking. No sooner had the Member got through than she took a box of cigarettes out of her purse and made for the door.

"What I am saying is that the Hon. Member is addicted.

"We must endeavour not to be examples of the problem we are trying to address."

'DON'T WORRY ABOUT THE GUNFIRE, MADAM. IT'S PEOP
BOOM!
BAM!
CRACK!
BING!
BANG!
BANG!
BOOM!
BOOM!
BANG!
BANG!
(THE TRIATHLON, OVERTIME BAN, FARE AND PRICE INCREA

ERYWHERE, SHOOTING THEMSELVES IN THE FOOT...'
M! BAM! BANG! CRACK! BANG!
COME
O
MUDA
Peter Woolcock
IRONG ATTITUDES—THE LIST GOES ON, DOESN'T IT?)

Bermuda Inc.

UNTIL RECENTLY, Bermuda's economy has adapted exceedingly well to change. It had to if the population was to survive. Everything from tobacco to pearl diving was tried in the early 1600s, supplanted by boat building which took off towards the latter part of the century. Guns and ammunition were a hot commodity during the American Civil War.

Later, vegetables of both an exotic and essential nature were exported to the United States. And, of course, the famous Bermuda onion was grown here, becoming immensely popular and profitable until this trade was destroyed by an unscrupulous Texan. The scoundrel took some of the onion seeds back to his home state, renamed his farm "Bermuda," and promptly began marketing his own "Bermuda onions." Shocking when you think about it. Why, it's akin to stealing the name *Bermuda shorts* for commercial gain.

It was inevitable given the limited space on which to grow things, not to mention the growing demands of the large country to the west, that agriculture wasn't going to be a viable industry forever. As agriculture gradually declined throughout the early 1900s, tourism took over as Bermuda's main source of income. With the financial assistance of the Furness Withy Shipping Company which supplied its passengers as guests, hotels were built at Mid Ocean and Castle Harbour to cater to well-heeled patrons from the east coast of the United States, who at the time thought of Bermuda as solely a winter resort. When the daughter of Queen Victoria, Princess Louise, graced the island with her presence, the die was cast, and others soon ventured regularly to this newfound oasis a few hundred miles off the coast of North Carolina, away from the cold and misery of a long and dreary American winter. Writer Mark Twain always remembered with great joy his sojourns down to the public washrooms on Warwick Long Bay, surrounded by tall grass and secret sand dunes. "Everyone is so friendly," he said wistfully in his later years.

Tourism is now the main income earner for the island. It has also become a bit of an obsession. Charts, graphs, and incessant newspaper articles record air and cruise ship manifests by the week, month, quarter, season, and year and are exhaustively analyzed. "This month's arrival figures are .000003512% down from the same time last year but up .000005366% from the previous month, mainly because a diverted planeload of passengers arrived from Barbuda last Tuesday after an engine failed on an American Airlines flight to New York . . . " and so on.

Lately, tourism figures are most discouraging and show little sign of changing in the immediate future. While cruise ship arrivals are up, air arrivals are down significantly from their peak.

And cruise ship passengers don't spend nearly as much as their jet-setting cousins. Maybe a few tee shirts or a key chain, then it's a marathon race back to the ship for a free lunch courtesy of the *Dreamward*.

This change in caliber of visitors may account for the decline in fortune of many Front Street merchants. At one time, elegant shops such as Trimingham's offered an array of excellent clothing and unique merchandise from around the world. Now the selection is about as stimulating as an evening with Tori Spelling.

Times have changed, which perplexes Bermudians greatly. They cannot understand why every single person in the universe is not aching to return again and again to pay $400 per night for a "deluxe" room in a "five star" hotel, which in most cases is anything but deluxe or five star, and where most members of staff are far more interested in yesterday's episode of *The Young and the Restless* than responding to your twenty-five calls for an ironing board.

Things weren't always so. Once upon a time a couple might have sailed to Bermuda for their honeymoon, fallen in love with the scenery and sincere natives, and made an annual trek to the island once a year for the rest of their natural lives. It was not unusual for people to never go anywhere else on vacation. But those were the heady sixties, seventies, and eighties when it must have seemed to islanders as if the good days would never end.

But they did.

You know those enticing ad campaigns I mentioned on television and in the magazines proclaiming the friendliness of Bermudians? Their warmth and charm? Their eagerness to serve? Well, there's a slight problem. Those Bermudians are all dead.

Well, practically. Like aging veterans from World War II, those remaining stalwarts who once truly loved to serve and considered paying tourists a gift from God are fast disappearing, to be replaced by their children and grandchildren who are more materialistic and far less inclined to attend to the needs of others. They also do not need the money quite so badly. It's as though the entire country is living in a time warp, refusing to believe that they must change course immediately if they are to maintain their heady economic accomplishments and lifestyle.

The Minister of Tourism, the Hon. C. V. (Jim) Woolridge, is no help, either. He should send his CV out for another job. He's been fired from his post more times than George Jetson and Fred Flintstone combined. Jim believes that the best way to improve tourism is for him and a legion of department employees to fly around the globe with a bunch of goons called gombeys in bargain basement costumes (for some bizarre reason, Bermuda's national symbol), flying first class, staying in the finest hotels and swanning around at promotional black-tie dinners.

More often than not when you see him in promotional television campaigns, he doesn't even bother to iron his wrinkled Bermuda shorts. Like his ideas to increase tourism, you can practically smell his stale underwear through the television screen.

To me, he is the proverbial wolf in sheep's clothing. I once saw a photograph of him surrounded by a group of schoolchildren. He looked as if he was about to eat one of them for his dinner. The result of all this strenuous activity on the part of Mr. Woolridge and a host of other curious looking creatures who work under him, is, understandably enough, a firm drop in tourism income. Now the government has resorted to subsidizing airlines in order to persuade them to start up service to the island, as is the case with the German airline Condor.

Because of changing attitudes amongst islanders, vacationers seeking old-fashioned island hospitality now find rude, obnoxious locals who are working feverishly on a scheme to somehow collect tourists' money without actually having to provide them with anything in return. It's a terrific idea and very cost effective. There is just one problem: it won't work. But don't try and explain this to most Bermudians working in the service industry. They can be as bullheaded as male sea lions during mating season.

Obtaining permission to enter Bermuda and spend your hard-earned money to support the economy can be a trip in itself. The government only wants you if you are rich, and they have no hesitation in saying so openly. To reside here for more than three weeks requires special permission from immigration. If you want to winter, you will need either a work permit or a financial statement proving you are self-sufficient or, failing that, a resident who will agree in writing to take responsibility for you while you are on the island.

Don't ever fall in love while you are off the island and expect to bring him or her back without the benefit of a marriage certificate. Immigration takes a very dim view of this practice. They are quite frank about it at times: Marry the person within the next few weeks or he/she must leave! Ah democracies, aren't they splendid?

Being of average means is practically a crime in itself. You don't stand a chance of being allowed to actually reside permanently unless you can prove you have assets totalling a million dollars or more, and even then it's iffy. Quite frankly, government would prefer that you go somewhere else, like Disneyland, Blackpool, or Bangor, Maine, where they are better equipped to cater to plebeian tastes.

Those tourists who do pass muster and receive divine permission to help support the economy are a source of enormous humor for locals. The sight of mopeds careening off roundabouts into oleander bushes is terribly funny as long as no one is seriously hurt. To me, it's positively inane to rent out scooters to elderly visitors who cannot drive motorcars back home let alone motorbikes on the wrong side of the road in as treacherous a terrain as this. But rarely is the point raised except after a particularly gruesome crash involving an elderly or honeymoon couple.

As beautiful a spot as this is, you must always remember that this is "Bermuda Incorporated" and the almighty dollar rules. The current Minister of Finance, Dr. David Saul, a man whose hunger for the limelight would make Madonna blush, actually declared this on television not so long ago. No room to consider safety. Restrictions on scooter rentals might eat into the revenue being earned by an important citizen.

But as I said, tourists on bikes have their humorous moments. The sight of them staggering out of Hamilton pubs, attempting to manoeuvre their mopeds down Front Street back to their hotels is wonderful, free entertainment. Often, regrettably, they do not make it home in one piece. There are so many scooter accidents involving tourists that I am told at one time the government placed a sign in the arrivals terminal of the airport stating the number of accidents to date, in an attempt to forewarn people of the dangers of riding a bike.

Driving a car can also be hazardous to your health if you happen to own one. Not a day goes by that you don't receive a jolt of some kind or other. The speed limit of 20 mph is deceiving. Doesn't it sound slow and safe? Uh-huh. The only snag is that nobody obeys it or any rules of the road for that matter. Ask a friend to tell you where you can pass another vehicle and where you can't and they will be hard pressed to answer. I couldn't. The answer seems to be *anywhere*. Blind corners are preferred spots.

One complaint you hear over and over nowadays from tourists is how expensive it is to vacation in Bermuda, to the point that locals rank nationalities according to their cheapness. Canadians are at the top of the list followed by the British in second place and the Americans in third. Germans and visitors from Japan are considered generous, but unfortunately, they do not come here in vast numbers. They are much more quality conscious when they travel, and air connections are not the best beyond North America.

From my own experience, it is the Bermudians who are the cheapskates. Why, they make Ebenezer Scrooge look like Santa Claus in comparison. The richer they are, the cheaper they are. Every Wednesday, if you are up early enough, you will see all the multimillionaires rushing off to the supermarket in their cars at breakneck speed because Wednesday is the hallowed "5 percent off day." Nothing they like better than a good battle in the produce aisle and grocery-cart gridlock in order to save a few bucks.

For some unknown reason, many male tourists are under the impression that to really look like a native and blend in, they have to dash off to Trimingham's or Smith's or A. S. Cooper's at the first opportunity and purchase the most garish sports jacket and Bermuda shorts they can find. I'm talking loud colors here. Red, orange, purple, pink, yellow, lime green—the brighter the better.

Granted, it's cool to look tropical, but some of the getups I have seen tourists in would have made Liberace cringe. Picture for a moment, if you will, an elderly Japanese businessman, usually the epitome of conservative taste 358 days of the year, walking down the street on his way to dinner dressed in the Bermudian equivalent of J.J. in *Good Times*. Now imagine hundreds of Japanese, Canadians and American men all dressed in similar fashion. It's hysterical. They think they look *marvelous, darling*. They actually look silly. All the shops know they look silly. All the residents know they look silly.

Bermudian men wouldn't be caught dead in such attire. They prefer more tasteful shades. Once tourists get their outfits back home to Missouri, those jackets never see the light of day again. Walk down any street in Middle America dressed like that and chances are excellent you will be surrounded by a group of five year olds and beaten to within an inch of your life.

The beach is another place to tourist watch between November and early May. Why? Because the only ones on it are tourists. Most Bermudians do not swim in the ocean or unheated pools during the winter under any circumstances even though the water is more than comfortable enough. How tourists don swimming trunks and frolic in the ocean under 75 degrees is completely beyond them.

Understandably, weather is important, perhaps more important than in places that do not rely on tourism for their survival. Once you have lived here for a year, you quickly learn that just because the sky is cloudless and blue at 8 a.m. when you leave for work is no guarantee it will be that way in half an hour's time, especially in the winter. Many a visitor can be spotted cycling back to their hotel from the other end of the island in torrential rain dressed only in shorts and tee shirt, drenched to the skin and looking miserably dejected.

Never have I seen the weather change as rapidly. Never have I heard people discuss the subject so much. It's as though some tourists actually believe that if they pester you enough, you can influence the heavens. "YES. ALL RIGHT! I'LL RING JESUS TONIGHT AND PLACE YOUR ORDER!"

Now I must tell you the story of author and resident, Tracey Caswell, lest I forget.

Tracey is a Canadian who married a Bermudian and came to live here some years ago. She is the perfect example of someone who has been on the island too long. (She is also so cheap she refuses to plug in her air conditioner, but that's another story.) Tracey, poor dear, had so little to occupy her time on the island while her hubby was at work all day that she became completely absorbed—no, *obsessed* is the right word—with moisture. Every moment of every day was taken up with thoughts of moist air, moist crackers, moist bed linens.

She finally felt compelled to write a book to warn other unsuspecting women planning to move to the isles of sun; a manual on how she personally coped with her newfound humid life a thousand miles from her homeland. The book is called *Tea with Tracey*. I suggest you buy a copy. It is more like *Moisture with Tracey*. The very first line in the very first chapter of her book: "Humidity is the instigator of a zillion problems." Her second line: "I blame everything on humidity." In fact, the whole first chapter is devoted to wetness—in the air, in her blankets, in her hair. Title of Chapter two: *The Enemy Within*. You guessed it. Mildew.

Tracey, dear, they're having a sale at Trimingham's on 100 percent cool cotton straightjackets next week. Be there.

Please don't end up like Tracey Caswell. Leave after a year or two while you still have your sanity.

To be fair to poor Tracey, the weather can be the pits. After three decades of bountiful tourism on the island, word is finally getting back to the mainland: visit Bermuda in the winter at your own peril. To counter this, hotels try and attract people with what they call a "temperature guarantee." If the temperature does not reach 68 degrees on any given day, then participating hotels and businesses offer discounts up to 20 percent. This has proven popular with those skinflint Canadians, but as you'd expect, there is much suspicion when the paper reports the temperature "reached 69 degrees yesterday" when it felt more like 65.

That said, you can still have a damn good time here if you come with the right attitude and don't despair if it isn't sunny and hot every day of your stay. Chances are it won't be. A good steaming bowl of Bermuda fish chowder and copious quantities of Dark 'n Stormies (Gosling's dark rum mixed with ginger beer) at the local pub should return even Connie Francis to high spirits.

A word or two of warning, however, should you venture into Hamilton after dark. Watch out for those gangsters with guns chasing innocent vacationers into Hamilton Harbor and always be mindful of that popular song you may have heard over cocktails back at your hotel.

Bermuda is another world.

WOMAN MUGS MALE VISITOR

A knife-wielding woman mugger propositioned a male tourist on Richmond Road, and then robbed him Thursday night, police say.

The man, a 31 year old visitor from Flushing, New York, told police he was walking along Richmond Road when a woman approached him, asked directions and then propositioned him.

When he declined, she pulled a knife and robbed him of his wallet before riding away on a scooter.

The wallet contained $30 in cash, plus credit cards.

Police believe the culprit is a black woman, about five feet four, who spoke in a high pitched voice and wore a crash helmet and visor.

CARTS ROW AT AIRPORT

The new departure terminal at the airport opened yesterday amid controversy over the positioning of luggage carts.

And in the meantime no luggage carts are available for passengers, many of whom are forced to carry their bags from the entrance of the terminal to the baggage area—a considerably further distance than in the old terminal building.

"It's a lot of carrying," said Mrs. Mett Nilsen, who was with her two children, age three and 15 months, en route to Norway yesterday.

The dispute is between government and the Sky Tops—Airport porters—who currently carry passengers' luggage from the sidewalk of the departure terminal to the airline check-in counters.

It centres on whether the carts should be positioned on the sidewalk outside the terminal building, or whether they should be available only after passengers check-in with the airline.

Shop steward and Sky Top Mr. Edmund Curtis, who is involved with the negotiations, said talks—which included wage negotiations—are going into their sixth month. He said the positioning of the luggage carts is the only outstanding issue.

"It would look like a supermarket," he said. "We don't need that. It's not Bermuda's image."

He said the Sky Tops are holding firm on the issue, and they are optimistic about the outcome. "Hopefully we will settle this soon," he said.

Mr. Graeme Seaton, Pan Am manager, said the new terminal was designed around the cart concept and noted the distances are much greater than in the old terminal.

"I think a satisfactory agreement can be reached with the Sky Tops to have the carts in a restricted area," he said.

GOLF BALL INCIDENT AT AIRPORT

Independent Senator Joe Johnson fired off a string of complaints about Bermuda Customs during the Motion to Adjourn in the Senate.

Sen. Johnson said he made several observations as he passed through Customs after arriving at the Civil Air Terminal from Boston.

He said he witnessed a tourist being told he would have to pay more than $300 duty on a box containing 40 dozen golf balls intended for a group of visitors.

Sen. Johnson said he overheard a customs officer tell the tourist that even though the golf balls were not for sale he had to understand that maybe they would be lost and sold to a Bermudian.

"We spend thousands encouraging tourists to come here and major hotels have repeatedly stated they depend on group business to a large extent . . . there should be some discretion," Sen. Johnson said.

He added the irony was that if the tourist had taken the golf balls out of the package and distributed them to the people in his tour group, he would not have had to pay anything.

ABRUPT HALT TO BERMUDA HOLIDAY

A Canadian tourist's holiday in Bermuda came to an abrupt halt last Friday when he was arrested for masturbating in front of a police officer.

Lyle Watling, 32, pleaded guilty in Magistrates Court yesterday to committing an indecent act in a Warwick Long Bay washroom at about 5.30 p.m.

Police Sgt. Alan Cleave, prosecuting, said a plain clothes police officer entered the washroom. He was followed moments later by Watling, who had been seen a few minutes earlier leaving the washroom.

In a toilet stall, the police officer looked up to see Watling peering over the partition wall apparently masturbating.

Sgt. Cleave said the officer then left his stall and opened Watling's to see that the man was masturbating. Watling was then arrested.

Lawyer Mr. Kim White said Watling was embarrassed by the incident and planned to leave the island today.

Senior Magistrate the Wor. Granville Cox fined Watling $200 and suggested that the washroom's partition wall be raised.

VISITOR IN INTENSIVE CARE

A visitor from England was still in serious condition in hospital intensive care last night, after he collided with a tree while driving his livery cycle on Friday night.

Mr. Kevin May is believed to have suffered a fractured skull and had two operations.

Officials at the King Edward VII Memorial Hospital said he was in serious condition last night in the intensive care unit.

The 35 year old man from Reading, England, had been driving east on Middle Road in Devonshire about 11.45 p.m. on Friday when he collided with the tree, said police spokesperson Insp. Roger Sherratt.

VISITOR DIES

A tourist searching for a golf ball at the Marriott Castle Harbour's course plummeted to his death yesterday, after he slipped and fell over a cliff.

Police spokesman, Sgt. John Instone, said Mr. Bryan C. Bruemmer, 64, of Wilmette, Illinois, was playing golf when he slipped near the eighteenth tee and fell over a cliff estimated to be 15 feet high.

Mr. Bruemmer suffered serious head injuries and was pronounced dead on arrival at [the hospital]. The accident occurred just before 3.30 p.m.

Marriott's Resident Manager, Mr. Charles Clist, said he was still "trying to get to the bottom of the matter," when contacted early last evening.

UNEXPECTED SWIM IN THE HARBOUR

A woman went for an unexpected swim on Wednesday after she lost control of her cycle and drove it off the dock and into the water at Ordinance Island in St. George's.

The visitor, 46 year old Evangeline Sadler, suffered only minor injuries as a result of the mishap.

Another visitor was not so lucky however, when she lost control of her cycle and hit a wall about 6.25 p.m. later that same day.

STARTING OFF ON WRONG FOOT

The bride and her mother went on a shoplifting spree just days after a Bermuda wedding, Magistrates Court heard yesterday.

Together they raided nine Hamilton shops, stealing 70 items worth some $1,600.

Yesterday, the pair, both Sri Lankans, were remanded on bail for social inquiry reports before Senior Magistrate the Wor. Will Francis decides what punishment to give them.

Sudharshini Ponniah, 22, of Ord Road, Warwick, and her mother Monica Chelliah, 43, both pleaded guilty to stealing goods from Marks and Spencer, Masters, Smith's, the Treasure Chest, and Trimingham's. They asked for offences at Davidson's of Bermuda, the Phoenix, Calypso and Bananas to be taken into consideration.

All the thefts took place on the same day, September 25, shortly after Ponniah's marriage.

Miss Patricia Harvey, in mitigation said Chelliah had led her daughter astray because she wanted souvenirs to take back as gifts to her homeland. Her husband, who works out of Sri Lanka, was due to send her money but it didn't turn up, she said.

Miss Harvey asked for Chelliah to be dealt with immediately so she could return home while a social inquiry report should be ordered on her daughter. But Insp. Duffy objected saying both should be dealt with equally and pointing out the danger that Ponniah could retract her admission once her mother was off the island.

Mr. Francis agreed, despite Miss Harvey's plea that Chelliah— who appeared in court wearing her sari—had only 30 pounds to her name.

AMERICAN WRITER HAD A DIFFICULT TIME IN PARADISE

Bermuda's friendly reputation has received a hefty dent from an American newspaper writer.

But the people alleged to have upset *Atlanta Constitution* columnist Lewis Grizzard cannot understand the fuss.

"I am certainly not calling him a liar, but these things seem very out of character," said Director of Tourism Mr. Gary Phillips.

Mr. Grizzard described Bermuda as paradise in his column, but said he was having a difficult time with Bermudians (sic).

"Many of the locals, most of whom make their living off the tourist trade, have no use for tourists," he claimed.

In particular he named the Mid Ocean Golf Club and the Sonesta Beach as places where he had had trouble. He said he was turned away from the golf club because his shorts were too short and then after he had bought a longer "ugly" pair, the starter "snapped" at him that he couldn't have a cart.

At the hotel, he claimed the night doorman became angry when he called for a cab. "You don't say 'taxi', I say 'taxi'," the doorman is alleged to have "spat" at him.

He also said a taxi driver was rude to him because he wanted to take a cup into his cab.

"Walking in Bermuda is very dangerous," added Mr. Grizzard. "If you are a Bermudian and you run over a tourist, you get a free ticket to the cricket matches or some other valuable premium." He concluded his column: "I'm leaving Bermuda today. When my plane is safely airborne, I am going to turn back and give Bermuda a well-known gesture. The beauty here just ain't worth the bother."

COMPLAINING VISITOR IS TO GET A MANAGER'S LETTER

Cambridge Beaches' manager Sen. Mike Winfield will contact a dissatisfied customer who asked that his refund for an aborted stay there be given to a local charity.

"I'll be writing to the gentleman directly," Sen. Winfield said ·yesterday. "There are variances as to what he says and what happened.

"Any problems of this type I deal with directly and personally."

Sen. Winfield was responding to a letter to the Editor printed in Tuesday's *Royal Gazette* from Mr. John Henry Parkin, who booked five days at the Somerset cottage colony in April.

Mr. Parkin and his wife refused to stay at Cambridge Beaches after finding their room "tatty, dirty inside and out, damp and extremely smelly . . . "

In addition, he said there were no porters available to take their bags—a situation resulting in the couple being taken in the gardener's truck.

"We sat in the front with all the gardening implements and my wife's new dress was covered in dirt," Mr. Parkin wrote.

The disappointed couple were given another room which, after a 20-minute search, they found. It was "worse than the first one," he wrote.

Mr. Parkin said he did not want the money back but that it should be donated to a local charity named by the Editor of *The Royal Gazette.*

Yesterday, Sen. Winfield said his cottage colony was "continuing to do a good job."

"We'll not rest on our laurels and we will correct anything we're doing wrong."

FRIENDLY BERMUDIANS 'A FICTION'

The notion that Bermudians are the friendliest people in the world is "a fiction," Independent MP Mr. Harry Viera charged yesterday.

"And we've got to start doing something about it," Mr. Viera said.

Speaking in Somerset at a public forum on Bermuda's tourism industry before Government's Commission on Competitiveness, Mr. Viera said the less than warm welcome visitors often receive begins at the airport.

"I've had better receptions in Prague when it was under the communists," the Southampton West MP told about 40 people who turned out at St. James' Church Hall.

Bermudians who travel anywhere from Australia to the Carolinas notice their hosts there "really knock themselves out," Mr. Viera said.

And while most Bermudians are still charismatic and friendly, "there is a substantial number who are not, and unfortunately a great many of them are working in the civil service."

He related complaints he received from visitors about rudeness at the hands of a clerk who sold ferry tickets.

But he also cited the private sector, from taxi drivers to the waiter who "doesn't drop the soup in your lap . . . but it's almost impossible in some cases to get a 'thank you,' or 'you're welcome'."

AN 'ISLAND OF STRESS'

Bermuda is definitely an island of stress, according to psychologist and traumatic stress specialist Ms. Christine Stubbs.

Ms. Stubbs, who is travelling to China next week to see how Orientals cope with traumatic stress, said Bermudians were highly stressed because of the island's size—22 miles long and less than two miles wide.

And she said living with parents or siblings suffering from alcoholism, drug addiction or mental illness is the major cause of traumatic stress in Bermuda's youngsters.

"I see a lot of traumatic stress here," she said. "The population is extremely vulnerable to stress because it is so small and there is no way to just get in your car and drive away."

Symptoms of traumatic stress in children include personality changes, headaches, sleeping problems, bed wetting, nightmares and poor performance in school, she said.

And highly stressed adults who do not get professional help may end up suffering stress-related diseases such as cancer and heart disease, she warned.

Ms. Stubbs, who was educated at Harvard University and is a guidance counsellor at Warwick Academy, said a lot of the problems with teenagers today are stress related.

"Violence in the home has a severe impact on young children. It is inevitable that stress will have an impact later on. That is one of the reasons why so many young Bermudian men become self destructive. They tend to do dangerous things to themselves," she said.

GUNMEN DROVE VISITOR INTO HARBOUR

A 25-year-old visitor took to the water when he thought gunmen were chasing him through Hamilton.

The only problem was, he chose the Government boat 'Friendship' to make his escape, untying it and drifting out into the Harbour.

Insp. Peter Duffy told Magistrates Court yesterday that police spotted the tender and discovered Illinois man Barry Immesoete on board.

"I had no choice," he told officers in a slurred voice. "They were shooting at me. Don't you see the bullet holes in the deck?"

Immesoete had apparently been drinking heavily, said Insp. Duffy.

Immesoete, on honeymoon with his wife, admitted removing the boat on Saturday night and was fined $100.

Miss Elizabeth Christopher, defending, said Immesoete had been chased by other tourists. He told police he was being shot at so they would take him seriously, she said.

SURPRISE! YOU'RE ON YOUR WAY TO COURT

When American Nicholas Pattakos was swept off his feet by his romantic girlfriend, he landed in a Bermuda courtroom.

Back in New York last Friday, she picked him up and drove him off on a surprise birthday trip, leaving him guessing where they were headed.

And when he realized they were boarding a flight to Bermuda, he was so carried away he forgot one small thing—the cannabis in his jeans pocket.

In Magistrates Court yesterday Pattakos admitted having 4.20 grams of cannabis, with cigarette papers, when he arrived at the Civil Air Terminal. Acting Senior Magistrate the Wor. John Judge fined him $450.

Pattakos, who celebrated his 29th birthday on the island, told the court: "My fiancée took me to Bermuda as a surprise. She took me for a ride and said 'I'm not going to tell where you're going until we get there.'

"We arrived at Newark airport, and when we got to the gate that was when I realized I was going to Bermuda. I forgot I had the cannabis.

"I thought we were going to Florida. If I had known I was going abroad I would not have brought it."

REPORTER'S NOTEBOOK

Our last 'Notebook's' revelation, that Bill Clinton's daughter was conceived in Bermuda, caused a few ripplings across the water.

We reported comments made by the President to a Bermudian couple touring the White House.

"Hillary and I are fond of Bermuda," he said. "In fact, Chelsea was conceived at Horizons [Hotel]."

A New York Post gossip writer this week picked up the story, which he reported with a glowing description of Bermuda as a "tropical island paradise."

He wondered if Horizons would put up a plaque saying "Bill Clinton slept here."

The story also reached John MacArthur, publisher of Harper's, the oldest continually-published magazine in America. His office called the 'Notebook,' urgently requesting a fax of the original piece.

"It's for his own personal use," an aide said mysteriously.

CRUISE OFFICIALS EMBARRASSED OVER MISTAKE IN BROCHURE

Chandris Celebrity Cruise Lines is promoting voyages to Bermuda with a picture of a child wearing a T-shirt proclaiming "It's Better in the Bahamas."

The picture runs on page 13 of a glossy new brochure produced by the company to promote its 1990 line of cruises on the purpose-built MV Horizon and the by-then refurbished SS Meridian cruise ships.

On a two-page spread touting the "Fine Art of Cruising" the picture runs between advice on money matters in Bermuda—most shops accept both US and Canadian currency, the brochure says—and a segment on "etiquette, Bermuda Style."

The picture shows a young child holding up the T-shirt promoting Bermuda's competition, while a man and woman look on adoringly.

Yesterday, Chandris' agent in Bermuda, Meyer Agencies president Mr. Henry Hayward said he had notified Chandris' head office of the mistake.

"They're not pleased about it—more than a million of those brochures have gone out to all their marketing offices and all the travel agents," Mr. Hayward said. "They must be very embarrassed by this."

COMPANY REPLACES SOCKS AFTER A MERE 48-YEAR GAP

It took him 48 years, but Mr. Calvin Fulenwider of Colorado finally decided a pair of Argyle socks he bought at H.A. & E. Smith's Ltd. during the Second World War just didn't become him.

So last Thursday he whipped back in and had them replaced.

"I saw they were size 12 and too big for him anyway, so I gave him a nice size 11 & a half," drawled veteran mens' wear assistant Mr. Harris Flood.

Mr. Fulenwider bought the socks when he was a US serviceman stationed at the Inverurie in 1942.

For reasons even he isn't sure of, the socks were never worn, but remained in a plastic bag at the bottom of various wardrobes for half a century.

Packing for his first trip back to the island since his young soldiering days, Mr. Fulenwider discovered the socks and decided to bring them along.

Mr. Flood said Mr. Fulenwider's socks would have cost about 12 shillings and sixpence in 1942.

The latest line in Argyle socks which he gave Mr. Fulenwider as a replacement cost $33.

"The old ones are still perfect, you could get some good wear out of them," Mr. Flood said.

Mr. Flood, who has been with Smith's since 1958, admitted the half century delay in the exchange was a little unusual.

But he has another customer who bought a pair of cashmere socks a couple of decades ago who has come back to Bermuda 18 times, still wearing those same socks.

"I guess he must have good feet," Mr. Flood said. "I've lived half my life in here. You see these things."

THE TRIBULATIONS OF LOCAL BEAUTY CONTESTS

Miss Bermuda Islands boss Mr. Terry Smith is to meet the Hon. Pamela Gordon, one of the show judges, today in the hope of satisfying her the show was run fairly.

Sen. Gordon, Minister for Youth, Sport and Recreation, has asked to see proof that scores were accurately entered into the show computer.

Angry contestants in the show have attacked the system of judging, and have started legal moves against Mr. Smith.

The record shows the catwalk often leads to a trail of anger and bitterness:

• 1973—Judy Richards, Miss Bermuda, launches an appeal after announcing she has nothing to wear for the Miss World show.

- 1975—Cindy Adams, Miss Tourism, hears politics robbed her of the Miss Tourism International title.
- 1977—Connie Frith, Miss Bermuda, falls ill while in the Dominican Republic for Miss Universe.
- 1978—Valerie Akinstall, Miss Hotels, quits after three months, tired and frustrated.
- 1979—Gina Swainson, Miss Bermuda, is runner-up in the Miss Universe show and says she was treated like a piece of meat. A few months later, she wins Miss World in London.
- 1980—Arretta Furbert, Miss Tourism, tells of chaos and insults during a pageant in Trinidad, and attacks her local organizers. Jill Murphy, Miss Bermuda, quits Miss World saying the local committee is not interested. She is replaced by runner-up (Miss) Minks, who says once is enough.
- 1982—Heather Ross, Miss Bermuda, is arrested and jailed in England on cocaine charges.
- 1986—Suzanne Koren, Miss Photogenic, says she won Miss Bermuda on points but was cheated out of the title.
- 1987—Shelley Bascome, Miss Bermuda, loses the chance to compete in Miss World after the organizers discover they made a mistake on her age. First runner-up Donna Lee Ingham, Miss Tourism, is told she cannot go.
- 1989—Miss Ingham sues contest organizer Wentworth Christopher.
- 1990—Miss Ingham's contract was broken, Supreme Court rules. Mr. Christopher must pay her $26,000, says the judge.
- 1992—Dianna Mitchell is crowned Miss Bermuda Islands after a three-year lapse in the contest. Disappointed contestants start legal moves against organizer Terry Smith after allegations of fixing, unfair judging rules and exploitation.

DESPERATE BOYFRIEND FORCED MISS TOURISM'S PLANE BACK

A pining boyfriend forced ex-Miss Tourism Donna Lee Ingham to return to the island by phoning a bomb threat to Eastern Airlines, a court heard yesterday.

Anthony Smith—who wiped tears from his eyes as the case was heard—said he "panicked" when Ingham boarded Flight 806 to New Jersey still owing him $3,000.

Smith, of Bob's Valley, Sandy's Parish, admitted making the false statement. Senior Magistrate the Wor. Granville Cox released him on $500 bail to return to court in two weeks pending a social inquiry report.

Defence lawyer Mr. Julian Hall said the 26-year-old fisherman was driven by desperation to call in the bomb threat and force Ingham to come back to the island.

"He has been extremely distraught since the relationship ended a few weeks ago," Mr. Hall told the court. "It was a momentary aberration of folly on his part.

"He's been going through a most difficult time in his life. His actions were due to his state of distress. They will not be repeated."

Crown Counsel Mr. Brian Calhoun said Smith—who lives across the street from Ingham—followed her to the Airport on Wednesday afternoon because she still owed him the money.

He said Smith called the airline shortly after 1 p.m. when he saw Ingham board the flight bound for New Jersey.

"He told the supervisor at Eastern Airlines there was a bomb on Flight 806 that was to go off in one-half hour," Mr. Calhoun said.

He said the pilot returned to Bermuda 40 minutes after take-off and evacuated the plane, while fire trucks from Hamilton and

St. George's arrived at the scene. When no bomb was found, the passengers reboarded the aircraft and set off for New York after 3 p.m.

THE BEAUTY QUEEN WHO CANNOT RETURN HOME

She carried Bermuda's hopes in the Miss Universe contest. She was brought up on the island. And, of course, she found romance here as an eye-catching teenager.

But now blonde Andrea Sullivan faces a life cut off from her family, friends, and the island she calls home.

For the 22-year-old former Miss Bermuda 1991 has been told she is not a Bermudian.

Sadly, she has fallen through a crack in Bermuda's strict immigration rules.

Miss Sullivan, now studying law near London, came to Bermuda with her British parents when she was eight.

But to become a Bermudian she said she needed to have been here before her sixth birthday.

The bureaucratic block has split her from her family.

Nineteen-year-old sister, Kirsty, who arrived here as a five-year-old, escapes the immigration ruling.

And her father, divorced from his first wife, has married a Bermudian and expects eventually to apply successfully for status.

Her mother, too, has also remarried a Bermudian, and could return.

CLUBS TOO HEAVY, SAYS KILLER CADDY

A Mid Ocean Club caddy, who spent six years in jail for killing a man, threatened a visiting golfer because his golf bag was too heavy, a court heard yesterday.

And when the golfer failed to pay him the usual fee after 16 holes, Warren Smith ran off with his clubs as a "so-called fee."

Smith, of Collectors Hill, admitted using threatening behaviour when he appeared in Magistrates Court yesterday. He was sentenced to a day in jail but the Wor. John Judge considered the day Smith already spent in jail, and released him.

Smith, 39, told the court he did not mean any harm to Marriott's Castle Harbour guest Ernest Clarke, but could not carry his bag any further than the sixteenth hole during a game on March 22.

"I've been a caddy since I was 11-years-old and I never carried a bag that heavy in my life," Smith said. "I asked him why they were so heavy and he told me you couldn't get the clubs anymore. I don't know if he said they were expensive. But that didn't excite me."

I went 15 holes not asking for any money, but I was lagging behind. Every hole after the eleventh felt like I was going 18 every time. I had to lay off." *

Smith said he asked for his fee at the sixteenth hole, but was only given $13. He told the court the usual fee was $23 for a single bag and $40 for two.

"I just gave the money back," Smith said.

Clarke told the court Smith pushed him on his chest and told him he just got out of prison for murder.

"He said he would do it to me or kill me," Clarke said. "He took my clubs and started running away."

But Smith said he told him about his conviction because he "didn't want to make any trouble over the money." And he said he only took the clubs "as a so-called fee."

"I didn't make no argument or nothing about money," he said. "I didn't want to upset his game. I can't even go to Mid Ocean no more. I've never been in trouble at Mid Ocean in my life."

Smith was acquitted of murder, but convicted of a lesser charge of manslaughter in May, 1984 for his March, 1983 killing of Kenneth Eugene DeGraffe.

Smith told the Supreme Court that he hit DeGraffe over the head with an empty rum bottle in self-defence. DeGraffe died seven days later.

REPORTER'S NOTEBOOK

Ooops! Tourism Minister the Hon. C.V. (Jim) Woolridge suddenly found he needed to delve into his complete repertoire of verbal gymnastics during a few toe-curling moments at the XL Bermuda Open last weekend.

And, unfortunately, the desperate contortions left the Minister in a less than honourable position...firmly on his backside.

Mr. Woolridge's angst occurred during the award-giving ceremony at the end of a closely contested doubles final which saw Grant Connell and Todd Martin edge out Jason Stoltenberg and Brett Steven.

While handing over a runners-up cheque to Brett Steven, Mr. Woolridge bungled his lines with rare aplomb. For spectators watching in mounting embarrassment, it was truly a case of: Oh No! As Mr. Woolridge congratulated a Mr. Brett "Steinberger" on his performance.

And then, Oh, My Gosh! As the Minister, amid a smattering of nervous giggling from the crowd, attempted a hasty correction: "I mean, Mr. Brett Stern."

And finally, I Just Don't Believe It! As Mr. Woolridge, giving up the ghost, blurted out: "It doesn't matter what tag I put on a donkey, the money is still spendable!"

After getting the cheque, Steven trudged off court, his face a mixture of wonder and bewilderment.

"Funny place, Bermuda," would be a fair translation.

"See you, Mr. Steinberger!" one wag in the crowd cried out.

DISPUTE OVER $1.50 A WEEK

Hotel workers and other unionized workers are being asked to strike over what amounts to about a $1.50 a week difference in pay, the top bellman at the Sonesta Beach Hotel said last night.

Mr. Raymond Russell said workers should be aware the current dispute over a new hotel workers contract has more to do with power than significant pay issues.

"Mr (Ottiwell) Simmons is trying to impress on the people of Bermuda that hotel workers have been given a bad deal with the Hobgood award," he said.

"But in fact the Hobgood award is not out of line with previous contract settlements. Given the economic hard times the island is in, it's the hotels that should be screaming."

Mr. Russell, who has opposed Mr. Simmons' (union) leadership in the past, said a comparison of five hotel worker wage settlements since 1976 showed the Hobgood award gave similar raises.

"Why should hotel workers ruin their careers for $1.50 a week?" he asked. "I don't want to go on strike for $1.50 a week. It appears to me Mr. Simmons is just trying to maintain power in his fight against this Hobgood deal, not to find a realistic settlement for the workers."

'YOUR BLOWING UP THE REEF GOT US MORE U.S. MED
WONDERING IF YOU'D SEE YOUR WAY TO BLOWIN

Perot
NOT FOR
PRESIDENT

Peter Woolcock

FANS GO WILD IN EL SALVADOR

Crazed soccer fans unleashed a horrifying barrage of dead cats, iguanas, and firecrackers during Bermuda's crunch World Cup clash with El Salvador, according to a news report yesterday.

Bags of urine and human excrement were also hurled on to the pitch—some landing on spectators' heads.

Sunday's mayhem erupted in the cheapest seating section in Cuscatlan Stadium, tagged "Vietnam."

Boisterous fans have apparently turned the section into a free-fire zone.

Despite their team romping to a 4-1 victory over Bermuda on Sunday, fans went wild, the Associated Press (AP) agency reports.

One man, a self-appointed caretaker for a group of foreigners, crushed empty beer cans to biscuit size and flung them into the air over the crowd.

He told an AP reporter: "It was pretty calm today. You should be here sometime when we lose."

When Bermuda took the field, the players were greeted by thousands of fans chanting an obscene Spanish epithet.

Spectators tossed fist-sized chunks of ice and beer cans, some empty, some not.

According to AP, dead cats and iguanas were also flung by their tails into the crowd and onto the field.

And firecrackers the size of a man's arm were tossed from the top of the stands.

Some made it to the field, others fell short, as did large strings of firecrackers hurled at random into the crowd.

Bags of water flew as well, along with empty beer cans and bottles.

Later, as the bags of water gave out, bags of urine were tossed, claims AP.

In addition, small bags of human excrement landed on the field, or on the heads of cheap-seaters who arrived late and sat in the lower rows.

Throughout the match, shouts of "Hoo Hoo Hoo Hoo," the chant of a student guerrilla group, floated down over the crowd.

To enter the stadium locals were asked to pay 20 colones, about $2.50—approaching the daily minimum wage for a labourer.

And they certainly made sure they got the most for their money.

Regulars say knifings are not uncommon in the Vietnam section, and shootings happen from time to time.

Police stay clear of the area, and foreigners are warned they go at their own risk.

BERMUDIANS BE CAUTIOUS

Callers from overseas offering all-expenses paid holidays in exchange for the purchase of anti-drug bumper stickers may be operating a scam, police said yesterday.

And police issued an advisory telling the Island's residents to "adopt a cautious attitude to this type of call and be very wary about parting with their money under these circumstances."

Police say they have received several reports about the calls, which originate from an office in Utah and inform the listener that they have won a holiday worth several thousand dollars.

But to collect, they're told they must place a purchase order for between 100 and 300 bumper stickers which carry anti-drug messages. The bumper stickers cost $4.99 each, the listener is told, and payment must be received in the US within two business days.

Some Bermuda residents have also received a similar offer together with a sample sticker through the mail.

A Police spokesman said yesterday that they have no evidence to suggest any criminal activity in connection with the offer.

"It may prove to be nothing more than a type of sales pitch with which Bermudians are unfamiliar," said the spokesman. "But we are advising people to be cautious."

HE WANTED A GOOD VIEW

An American expatriate artist who wanted to see Hurricane Emily close up last Friday wound up taking an unwanted trip across Hamilton Harbour in a nearly-sunk boat.

"Had I thought about it, I wouldn't have done it," said Mr. Tom Burke, who arrived in Bermuda three months ago to take a job as art director at Advertising Associates Compton Ltd.

Having bicycled in early for work that day, Mr. Burke only learned Emily was on the way once at the office. The New Yorker had never seen a hurricane, and he wanted a good view.

"The idea of staying inside didn't appeal to me," he said. "I just waited until it started blowing then I went out into it."

So off he went to Albouy's Point for a ringside seat. On the way, struggling along Front Street, he was struck by a flying sign and other pieces of debris.

Once at Albouy's Point, the wind was so fierce he said he got stuck up against one of the railings and couldn't move.

"Picnic tables, boats—all manner of things went flying by," said Mr. Burke.

As the second wave of Emily began to drop off slightly, he noticed a loose boat, about 18 feet long, drift along. It was sunk up to the gunwales. Mr. Burke thought he could jump into the boat, grab the line, jump out and tie her up again.

He jumped in all right. And he got out too—about 20 minutes later on the other side of the Harbour!

"I felt a little foolish," said Mr. Burke. "It didn't make a lot of sense I guess. I didn't have time to leap back."

So he just hunkered down low and rode it out. The boat was "fairly sluggish" he said on account of it being full of water.

Said Mr. Burke: "It was just one of those bizarre things."

COURT TOLD OF SLEEPING TAXI DRIVER

A 40-year-old taxi driver, who crashed his taxi causing a passenger to break an ankle, was disqualified from driving for six months after being found guilty in Magistrates Court for driving without due care.

Alfred Matthews, of Berkeley Road, Pembroke, was also fined $120 for the offence on September 23, 1984, when he crashed his taxi into a stone wall, breaking an ankle of his passenger in the front seat.

Matthews claimed he was asleep in the passenger seat with someone else driving the car when the accident occurred. But testimony from passenger Morris Pringle contradicted that statement.

Pringle, 19, of Somerset, told Magistrate the Wor. Ephraim Georges that Matthews got lost, fell asleep and invited him to attend a party during the early morning ride from Crawl Hill to Scaur Hill where the accident occurred.

Pringle said that Matthews behaved very strangely throughout the fare, driving off the road several times.

He said Matthews took the South Shore route to Somerset but missed one corner and ended up driving down the Tribe Road toward Elbow Beach before realising his error.

At one point—passing some parked cars—Pringle said Matthews asked him if he would like to go to a party. But Pringle said he just wanted to go home.

Pringle told the court that Matthews drove on but "was falling asleep on and off." Just before the Southampton Princess, he said Matthews asked him if he could rest a while. Pringle, who said he wanted to get home safely, agreed and they stopped by the road for about five minutes.

When the taxi set off again all was well until Scaur Hill when the car slid into a tree.

"We both got out of the car but nothing was said between us," Pringle said. He then walked over the hill and caught another taxi which took him to his Heritage Road home.

Under questioning from Inspector David Chew, prosecuting, Pringle revealed that his ankle was broken in the crash.

Matthews maintained he had never seen Pringle before.

He told the court: "I was driving the taxi and was tired so I went to sleep at Crawl Hill in the passenger side. I took off my shoes."

He said he believed that someone then drove the car and smashed it. "The next thing I heard was a loud crash and the engine revving," he said.

"I then heard someone say 'Get out, she's going to blow up.' I didn't see anyone but the voice came from the driver's seat."

He looked around the car for the driver because "my ear was bleeding so the other person had to be worse off than me."

Matthews admitted he had "a couple of beers" at a cricket game before midnight. He said he had a sobriety test which put his blood-alcohol content within the acceptable standard.

Mr. Georges said he believed "beyond doubt the account of the youngster."

He handed down the fine of $120 and the six month disqualification, half of the maximum sentence, saying: "It was a very unfortunate episode, but we can't have people who drive taxis in that condition. It is most irresponsible."

ALL ABOARD FOR SWELL FOOD!

Stories about what we did in the hurricane [Emily] are getting a bit boring now, five weeks after the event, but the one I heard this week really has to be shared.

It seems some guests on board the cruise ship *Atlantic* were more concerned with their stomachs than their safety when she broke free of her moorings in Hamilton Harbour.

Despite being advised to seek refuge at the height of the storm, they refused to leave the dining room.

Instead, they steadfastly waited for their meals—telling worried crew they didn't want to lose their place in the breakfast queue.

APRIL FOOL'S NO JOY AT DELIVERANCE

April Fool pranksters went too far on board the replica of the Deliverance in St. George's.

And the charity which opens the boat to visitors does not see the funny side. The pranksters tampered with clothing, wigs and limbs of the dummies on board and re-arranged them in compromising positions.

"I don't think it was really a prank. They did some damage," complained Mrs. June Spurling, chairman of the Junior Service League committee which owns and operates the replica sailing ship for charity.

"We think three foreign sailors were responsible," said Mrs. Spurling. "They paid to come on board but spent more time on board than usual. The next tourist who went on board came down and told the ticket-hut lady what had happened."

Junior Service League workers have tidied up the exhibits but will have to wait for new wigs to be delivered from abroad. The vandals stole some wigs and an old Bermuda map replica. The total cost to the charity of their April Fool's joke has been put at $50.

Police have been informed and spokesman said: "It appears to have been some sort of a prank, but it's a theft nevertheless."

LETTERS TO THE EDITOR

OIL ON THE BEACHES

Dear Sir,

Having just dried myself from the waters of the South Shore, I have taken sullen note—there are spots, black, sticky never-leaving spots all over me!

Oh, my white gown is now slave to the likes of Lestoil, Top Drum and Lysol Heavy Duty Cleaner.

Tell me, dear sir—How is a fair maiden to enjoy the finest treasure of Bermuda when in her beach bag there is a year's supply of tar remover?

Open up your eyes and see the threatened beauty, before it is lost.

Lady Kassandra's Point of View
Huntington, Long Island

WHY THE BLACK HURRICANES

(The following letter was written by the Gazette's cartoon artist, Peter Woolcock.)

Dear Sir,

Having just returned from holiday, I duly noted the slight hoo-ha caused by my having drawn the hurricanes black in a recent cartoon.

My reason for so doing was simply that the storms in question had all been born in and around the Caribbean area. May I assure Mr. Ible that if and when we are hit by a hurricane emanating from the North Sea or Bay of Biscay, I shall have no hesitation in depicting it as white.

Meanwhile, sincere thanks to those who came to my defence in my absence.

Peter Woolcock
Pembroke

HORRIFYING FREESIAS

Dear Sir,

I was horrified to learn from this morning's paper that freesias come from South Africa. They should all be uprooted and destroyed.

The Phantom
Bailey's Bay

FOR THE RECORD

A report on Saturday stated that P.c. Glenn Wordsworth had been awarded $200 by the Criminal Injuries Compensation Board for injuries sustained in the line of duty. While the Board did make the award, no cash was paid out because by law the minimum award payable is $300.

A story in yesterday's newspaper on Dr. Vincent Bridgewater's appeal for more Government funding for drug rehabilitation incorrectly reported two facts: Addiction Services counsels about 7,000 people a year, not each week; and the cost of sending one person to Montreal for drug treatment is $1,800 a month, not $18,000.

'...-PARKED, REID STREET, FEBRUARY '87...'

FOR DISREGARDING MINOR OFFENCE SUMMONSES.

Crime and punishment

WITH THE possible exception of Saudi Arabia, theft is a problem societies face throughout the world, no matter how advanced. My, how the threat of losing a limb controls widespread wayward behavior. What a difference it might make to Western murder statistics.

Personally I've never felt that a warm, cozy, modern bed-sitter with color television, games room, exercise equipment, free education, and complete medical coverage is enough of a deterrent. Why doesn't the legal system go all the way and offer to set up trust funds for the children of convicted killers? That way everyone in the criminal's immediate family can benefit from the taking of an innocent life.

In Bermuda, murder and violent crimes are rare thanks chiefly to the absence of guns. Police are prohibited from carrying them, too. Even carrying bullets or a flick-knife is illegal. But keep in mind, natives do become restless easily. There are only so many walls you can muster up enough enthusiasm to sit on each day, so mischief making of some kind is bound to occur.

The shout of "Hey white boy!" or "Hey, look at de white byes in dat jeep!" are oft-heard greetings demonstrating enormous intelligence at work. Bermuda's population is 60 percent black. Shout the same thing at a group of black boys and serious legal trouble will ensue. Jim Woolridge, Minister of Tourism, would be the first to publicly complain. In his eyes, it is perfectly acceptable to denounce the legalization of homosexuality. Upon the passage of that bill, he was quoted as saying he feared Bermuda would turn into a "fairyland," but utter just one word against a black man, and he'll demand you be thrown off the island forthwith.

Crime on this part of the globe usually rears its furtive head in the form of thievery: household and business break-ins and employee theft. At numerous island businesses, countless employees have made convenient transfers, often involving hundreds of thousands of dollars. With rare exception, the person caught is given little more than a slap on the wrist with the penance of probation and a firm promise not to do it again. The judicial system may be Draconian towards other lawbreakers, but when it comes to theft on the job there is, curiously enough, an apparent disinterest in punishing anyone for something as "tedious" as money.

Bermuda is so well off that today a large proportion of the population dislikes the concept of work entirely. It cuts into their recreation time. They would prefer that someone simply hand them money. Try finding a repairman to come to your house with just one call, and you will quickly discover what I mean. If you need a plumber to fix a leak under your kitchen sink that has provided you with an unanticipated indoor swimming pool, plan on making at least three calls to the same company before you see any action.

Proprietors of local businesses usually don't need your money bad enough to act quickly, and their employees will display about as much compassion and understanding toward your domestic dilemma as the IRS. Why should they? Their jobs are not at stake.

On the novel occasion when a Bermudian is actually fired for poor performance, there is always another position waiting for him around the corner, even with a negative reference. Most black Bermudians have tenure in their jobs no matter what profession they happen to be enjoying due to a union that virtually holds the government and country to ransom if it doesn't get its own way.

Practically all workers in the service industry belong to this union, particularly hotel employees, and they afford the leader of their cult, Ottiwell Simmons, who is also a Member of Parliament, the type of misguided and fallacious adulation once shown toward Idi Amin. (Come to think of it, Mr. Simmons does bear a striking resemblance to the former Ugandan dictator. And didn't I read somewhere that Idi went into exile and hasn't been seen in years?)

As with Mr. Amin when he was in power, Mr. Simmons is omniscient to his followers. When asked by the local paper once what his New Year's resolution was, he replied with divine confidence and not a moment's hesitation, "I think resolutions are for people who have a bad habit that they've got to break. I don't think I have any bad habits." No, but some oratory lessons wouldn't hurt.

While Mr. Simmons is busy sabotaging the country's future, conscientious Bermudians are sometimes forced to work two jobs to make ends meet. Their lazier brethren have taken up house break-ins to cover monthly expenditures. While other countries face theft in the form of bank robberies, muggings, pickpockets, telephone con men and, of course, stockbrokers, residents of this island are burdened with a far more insidious and horrifying pattern of evil, criminals who will stop at absolutely nothing in order to satisfy their ribald lust for thy neighbor's coveted possessions. I could only be speaking now about the notorious Bermuda triangle of evil: the dreaded chocolate milk thief, the fruit thief, and the Jack the Ripper of Bermudian criminology, the infamous Cracker Jack bandit; men who strike fear into the hearts of corner shopkeepers and popcorn aficionados from Queen Street to Salt Spray Lane.

Villains who practice the trade come up with exceedingly creative ways to take something that belongs to somebody else. Not long ago you could go out for the day leaving the doors and windows of your home wide open. Unfortunately, the local hoodlums, after decades of study, worked out that this would be the most opportune time to ransack your lair and remove anything of value. Stereos, televisions, computers, family heirlooms—all are typical targets of the Bermudian break-in artist. However, I know of a case where they made off with all the liquor, a frozen turkey, and even a working goldfish bowl. Later, a discarded bottle of port from the same house was located by police in the bushes revealing that the thief or thieves in question did not have a taste for Warre's '77.

The newspaper articles that follow illustrate the eccentricities of thievery in Bermuda. Cold hard cash is at the top of the wish list, and Bermudians oblige by keeping thousands of dollars on their bureaus, in drawers, under the bed, anywhere it seems but in the local bank. Apart from cash, items which you'd never imagine would be worth a few years in jail for are prime targets, such as eyeballs, fruit, bingo machines, towels, and even electricity.

Shocking, isn't it?

ACCUSED CHANGES HIS PLEA

In a bizarre twist more than an hour after originally pleading not guilty, a defendant accused of stealing a glass of milk from the Inverurie Hotel had a change of heart and reversed his plea to guilty before Senior Magistrates Court on Monday.

But Randolph William Allen's change of heart did little to change his fate. Mr. Cox allowed the reversal after Allen repeatedly interrupted proceedings some 70 minutes after his case had first been heard. But the chief magistrate still ordered that Allen be detained for two weeks until a psychiatric report could be carried out. Earlier, Mr. Cox had ruled that Allen, who police say has no fixed address, be remanded in custody for two weeks until his day in court.

Allen has previously spent two six month prison terms for separate convictions involving thefts at the MarketPlace. He also has a string of convictions relating to vagrancy.

Police Sgt. Cyril Plant, prosecuting, said the assistant manager at the Inverurie Hotel in Paget had caught Allen leaving the hotel kitchen with a milk container shortly after midnight on August 27. Allen managed to escape before police later picked him up.

Originally, Allen said he was innocent, claiming the assistant manager had misunderstood his intentions—that he was only looking for a glass of water.

"I'm sort of guilty with an explanation," Allen started out when asked to enter a plea. "The manager had the wrong impression."

"You had no milk?" Mr. Cox asked.

"No. I'm not guilty."

Allen repeated his assertion of innocence and Mr. Cox ordered a trial for September 11. Sgt. Plant asked that the defendant be remanded in custody as he had no fixed address.

"I have a place to stay," Allen argued. "I just don't like telling the police. They keep coming around and hassling me. I would rather not give out my address if you don't mind."

Mr. Cox ordered that Allen be held.

Later on, after apparently thinking over his plea, Allen began asking Mr. Cox: "Excuse me, Sir, can you hear my case today?"

That then led to Allen finally crying out that he wished to change his plea to guilty during a lull in another case. His plea caught Mr. Cox's attention. But before the Senior Magistrate could hand down a sentence, a self-described cousin of Allen asked to approach the bench.

"He's not well," Allen's cousin told Mr. Cox. "He's mental-like."

Mr. Cox suggested that Allen be enrolled at St. Brendan's for treatment and then ordered the psychiatric report.

MAN STOLE VODKA

A 38-year-old Pembroke man was last Thursday fined $50 for stealing a bottle of vodka from the MarketPlace on Church Street.

Lionel Herman Outerbridge, of the Salvation Army Shelter pleaded guilty to taking the $12.50 bottle of alcohol on July 19, but insisted that he intended to pay for it.

"I put it in my bag so that it wouldn't break, that has happened to me before. After I passed the cash register, I was approached by this man and taken to his office where he called the man," Outerbridge said. "I was going to pay, I had the money on me."

Police prosecutor, Sgt. Earl Kirby, said that Outerbridge had several prior convictions of dishonesty, theft and alcohol related offences.

"Outerbridge," he said, "put the vodka in his shoulder bag and walked right out the store."

A search produced $16.25 on Outerbridge.

Acting Senior Magistrate, the Wor. John Judge, sentenced Outerbridge to one month in jail, but suspended it for a year and fined him $50.

TRYING TO OVERCOME HIS BEHAVIOURAL PROBLEMS

A sweet-toothed man who threw a rock at a police car—and then a bottle at a policeman—was sentenced to a year in prison on Wednesday.

Ewing Burnell Wilson, 36, pleaded guilty in Magistrates Court to assault, violently resisting arrest, and three charges of breaking and entering, when he stole chocolate and cakes.

Sgt. Peter Giles, prosecuting, said police officers driving along Frog Lane, Devonshire, in August saw Wilson remove a rock from a plastic bag. He threw it at their vehicle and missed.

An officer stopped to talk with him, and Wilson swore and threw a bottle at him.

It missed the officer and hit the police car. During a struggle another officer received scratches from Wilson.

When Wilson was arrested, he kicked the vehicle causing damage costing $665 to repair.

Wilson broke into a home in June and took chocolate bars, potato chips and other foods, said Sgt. Giles. He had also got into the Bermuda College where he stole cakes and coffee, and The

Avocado Lodge Nursery where 11 chocolate bars were taken. Each time the goods were worth $6, said Sgt. Giles.

When Senior Magistrate the Wor. Granville Cox asked Wilson if he had anything to say, Wilson said: "I'm trying to overcome my behavioural problems. I'm not aware of a lot of things I do. I'm trying to make a step in the right direction."

Mr. Cox sentenced Wilson to a 12-month prison term for unlawful damage and three months each for assault and violently resisting arrest. Wilson also received 12-month sentences for the three breaking, entering, and theft charges, all terms to run concurrently.

SWEET-TOOTHED

A sweet-toothed thief made off with $23 worth of Cracker Jacks and potato chips from a Parsons Road, Devonshire, store over the weekend.

Caribbean Variety was entered sometime between Friday night and Saturday morning.

PLANT COST HIM FIVE DAYS

Digging up plants on Front Street put a Pembroke man in jail for five days yesterday. Ralph Ingham of Pond Hill Road pleaded guilty to stealing a plant from the flower-beds opposite Chancery Lane.

P.c. Earl Kirby said Ingham was digging with a shovel in the beds and uprooting flowers. Police approached him as he was walking away with a small plant in his hand.

When questioned, Ingham said he liked gardening and would give the plant a good home. When arrested, he said: "Does this mean I can't have the plant?"

Senior Magistrate the Wor. Granville Cox fined Ingham $50 or five days in jail. Ingham opted for jail because he said he didn't have the money.

REQUEST FOR CASEMATES

Convicted thief David Dill threw the Supreme Court for a loop yesterday when he appealed his sentence of corrective training and requested a term in Casemates Prison.

And his unusual appeal was granted when Puisne Judge the Hon. Mr. Justice (Austin) Ward sent him to jail for six months each for breaking and entering a Warwick home and stealing $270, and for stealing a motor cycle.

The 21-year-old's lawyer, Mr. Tim Marshall, said his client felt the sentence of corrective training—which can run between nine months and three years—was "too harsh" because he was unsure how long it would run.

"At first blush this may seem an unusual course of action to take, but my client is terrified of doing another term of corrective training for he is not guaranteed he will be out in nine months," Mr. Marshall said.

PSYCHIATRIC REPORT FOR A FRUIT THIEF

A psychiatric report was yesterday ordered for a man who broke a $175 display window to steal $10 worth of fresh fruit.

Charles Christopher, 27, of Scott's Hill Road, Somerset, pleaded guilty to the breaking and entering charge when he appeared in Magistrates Court.

P.c. Earl Kirby, prosecuting, told the court Christopher broke into The New Garden Patch in Somerset, smashing the display window to gain entry, and stealing a small amount of fresh fruit.

He said Christopher initially denied stealing the fruit but admitted knocking it over.

When Senior Magistrate the Wor. Granville Cox asked Christopher what he had to say for himself, Christopher said: "I've been up for something like this before. My mind just wanders like this sometimes. If I hadn't done that the other night, I'd feel better now."

Mr. Cox ordered the psychiatric report and released Christopher on a personal bond of $350 with a surety in like amount. Christopher will reappear in court on September 17.

CHOCOLATE MILK TAKEN FROM SCHOOL

A thirsty thief with a sweet tooth struck at Prospect Primary School over the weekend.

Police spokesman Sgt. John Instone reported school officials noticed the break-in about 8 p.m. on Saturday night. Twenty-four cartons of chocolate milk were reported missing.

TEENAGER 'FELT NICE' AND DECIDED TO STEAL

A young man felt so good he decided to steal some chocolate, a court heard yesterday.

Richard Stanley Lee, 18, of School Lane, Sandys Parish, admitted breaking and entering at the Somerset MarketPlace store.

Sgt. Peter Giles, prosecuting, told Magistrates Court Lee forced his way through an air conditioning unit outside to enter the store.

"He said he was feeling nice and going to steal chocolate when questioned by police," Sgt. Giles said.

Miss Charlene Scott, defending, said Lee committed the offence on the spur of the moment.

But Acting Senior Magistrate, the Wor. Ephraim Georges, expressed concern at Lee's tendency to steal.

"At his tender age he has a dozen offences committed when he was a juvenile," Mr. Georges said.

"He has a marked propensity for this type of thing and should be remanded in custody until he is sentenced."

BURGLAR CLAIMED TO BE POLICEMAN, COURT TOLD

Burglar, Maurice Burrows, came up with a novel excuse when a householder disturbed him hunting through his wife's jewellery at 5 a.m.

"I'm a police officer conducting a search," he said before fleeing, Magistrates Court was told yesterday.

Twenty-five year old Burrows, who has a police record dating back to when he was 16, was remanded in custody while a psychiatric report is conducted.

Burrows, who claims he lives with his father in Roberts Avenue, Devonshire, pleaded guilty to housebreaking at the home of Peter Blaney in Friendship Lane, Devonshire, and to burglary with intent to steal at the same home.

Sgt. Alan Cleave, prosecuting, insisted Burrows was of no fixed address as his father had kicked him out and had recently discovered him sleeping in bushes.

Sgt. Cleave said Burrows went to Blaney's house on February 24 and let himself in through an unlocked sliding door. He took a piggy bank containing just $2 and left it outside.

Two days later he returned to the same house and again let himself in. This time he woke Blaney as he went through the jewellery box.

When asked by Senior Magistrate, the Wor. Granville Cox, if he had anything to say, Burrows replied: "Could you overlook some of my case history?"

Mr. Cox told him he couldn't. "Even if I could, what would you do?" he asked.

"I'd be grateful," answered Burrows.

He will be sentenced on March 14.

UNDERWEAR THIEF IS REMANDED

A 26-year-old with a "fixation for stealing women's underwear" yesterday admitted taking several hundred dollars worth of lingerie within three months.

Dwayne Bean, of Radnor Road, pleaded guilty to two counts of breaking into Hamilton Parish homes and taking jewellery, cash and underwear and three counts of stealing clothing and underwear.

Duty counsel Mr. Kim White said Bean "quite clearly has a psychological problem—a fixation or delusion—which manifests itself in the taking of women's underwear."

Mr. White said Bean needed psychiatric counselling.

"All of the complainants would be quite happy for Mr. Bean to undergo counselling," he said. "It is the victims of these crimes that are asking this. It is the clear direction of their decision."

Sgt. Alan Cleave, prosecuting, said the Hamilton Parish man took $15 cash and $76.76 worth of underwear on April 19; $10 cash and a gold chain and pendant worth $85 during the month of March; ladies' underwear worth $99 on April 2; $59.50 worth between February 26 and 27; and $180 worth of clothing and underwear between April 23 and 24.

Sgt. Cleave said police went to Bean's home on April 27 where they found a pile of women's underwear hidden beneath a dresser in his room.

Senior Magistrate the Wor. Granville Cox remanded Bean in custody for two weeks pending psychiatric and social inquiry reports.

WRONG PAIR OF SLACKS

A man who said he did not pay for a bottle of vodka because he had donned the wrong pair of trousers was fined $30 in Magistrates Court yesterday.

Gerald Outerbridge, a 60-year-old Hamilton Parish resident, pleaded guilty to stealing the $15 bottle of vodka from the Shelly Bay MarketPlace.

Prosecuting, Insp. Peter Duffy said Outerbridge was seen lurking in the liquor department by a manager at the supermarket on the morning of January 4. The manager saw him take a bottle of Smirnoff vodka, put it down his trousers and then walk out of the store.

The manager followed Outerbridge into the parking lot, confronted him and called the police, Insp. Duffy said.

Outerbridge told the Court: "I am no thief. I just had the wrong pants on—the money was in my other pair of pants."

THIEF IS JAILED

A couple of housebreakers hid the spoils of their theft in St. Peter's Church graveyard after fleeing a police sergeant's home with corned beef, beer and mayonnaise, Magistrates Court heard yesterday.

But alert neighbours called the police and were able to describe the thieves resulting in their immediate arrests.

Dean Burgess, 27, of Khyber Pass, Warwick, and his 21-year-old girlfriend, Bernadette Rice, of Cove Valley Road, St. David's, admitted breaking and entering the St. George's home of Sgt. Ronald Boggan on September 15 this year.

Neighbours gave a description of each culprit to police, who netted the pair just minutes after they escaped through the window, prosecutor Sgt. Peter Giles said.

Rice admitted her part to police in a statement, explaining she held open the window for Burgess, who after stealing $26 worth of food and drink, handed the items to her.

The property was recovered from St. Peter's graveyard with Rice's assistance.

WHO TOOK THE CALL?

Police are investigating to see who took a phone call in Hamilton—or rather, who took the whole call booth.

The four foot high structure went missing from Angle Street last week, and it now seems no one even noticed it was gone for up to two days.

Not only the booth, but the phone and the coin box went missing as well, Police spokesman Sgt. John Instone said yesterday.

"We can only assume the person wanted the money out of the coin box," he said. "Of course, we have no idea how much was in it."

Police say the 60 lb. phone booth disappeared sometime between Wednesday and Friday but are not sure exactly when.

"I take it the phone isn't used all that much," said Sgt. Instone.

PLEASE RETURN THE BINGO MACHINE

St. Theresa's Cathedral has issued an all-points bulletin for their missing bingo machine.

The Cedar Avenue cathedral is hosting a Bingo night tonight and Father David Doran is desperate to get the machine back.

It went missing last week when someone borrowed it for their own Bingo event.

Since then, as Saturday night Bingo neared, Father Doran has been down to Magistrates Court to see what organization had a Bingo night last week. He has also made announcements for the machine at schools.

His efforts, so far, have been to no avail.

"I don't know who to call, and we've got Bingo tomorrow night. I've been trying to be a detective to trace this thing down, but I can't find it."

Anyone with information about the missing Bingo machine is asked to call Father Doran at 292-0607.

THIEF GETS SOME UNUSUAL ITEMS

A Tuesday afternoon break-in at a Southampton home netted a thief or thieves some unusual items, Police reported yesterday.

The theft from the Middle Road home included 30 pounds in sterling, one 14kt. gold chain with five 14kt. gold pendants in the shape of a boy's head, a Brazilian fist, an eyeball, an outlined map of Bermuda, and an oriental replica of a boat.

Police have asked anyone who has seen these items or who knows of their whereabouts to contact the Somerset Police detectives at 234-1010.

THIEF CAMPED OUT IN SCHOOL

A thief camped out at the Devon Lane School between last Friday and Monday. After breaking in, he cooked a quantity of food on a stove and slept unnoticed at the school for one or two nights. Nothing other than the food was reported missing.

ALABAMA 'DID ME IN'

A 31-year-old Pembroke man began sobbing uncontrollably in Magistrates Court after trying to tell the magistrate he was a good man before he visited Alabama. "All my convictions are a result of what happened to me in Alabama," Kareem Kenyatta told the Wor. Granville Cox. "I'm currently well but I still have this taint of evil."

"What happened in Alabama?" Mr. Cox said.

"I don't know. It was horrible." At that point, Kenyatta began sobbing loudly and a police officer led him from the room.

Mr. Cox postponed sentencing Kenyatta, who was charged with breaking a window at Warwick Holiness Church on May 9 and breaking into Bermuda Motors two days later.

Kenyatta, who lives at Brangman's Home and attends St. Brendan's [psychiatric] Hospital regularly, pleaded guilty to the offences. He will be sentenced on June 10 with reference to psychiatric reports on him.

REMANDED IN CUSTODY

An unemployed restaurant musician was remanded in custody yesterday charged with stealing a six-pack of light beer and some crackers worth a total of $4 from a house.

Carlos Richardson, 22, of Flatts Hill, Smith's Parish, denies breaking into the home of Patricia Ann Price on February 5.

Richardson, who is represented by Miss Charles-Etta Simmons, elected to be tried in Supreme Court.

Senior Magistrate the Wor. Granville Cox remanded him in custody until February 27 after P.c. Peter Giles, prosecuting, opposed bail.

TOWEL THEFT CASE DISMISSED

A St. George's man accused of stealing eight towels from the Grotto Bay Beach Hotel, had the case against him dismissed in Magistrates Court yesterday.

Senior Magistrate the Wor. Ephraim Georges declared there was no case because of the evidence given by prosecution witness Mrs. Phyllis Tuzo, the laundry supervisor at the hotel.

Mrs. Tuzo told the court she informed the defendant, Windell Hayward, where to find old towels and gave him a plastic bag to put them in.

The Magistrate told the court "the item must be taken without permission of the owner" for a theft to occur.

BROKE IN, HAD A MEAL, FELL ASLEEP

A Southampton man who stole food from a friend received a suspended jail sentence and $500 fine yesterday in Magistrates Court.

Richard Stanley Burrows, 30, of Camp Hill Road, admitted the offence to Senior Magistrate, the Wor. Will Francis, and said he had a problem with alcohol.

Police prosecutor Sgt. Peter Giles said that on April 25 Burrows went on a drinking spree in St. George's. He then went to Ronald Panchard's house on Broad Alley and demanded food.

Mr. Panchard refused to feed him.

Sgt. Giles said the next day Mr. Panchard returned home to find three window panes removed from a kitchen window, and the gas stove was on but unlit. The refrigerator was open, and food was on the table and in the microwave. Mr. Panchard heard snoring coming from his bedroom, and found Burrows lying on the bed asleep, wearing only his underwear.

The spoiled food was valued at about $50.

Mr. Francis fined Burrows $500, and ordered $80 of the fine was to go to Mr. Panchard. He also gave Burrows a six-month prison sentence, suspended for one year.

UNREPENTANT MAN JAILED FOR ATTACK ON 93-YEAR-OLD

A four-year sentence was handed down yesterday to a man who lifted 93-year-old Eldon (Smiler) Tucker off the street, carried him into a secluded spot and robbed him of his empty wallet.

Thirty-six-year-old George Keith Joell showed no remorse in Supreme Court for the robbery, which he admitted, and smiled as he was led out of Supreme Court.

"Why didn't you pick on someone your own size?" Chief Justice the Hon. Sir James Astwood asked Joell, who was unrepresented. "Look at the size of your biceps."

But the only words Joell spoke in his defence were, "I was going through a phase when it happened."

SHARP SHOCK

When Belco [Bermuda Electric Light Company] cut off Murphy's electricity supply, he quickly found a solution.

He just ran an extension cord from the adjoining pump house which fed the apartment upstairs, Magistrates Court heard.

But yesterday the judge told Murphy he was in for a shock—"and I don't mean an electric shock either"—as he fined him $250.

Murphy, 41, of Grotto View Hill, Smith's Parish, pleaded guilty to fraudulently extracting electricity. He was estimated to have taken around $20 worth.

Sgt. Peter Giles, prosecuting, said the neighbour suspected Murphy had been using her electricity and called police who arrived at 6 a.m. on September 2, armed with a search warrant.

"He was asleep and police found, and took possession of, an extension cord connected to a refrigerator in his house. The cord ran through a window into the pump room where it was plugged into a wall outlet.

"The fridge was working and other cords were plugged into the extension, giving power to the accused's apartment."

Sgt. Giles said Murphy told officers he thought the neighbour had consented. "He said he had been intending to go to her and offer money."

Murphy told Mr. Georges: "The other tenant agreed. It was the man who owns the apartment who complained."

But Mr. Georges told him: "Whoever gave you authority doesn't have permission. It doesn't legalize it, it is wrong."

CHECK THIS CHEEKY THIEF!

An ungentlemanly thief burst into a young couple's car while they were necking in the back seat and snatched the woman's handbag on Saturday night.

It happened at midnight in the Montpelier Road car park of the Arboretum.

The culprit, who got away with $145 cash, is described as dark-skinned and wearing a check shirt.

OUTBURST COSTS THEFT-CHARGE MEN THEIR LIBERTY

Two men charged with stealing avocado pears and lemons from a farmer's field were remanded in custody until today by a Magistrate after creating a disturbance in court on Friday.

"They don't seem to be in any fit state to take part in these proceedings," Magistrate the Wor. Ephraim Georges said.

The two—Calvin Ming, 40, of Hermitage Road, Smith's Parish, and O'Brien Hayward, 42, of Bailey's Bay, Hamilton Parish—were charged with stealing the produce, valued at $55.80 from a field in Hamilton Parish.

The pair, who were not represented by a lawyer, had entered not guilty pleas to charges of theft.

They had just chosen a Supreme Court trial by judge and jury when Hayward began to shout: "I want my pears. I love pears too."

Mr. Georges ordered the two to be ushered out of the courtroom until other cases were heard, saying they were "creating a disturbance."

The two, who were previously in custody, will remain there until the question of bail is raised in court today.

STOLEN GROUPERS UNSAFE TO EAT

Groupers involved in a major research project have disappeared recently from the Coney Island Park. And the Department of Agriculture, Fisheries and Parks warns that the fish are not safe to eat.

"Alarmingly, there have been cases of interference with experiments taking place on the site, by people apparently bent on eating fish which are the subjects of the experiments. These fish are involved in a major research initiative which involves treating the groupers involved with hormones—pharmaceuticals which are hazardous if consumed."

The fish thefts are among a number of incidents at the Coney Island Park in recent weeks. Quantities of ice have also disappeared after break-ins at the site and Fisheries' vessels have been vandalised.

"Anyone found trespassing on the Fisheries' facility will be prosecuted," the Department said this week.

NOT BELIEVED

Senior Magistrate the Wor. Granville Cox said he didn't believe a Devonshire man who said the $150 dress he admitted stealing from Trimingham's was for his wife.

Derek Winfield Simons, 33, admitted the stealing charge in Magistrates Court.

He said theft was "uncharacteristic of my nature" but also told Mr. Cox: "I still want the dress."

"Who's this dress for?" asked Mr. Cox.

Simons, of Middle Road, Devonshire, said it was for his wife.

"And she must have this particular dress?" Mr. Cox asked.

Simons said he knew his wife's size and taste.

"I don't believe you," said Mr. Cox, and fined Simons $150.

Prosecuting, Police Inspector Peter Duffy said store security saw Simons take the dress and put it into a trash bag before leaving the Front Street store on March 18.

PRICE PROTEST HAS COURT SEQUEL

A 32-year-old man was arrested after staging an unusual protest about prices in Bermuda.

Ricky Tyrone Thompson, of Brunswick Street, Hamilton, went into a Front Street ice cream parlour and asked for an ice cream, Sgt. Rex Osborne told Magistrates Court.

Told it would cost $1.75, he started cursing, saying he would only pay $1.25. He then picked up the cash register, which had to be wrestled away from him.

Continuing to shout abuse, he was arrested and charged with threatening behaviour.

Thompson admitted the offence and had his case adjourned until November 13 for social and psychiatric reports.

"We'd have a very exciting time if everybody objected to prices in Bermuda," Magistrate the Wor. John Judge told him.

SCHOOL THIEF SENT TO JAIL

A 53-year-old man who stole a school whistle and a pair of scissors from Saltus Cavendish School received a six-month jail sentence in Magistrates Court yesterday.

Cyril Tucker, of no fixed abode, has a long record of breaking into the school and stealing items, Police prosecutor, Sgt. Earl Kirby told the court.

Senior Magistrate, the Wor. William Francis, told Tucker he was a "real problem to the school" before sending him to jail.

MAN STOLE $55 WATCH

A social inquiry report has been ordered for a Warwick man who stole a watch thinking it would compliment his other jewellery.

Clifton Caines, 31, of Sandymount Drive, pleaded guilty in Magistrates Court to stealing the watch from Warwick Shell Gas Station.

Prosecutor Sgt. Cyril Plant said that on January 25, Caines entered the station and stole a $55 watch displayed by the cash register.

Caines was arrested and taken to the Hamilton Police Station where he admitted stealing the watch.

Sgt. Plant added that when asked by police why he stole the watch Caines said: "I thought it would look good with my ring so I put it in my pocket and walked out."

He told Magistrate the Wor. Cheryl-Ann Mapp: "My fiancée and I had a misunderstanding and I walked out of the house, went to the gas station and took the watch."

Mrs. Mapp bailed Caines in the sum of $300 with a surety until sentencing on April 4.

SOCIAL INQUIRY

A social inquiry report was ordered yesterday for a 26-year-old unemployed Pembroke mother facing theft and fraud charges.

Elizabeth Louise Smith, of Mount Hill, pleaded guilty in Magistrates Court to stealing a Bank of Bermuda cheque worth 10 cents.

She has also admitted forging a cheque of $42.14, fraudulently altering a cheque, and attempting to defraud.

Senior Magistrate the Wor. Will Francis put the case off until February 10 for a report to be prepared.

MOTHER OF THE YEAR UP FOR STEALING

Mother of the Year in 1987 Anita Brown was charged yesterday with stealing more than $350,000 from her employer, BDC.

Brown, 35, of Valley View Crescent in Hamilton Parish, was not required to enter a plea to 54 counts of stealing, forgery, uttering cheques under false pretences and others when she appeared in Magistrates Court.

Brown is alleged to have stolen $350,000 from the company between November 30, 1986 and June 16, 1989.

She will return to court in three weeks for mention.

COURT SAYS MAN'S JAIL TERM 'NOT EXCESSIVE'

The Court of Appeal on Monday turned down a 37-year-old Sandys man's request to have his three-year prison sentence for "stealing a $1 cup of soda" reduced.

Mervyn Wilbur Smith, who represented himself, argued that the sentence was harsh and excessive.

But before he began, the Hon. Mr. Justice da Costa warned Smith that if he persisted with the appeal, his sentence may be increased.

"You have run almost the gamut of crimes," Mr. da Costa said as he looked over Smith's criminal record. "You hold contempt for law in this country. You've been getting off lightly. But you have absolutely no respect for people's property. So it is for you to make up your mind. But it is a real danger you face."

Puisne Judge the Hon. Mr. Justice Ward sentenced Smith, an admitted drug addict, in May to three years in prison for breaking and entering Sandys Boat Club in February, and a year for possession of an instrument used for housebreaking.

The case was sent to Supreme Court for sentencing after a magistrate convicted him of the two charges.

But yesterday Smith said he was not in his "right frame of mind" when he pleaded guilty to the charges in Magistrates Court. Insisting that he found the club door open and just took a cup of club soda, he said he did not have time to represent himself "fairly."

"I understand my record is deplorable," Smith said. "I've had a problem with drug addiction for a long time. I think my disregard for the law, as you call it, is due to this."

Interrupting, Mr. da Costa said drug addiction is no excuse. "It is not a mitigating factor," he stressed. "It is an aggravating factor."

Smith said he also thought his sentence was unfair because there were others who committed more serious crimes and they received the same sentence. "There are chaps that have been given three years for breaking into tourist-accommodation and taking $20,000 worth of items," Smith said. "All I'm up for is taking a cup of soda worth $1.

"I'm not saying I want a break. I'm asking where's the justice?"

Handing down the court's decision, Mr. Justice da Costa said: "We're of the opinion that the sentence of three years was a proper sentence for breaking and entering and stealing. It's far from being harsh and excessive."

CONVICTED ROBBER RECALLED TO COURT

Convicted robber Winton Edwards was yesterday recalled to court to have his 12 month prison term substituted—with a one year jail sentence.

Puisne Judge the Hon. Justice Ward told Edwards he had made a mistake in the original sentence and should have taken a six month suspended sentence into account.

But he started the proceedings by telling him: "Let me put your mind at rest. I have no intention of adding to your sentence."

LETTERS TO THE EDITOR

WEATHER

Dear Sir,

Those interested in records for sustained bad weather might like to look at the statistics for April, 1960. In my memory, which may exaggerate a little, it rained steadily for the whole month.

It was then that an unfortunate visitor was heard to say as he was departing at the Airport: "I might just as well have stayed home, put on my best clothes, stood in the shower and torn up $20 bills."

Andrew Trimingham

Paget

GOVERNMENT

Dear Sir,

This evening ZBM Channel 10 broadcast an interview with our Premier and Tourism Minister by a New Orleans television station. It was one of the most embarrassing moments of my life to see these government ministers looking like a pair of frogs on a lily pad, waiting for the next fly to come by.

The Premier's jacket was bursting at the middle and he looked quite uncomfortable in contrast to the interviewer who was very relaxed and immaculately dressed.

If the government thinks interviews like this are going to benefit tourism they are wrong. They make us look like a banana republic desperate for American dollars.

I hope this was the only interview of this sort.

EMBARRASSED

City of Hamilton

CONTRIBUTING TO CRIMINALS

Dear Sir,

Criminals think that they will not get caught. If caught, they think that they will not get convicted. If convicted, they think that they will get a light sentence.

We, the non-criminals, have contributed greatly to their way of thinking.—PAPADAKIS (The Howls of Justice)

John Tartaglia

City of Hamilton

FROTHING AT THE MOUTH

Dear Sir,

As I was walking down the road this afternoon I saw a horse and carriage coming towards me. It looked more like a wave of soap suds and foam because the horse was frothing at the mouth so bad because the ignorant driver had neglected to give him a drink for I don't know how long.

"Halt" I shouted, and stood fast in his way, one arm raised with my fist clenched, the other arm hid behind my back grasping my whip. But oh, the driver recognized me and knew what was coming alright, for he reigned in the halter, jumped out of the carriage and belted down the road like the coward he was.

But to be sure, I was up for the chase. These ignorant cowards cannot outrun me. He ran fast, the brute, but I caught him after five miles and when I did I gave him a taste. Yes, I whipped him, but good. Then I stood behind him as he fetched a bucket of water and watched him feed it to his poor thirsty horse. I then gave him a lecture and a stern warning not to treat a horse or any other animal so horribly ever again, and whipped him a second time to ensure he understood.

So here is the message to all of you: Don't mistreat a horse, a dog or any animal ever; because, by jove, if you do then just look over your shoulder, and there I will be like a nightmare, with my trusty whip; and when I crack that whip, I assure you it stings! You will never forget it! Ask around. Those who have felt it will tell you.

Sarah T. Sweepclean
Harrington Sound

FOR THE RECORD

Mrs. Antoniette Talbot of Jingle With Us Singing Telegrams says she will perform for anniversaries and other celebrations of friendship, but will not perform for birthdays, because of religious reasons. An article printed yesterday reported that she did.

The Harold Madeiros who dumped trash at the National Trust's Hughes Nature Reserve is not the same Harold Madeiros who recently moved from Bostock Hill East Paget, after living there for a period of 15 years.

QUOTE OF THE DAY

"The other day I weighed the report and it was six pounds and ten ounces of verbiage...but I don't say that in a derogatory way."

Dr. Clarence Terceira (Minister of Education).

Appetizing thoughts

WITH THE possible exception of Kate Moss, just about everyone enjoys a well prepared meal.

Bermudians certainly do. After all, apart from drinking, they have little else to occupy their valuable time. Unfortunately, provisions are exorbitant. A tube of toothpaste and a carton of milk will set you back the better part of ten dollars. Lunch for two in Hamilton, just a hamburger and two pints of Websters, can cost upwards of forty dollars. Bermudian multimillionaires are rarely able to afford this special treat except on Wednesdays after the shopping is completed.

Groceries and rent are the two most expensive aspects of living in paradise. Don't expect a house with a view for under $3,000 a month unless you strike it lucky. A taxi into town will set you back at least ten dollars. If you're bored with the beach, swimming, golf, and tennis, there isn't much else to do. The only way you can "take off" for the weekend is to buy an airline ticket out. Again, not cheap.

With all of these restrictions, is it any wonder some people go a little crazy when they head out for dinner? The anticipation, the excitement, the personal loan taken out on your neighbor's scooter to avoid being invited into the kitchen to scrub the dishes.

There is no real national cuisine to speak of. Bermudians have very catholic tastes when it comes to diet. However, there are several unique Bermudian dishes which brave visitors might wish to sample provided you place a bucket nearby. Let's see . . . there's cassava pie which consists of meat, the root of cassava, and sugar; then there's something called Pawpaw Montespan, a blend of meat, cheese, and underripe papaya in a casserole; fish cakes; codfish with bananas; and, oh, I mustn't forget, the most scrumptious curried mussel pie.

Perhaps you should begin your culinary adventure slowly with fish chowder or red bean soup which, provided it is not made with three-week-old ingredients, is quite tasty. I recommend topping it off with healthy dollops of delectable sherry peppers and black rum. Failing that, the best-known Bermudian dish can be found at only one well-known establishment and nowhere else: Kentucky Fried Chicken. Bermudians go wild over it, causing lengthy queues to the back of the restaurant.

Local establishments have just about every cuisine you could possibly want, although the past few years have seen a marked decline in quality and consistency without a concurrent drop in price. Alas, with such a wide choice, difficulties do arise.

I recall the time a despondent customer discovered a reluctance to serve French fries on the part of one Chinese restaurant on Reid Street. He found a novel way to express his chagrin. Also, if you are an early riser and require a filling breakfast, I trust you have a taste for something other than maple syrup on your pancakes. Oh, and don't forget to ask for extra cockroach legs with your pork fried rice or, if you prefer spicy food, fingernail clippings in your takeout chili. Makes it nice and crunchy.

Under no circumstances should you worry about your health while dining out. Let me put your mind to rest at the outset. Your interests are fully protected. The Bermuda health department is on the case.

Ah, the delights of dining in the tropics. Whether it's The Hog Penny, a sad attempt at a British pub (that is always out of draft British beer), or in your sumptuously furnished room at the Belmont Hotel (Not!), there is so much culinary pleasure awaiting you that I am about to burst with pride.

TAKE-OUT DINNER IS A SHOCK

A take-away dinner party turned sour after cockroach legs were found in the food.

Disgusted customers Mr. and Mrs. Jim Paul, of Smith's Parish, and their landlady Mrs. R.A. Hollis decided to get together for dinner on Monday night and bought nearly $50 worth of food from the New Queen restaurant in Hamilton.

But as they began to satisfy their taste buds, Mrs. Hollis discovered her chicken fried rice was contaminated with cockroach legs.

"We immediately stopped eating," said an angry Mr. Paul yesterday.

But the dinner party horror did not stop there. The trio decided to give up on the Chinese food and eat some lemon pie since it was probably not made at the Chinese restaurant.

"But we found a blond hair in it," he gasped. Mr. Paul said they were totally disgusted about the situation, and could not think of eating anything else that evening.

He called the manager/owner of the New Queen restaurant Mr. Ken Fong to tell him what happened, but said Mr. Fong was uncooperative.

He said Mr. Fong offered to give him back the $47.50 if he returned the food to the restaurant. But Mr. Paul refused and said he thought Mr. Fong should drive down to Smith's Parish to pick it up.

"Why should I ruin my evening with company to drive to Hamilton to return the food," he said. "I should have some rights as a customer."

But Mr. Fong disagreed, and told *The Royal Gazette* he would have gladly refunded the money if their accusations were true. Mr. Fong said Mrs. Hollis placed the food order at 5.45 p.m. and picked it up about five minutes later.

He said at around 9 p.m. he received a call from Mr. Paul complaining about cockroach legs in the food.

Mr. Paul said the reason they called the restaurant some hours later was because he and his wife were putting their four children to bed for the night.

"All they had to do was bring back the food to prove something was wrong and we would have refunded their money," he said. He said Mr. Paul also threatened to go to the Health Department and the Press with the story.

"If he wants to take it to the Health Department I cannot stop him. Besides if something is wrong we want to correct it," Mr. Fong said.

Chief Environment Officer Mr. Patrick Mayers said a Health Department representative had picked up the food from the Paul's residence yesterday afternoon.

"We are investigating the situation. We have no further information at this time," he said.

COOK NOT TO BLAME IN OVEN CLEANER CASE

A cook in a restaurant that served a customer oven cleaner in a syrup jar was not responsible for the accident, a Supreme Court judge decided on Wednesday.

Evidence in the case showed Mr. Tony DeSilva went into the Arcade Restaurant on September 14, 1985, and ordered a breakfast of bacon, pancakes and maple syrup.

But instead of syrup, someone had filled the syrup jug with oven cleaner, which was stored in bulk in a similar container and in the same place as the syrup.

The restaurant admitted liability for the act, but owner Mr. Junio Ming asked the court to decide whether the cook on duty, Mr. William Moniz, was responsible.

Mr. Moniz, who was 73 at the time, underwent an operation to remove cataracts from his eyes shortly after the accident. But he testified that he was sure he hadn't poured anything into the syrup jug that morning, and Mr. Ming confirmed that evidence.

Other employees said many people shared the responsibility of filling the syrup jugs.

"The court must determine whether (Mr. Moniz) was negligent," Acting Puisne Judge the Hon. Mrs. Justice Wade wrote in her decision.

"The court believes (Mr. Moniz), who represented himself as a truthful witness, when he told the court that he did not pour anything into the porcelain (syrup) jar that morning.

"There is not sufficient evidence to convince me that he did the act of pouring the oven cleaner in the jar which was served to (Mr. DeSilva)."

'NO DINNER' MAN IS FINED

A St. George's man who slapped his wife and threw her to the ground because she failed to have his dinner ready when he came home from work has been sentenced. Phillip Bailey, 48, of Cut Road, was fined $300 and given a three month jail term suspended for 18 months when he reappeared in Magistrates Court.

Mr. Cox said the sentence would deter Bailey, but added he had considered a prison term. Bailey, a bus driver, started shouting at his wife when he returned to his home at 8 p.m. on November 27 and found his dinner uncooked.

He slapped her and pushed her up against a wall, and then took her outside and threw her to the ground. Bailey's sentencing had been delayed, pending social and psychiatric reports.

STEAK THIEF IS JAILED

A 34-year-old man with "an appalling record" was sent to prison for two months after he was found guilty of stealing seven steaks from a Hamilton supermarket.

Edward Paynter of Cut Road, St. George's, denied the charge and told the court the two floor managers who testified against him were "liars."

But Acting Magistrate the Wor. John Riihiluoma said the two Shopping Centre employees had no reason to lie about Paynter.

Floor manager of the Victoria Street business, Helen Francis, said she watched Paynter walk out of the store with the steaks in his shoulder bag.

She said she had called another manager, David DeSilva, and told him of the incident. He then waited for Paynter outside the store.

But DeSilva told the court Paynter did a "u-turn" when he saw him outside. And Francis said she followed Paynter when he walked back into the store and watched him throw the steaks onto a shelf in the second aisle.

Paynter told the court he had a wife and two children to feed.

"I'm innocent," he said. "And I don't want to go to jail because I have to put food in my children's mouths."

But Mr. Riihiluoma said Paynter, who has a string of similar previous convictions, had "an appalling record."

"You've only been here for about a year and you've been before the courts for stealing several items," said the judge. "You've got to learn."

SEAFOOD SCAM

Buying 50 lobster tails and 200 shrimp on credit for a non-existent party at Senate President the Hon. Albert Jackson's home resulted in a $100 fine for a Somerset man.

Wayne Crane of Cambridge Beaches Lane pleaded guilty to false pretences in the November 23 incident in which he told K.C. Enterprises he was buying the food with Sen. Jackson's authority. The bill came to $1,125.

Sgt. Rushe said Crane told the store owners the food was for a private party at the Jackson's Southampton home and that the Senator would pay for it later.

Sgt. Rushe said subsequent inquiries revealed Crane did not have the Senator's authority to buy in his name nor was there any such party. Crane was arrested on December 2.

Yesterday, Crane told Mr. Cox that he took the wholesale food to sell to friends at retail prices.

At the time of his arrest, he had paid back $625 to K.C. Enterprises with the full amount reimbursed in the last week.

"I would never do that again," he told Mr. Cox, adding that he did not make money on the scam.

TAKE-OUT COST MAN YEAR IN JAIL

When a Chinese restaurant refused to give a Pembroke man french fries, he made off with three dinners and then damaged a car, a court heard yesterday.

George Keith Joell, 36, also admitted violently resisting arrest and assaulting a police officer when he appeared in Magistrates Court.

Sgt. Earl Kirby, prosecuting, said the incident was reported to police by Chopsticks restaurant manager Mr. Nigel Wilkinson.

"The defendant entered the premises and demanded a take-out of french fries, which the restaurant does not sell," Sgt. Kirby said.

"But when Joell became belligerent and continued to demand french fries, Wilkinson called police. Joell then grabbed three take-out dinners worth $22.95, and left the restaurant, with the manager in hot pursuit."

Joell still had the dinners with him when he was stopped by police.

He was arrested and when the officers tried to put him in the car he kicked in the windows and damaged the door, causing $1,114 worth of damage.

At the Hamilton Police Station Joell attacked a police constable and tried to kick him in the groin. The officer dodged Joell's kick but was hit on the leg.

He remained uncooperative while in custody, Sgt. Kirby said.

Senior Magistrate the Wor. Granville Cox sentenced Joell to one year in prison.

JULIE FONG'S 'BUSY' LAST NIGHT

Julie Fong's Restaurant owner Mrs. Julie Connolly said the establishment was busy last night, in this the first week open after being closed by Health Department officials.

But Mrs. Connolly said she has no further desire to speak with the Press.

"Every day I open the paper I see my name in it. I wish you people would just leave me alone," the restaurant owner said.

Julie Fong's was closed earlier this month after officials found the restaurant was roach infested. Since that time, the business has been scrubbed out and insects exterminated.

After two failed attempts for clean bills of health, the green light was finally given on Tuesday after a third inspection. Chief Environmental Health officer Mr. Patrick Mayers said the restaurant would undergo normal periodic inspections, and Mrs. Connolly said the restaurant would be kept clean.

REPORTER'S NOTEBOOK

A Southampton woman found a unique way to handle the pre-Christmas shopping frenzy.

Mrs. Lucille Butterfield was grocery shopping at the busy Heron Bay MarketPlace on the Wednesday before Christmas when she became separated from her shopping cart containing her purse.

"Everybody freeze," a source recalled Mrs. Butterfield shouting.

Amazingly, shoppers stood still while the woman retrieved her cart and purse.

WOMAN IS DISGUSTED AFTER FINDING FINGERNAIL IN HER CHILI

A cup of chili on a breezy day may tempt some, but definitely not Miss Leslie-Ann Phillips after she found a finger nail in what she thought would be a nice lunch.

Miss Phillips, who works at the United Parcel Service, went next door to the Donut House this week to order lunch for herself and some fellow employees.

"I ordered the cup of chili and took it back to the office to eat," Miss Phillips said.

"I had gotten down to the bottom of the cup and as I was chewing, I felt something really hard and I spit it out in a napkin," she added.

Miss Phillips was too afraid to look at what she knew was something that was not supposed to be there so she took the napkin to a friend in the office for inspection.

"My friend told me that it was a fake fingernail with bronze nail polish on it. It still had the glue on the inside," Miss Phillips said.

She added that she showed the nail to the rest of her fellow workers and then marched back to the Donut House clutching the nail as evidence.

"A woman who works at the Donut House told me that none of the girls that work in the shop wore fake nails."

Miss Phillips also said the woman suggested that it could have come from Butterfield and Vallis food service division because that was where they get their meat and red beans for the chili.

"The woman looked at me and asked whether the nail could have been mine and I showed her that all my nails are purple, and real," Miss Phillips said.

In a quest to find out exactly how a nail did get in her chili Miss Phillips called Butterfield and Vallis and the owner of the Donut House Mr. Fred Pereech.

"Mr. Pereech also said the nail must have come from Butterfield and Vallis, and when I told him how dirty it was he said that when you boil something six or seven times it is 100 percent bacteria free.

"And then he told me I would get reimbursed for my troubles," a disgusted Miss Phillips said.

But a worker at Butterfield and Vallis said only men work in their meats department.

Miss Phillips added: "When people serve food, I don't care where they work, they should wear gloves.

"You're handling people's food with your hands, anything can happen."

Miss Phillips also said that the nail was handed over to the health department.

'PIZZA' CALL ALMOST SPARKS TV WAR

A cheeky caller gave ZBM sports anchorman Mike Sharpe much food for thought—and nearly started a bizarre tv war.

The prankster amazed viewers by ringing Mr. Sharpe's new Sports Voice programme, and quipping: "Is that Four Star Pizza?"

It left ZBM bosses smelling something fishy, and suspecting rivals VSB [TV] may have been taking the mickey, or even the Michael.

But if that was the pasta joke, their presenter had more to swallow the following night.

This time it was a case of love on the air as a dialling damsel declared her affections for the TV sports announcer.

"I love you too," he replied, quick-as-a-flash.

One rumour probed by ZBM was that a VSB employee was the Four Star Pizza caller.

A ZBM journalist thought she recognised the voice, but inquiries drew a blank.

And VSB journalists have strongly denied having anything to do with the prank.

REPORTER'S NOTEBOOK

Accompanied by houseguests from overseas, a local shopper recently rolled his trolley up to the check-out counter at a major supermarket and unloaded the contents.

Things were going smoothly until the cashier came to an item marked $1.50. She stopped, turned to a fellow cashier on another register and, holding the item aloft, sang out: "Is $1.50 the right price for this? I thought it was $3 for two."

The visitors are still recovering!

LETTERS TO THE EDITOR

TONGUE TWISTER

Dear Sir,

I thought "Peter Piper picked a peck of pickled peppers" was a good one. But, needless to say, Senator Jerome Dill's (today's Royal Gazette) statement that Bermuda has been "perniciously and precariously perched on a perfidious precipice" took the cake.

Who was he talking to? Certainly it was not to the ordinary guy, as I am sure that his tongue-twisting tidbit left a lot of people wondering just what in the world he was talking about.

Will all those who took to their dictionaries, please stand up!

Pat Ferguson
City of Hamilton

WE HAVE ENOUGH LAWYERS

Dear Sir,

How many lawyers shall we end up having in our Houses of Parliament for Pete's sake? They keep coming at us in squads, mainly men of course.

What do we need them all for, Mr. Editor? Most of the lawyers I have met wouldn't know the difference between a recession and an outbreak of foot-and-mouth disease.

Moya Boyd
Somerset

CONSCIOUS OF FRAUD

Dear Sir,

It's good to see that our stores are becoming truly fraud conscious these days—but in real Bermuda style!

I made a purchase at a Reid Street store yesterday, for which I intended to pay by cheque. The assistant correctly asked if I had identification to support the cheque. I replied that I did and immediately began to search my bag for the required evidence. She stopped me immediately, and kindly told me that she didn't need to see my I.D.—she just needed to know if I had any!

I guess that's why Bermuda is 'Another World'—it's still so cute!

Maureen Bolland
Warwick

FOR THE RECORD

A divorce list provided to *The Royal Gazette* by the Supreme Court office on Monday erroneously included the names of Rosenell Caesar and Wendell Kenneth Eugene Caesar. The names on the list were published in yesterday's *Royal Gazette*. The Caesar's names should not have been included.

'THAT BUMP OVER SO.

ET BRIDGE WAS FUNNY, WAS'NT IT, DARLING?

Creature comforts

FOR AN island that is essentially tropical (it is actually subtropical, but let's not split hairs), Bermuda has very few bugs or critters or things that go SS*sssss* in the night. Virtually every other tropical spot from Barbados to Bora Bora has at least one thing to fear. Though you might never see the "thing" in question you know it is out there somewhere, and that is often enough to make meek writers from Canada squirm in their beds from dusk until dawn.

Bermuda and the Hawaiian islands are rare in this respect. There are no snakes, not even of the grass variety. Notices posted at the Bermuda airport proclaim this snake-free environment and urge you to cooperate. Violators (and believe me, they exist) are prosecuted if they attempt to import the slithery things.

Once every few years, a snake is spotted somewhere, and it is always because some idiot thought it would be "neat" to bring one back home for his girlfriend or as a pet. Only recently a customs agent got the shock of his life when he opened up a returning resident's suitcase to find a python coiled up comfortably under some underwear. An official inquiry was considered when it was discovered the underwear was not nearly presentable enough for a Bermudian citizen to travel abroad.

The majority of Bermudians are absolutely petrified of snakes. The mere thought makes them visibly shudder. What we do have is more than tolerable. Spiders, ants, chameleons of all sizes, gigantic toads, wasps and bees, and the cutest little frogs no bigger than the tip of your baby finger, nestled in bushes outside your windows, responsible for the harmonious nocturnal chirping that many visitors mistake for crickets. Rainfall is an aphrodisiac to them (the frogs), and the intensity increases tenfold.

Naturally there is an abundance of birds of myriad colors, more than three hundred varieties in all. Most prominent is the bright yellow-breasted kiskadee renowned for its unrivalled ability to know when it is Sunday morning and exactly who is still in bed with a raging hangover. Guaranteed one will land directly outside your open window on a bushy hibiscus and begin its tortuous and unrelenting shrill song consisting of one, two, or three monotonous notes. Believe me, the Partridge Family had a bigger repertoire.

Inevitably the arrogant bird enrages you so much that, unable to stand it any further, you fly out of bed, grab the nearest slipper or heavy object, and run outside to knock it senseless. The species is so plentiful the odd one will never be missed, but don't bet any money on making contact for they are very quick. Still, if you hurl granny's false teeth at one, it will fly off and leave you in peace.

Apart from an assortment of other harmless creatures, that's really all there is in the way of animals. No squirrels or skunks or porcupines, no badgers or foxes or weasels nor anything resembling a Member of Parliament. Once in awhile, some exotic creature will land on the island en route to somewhere else, but they do not usually stay for long. In no time at all, the creature comes to the conclusion that dating is going to be difficult.

The one life form that does take some adapting to and is capable of striking fear into the hearts of many is the dreaded Bermudian cockroach. During the summer months it spreads its hideous brown wings and actually takes flight . . . around your house! I still have not become completely used to them. Debbie Allen must be on contract because like the kiskadee, the flying cockroach choreographs its appearance with prescient consideration, usually the exact moment you decide to turn out your bedside lamp for the night.

Why is this the worst possible time? Because in my case, if I see one, I cannot rest until I catch it, kill it and flush its terrifying carcass down the toilet. Normally you have only one chance to catch him. Once he is aware you are in pursuit, he will move faster than a priest's hand on an altar-boy's zipper.

But I digress.

If there are sixty thousand people living in Bermuda, then surely there must be as many stray cats. They are everywhere. In your backyard, sleeping outside hotel lobbies and guest bedrooms, behind restaurants, roaming golf courses, main roads, sleeping on rooftops, and on the tops of anything that is comfortable looking.

It's mind-boggling that so many homeless felines can be in one place. Some are lovely, amiable animals and make terrific pets if they arrive on your doorstep seeking lodging and public assistance; others, with their gaunt, wasted appearance look like abortions on paws. At dusk they gather from miles around to pay homage to their great leader, union chief Ottiwell Simmons.

It's not only cats. There are also a good number of dogs. As you might expect, living in such close quarters with so many dogs and cats means there are strict laws applying to their behavior, which must be adhered to or there will be serious trouble. Contravene the tiniest rule and you'll find yourself standing in front of a judge.

If you own a dog, you are prohibited from breeding him without a licence. Should Rex stray down the road for an all-nighter, you could be in for a shock. Allowing him to mate with another of his species without the proper permission is a fineable offence. It matters not the slightest that you weren't a party to his illicit fling. You are expected to keep control and prevent him from leaving home period - take his car keys, ground him, or at least offer a stern lecture on safe doggy-style sex! (Not that I would personally know what that means.)

Nor is Rex allowed to bark whenever he feels like it. Keep your neighbors awake for one moment and you'll have to answer for it in court. Fines are severe. Rex cannot chase cats, accompany you into town unless on a leash, nor relieve himself on public property.

Many people find that the best protection is an invisible fence. A device is fitted around the animal's neck and an electric wire buried underground on his property. If Rex puts one stray paw over the line—ZAP! Just remember the same will happen to you if you remove your pet's collar to give him a well-earned scratch. A former shampoo girl-turned-charming wife of a well known doctor on Belmont Road, once relayed to me how she forgot she had her Labrador's collar in her hand as she proceeded through the gate to her neighbor's house for a chat. She did not make the mistake twice.

As for me, I have always been an animal lover. My sweet black pussy, named Rasputin, chose me at the SPCA three years ago, and I have been with him ever since. He's very good to me, too. Let's me feed him Fancy Feast whenever I want.

IT'S OFFICIAL: HORSE IS AN ANIMAL

A man accused of riding a horse after too many to drink was allowed to walk free from court yesterday when a magistrate ruled: "A horse is still an animal."

Senior Magistrate the Wor. Granville Cox concluded a horse could not be considered a vehicle as it has no wheels.

Kenneth DeSilva was charged with impaired driving on December 22 but sentencing was adjourned until yesterday.

"I have no difficulty in deciding that a horse is not a vehicle," Mr. Cox said. "A horse is still an animal. Until the law says something else I am dismissing the information."

Insp. Peter Duffy tried to prompt Mr. Cox in his decision saying the Oxford Dictionary definition of 'vehicle' is "a conveyance for transporting passengers from place to place."

Conveyance, he said, means anything used to transport people—a vehicle.

Mr. Cox advised 26-year-old DeSilva to change his plea to not guilty, and the court would drop the charge.

DeSilva, of St. Anne's Road, Southampton, was arrested by police in October after he fell from his horse during an early morning trot down Turtle Place in Southampton.

Officers had just finished a conversation with him and had noticed his speech was slurred.

DeSilva trotted off down the middle of the road when officers stopped him again. And on he went again when police finally decided he was too drunk to ride. They stopped him and were in the middle of telling him to get down from the horse when DeSilva fell off.

The officers said they were going to arrest him on suspicion of impaired driving and said he would have to come to Hamilton Police Station for a breathalyser test.

"Sure, get the horse to blow as well," DeSilva said. "I'm not drunk."

SHAKIN' THE AG SHOW BACON

The Director of Agriculture and Fisheries yesterday defended a $3,000 Government-funded trip he took to Las Vegas last November, saying it paid off by securing a new act for this year's Exhibition.

Mr. Ed Manuel said the recruitment of Robinson's Racing Pigs was well worth the five-day trip to International Association of Fairs and Exhibitions convention in Nevada though then-Senator David Allen claimed it was a waste of taxpayers' money.

"The trip was definitely worth the money involved," Mr. Manuel said. "We developed an awful lot of beneficial contacts and were looking for acts not just for this year but for years to come."

Mr. Manuel would not disclose how much money the show will cost to bring to Bermuda, but said he thought it would be a popular event.

"There will be a set of races two times a day, and each race will have two heats," Mr. Manuel said. "The best from each will be in the final on Saturday."

Robinson's Racing Pigs will bring the portly porcine beasts from Florida for the event scheduled each day of the three-day show starting on April 20 at the Botanical Gardens.

Because taking them back to the United States would involve a 60-day quarantine, the pigs will be sold to local farmers for raising, Mr. Manuel said.

Promoting pig racing as a travel attraction was the brainchild of Mr. Paul Robinson and his wife Carlotta, together with Mr. John Capobianco of Creative Outlet, Tampa - a company which handles special events for fairs.

Pig lovers Mrs. Gwen Norton—Mrs. Robinson's mother—and Mr. Capobianco will bring the pigs to Bermuda on April 18.

TOMFOOLERY

You might call this one "the revenge of the Toms" or "how the pedigreed are fallen."

Just last month, local cat breeder Mrs. Morag Smith introduced 'Living' readers to her family of prize Abyssinians. Proud mother Adqwesh Rosy Primrose (Rosy P for short) and her significant other Tommy Juice (commonly called TJ) were seen cavorting with their adorable litter in a special enclosure where the cats were kept when the Smiths were not around to supervise.

Since that time, three of the four kittens have been sold, in spite of their cool $300 price tags (the fourth has elected to remain with the Smiths indefinitely). The Smiths themselves talked optimistically of starting another litter sometime early next year.

Unfortunately, there has been a new, and less welcome, development in the Abyssinian saga.

It seems that mother Rosy P had occasion to sneak away from the family's Southampton home recently. The disappearance was short-lived, but still long enough for Rosy to fraternise with the neighbourhood Tom.

To the astonishment of both family and vet, the recalcitrant Rosy, who was at the time still nursing her first litter, was found to be once again with kitten. Four kittens in fact.

"One of her nicknames had been the 'Tart of Rebecca Road'," Mrs. Smith said this week. "I never realised how apt it was until now."

Luckily, though, since word of the impending arrivals leaked out, a number of family friends have rallied round and expressed interest in acquiring one or more of the exotic half-castes.

"As soon as all this is over, she's going on the Pill," Mrs. Smith said.

BERMUDA BREEDS A TOP ROACH

A Bermudian cockroach who grew sleek and fat amid high society in Riddell's Bay just missed out in his bid for glory at the Combat Quest For The World's Largest Cockroach.

The high-living roach, found drowned in a pool by Warwick resident Mr. Edward Lawrence, succeeded in putting Bermuda on the map as a breeder of extraordinarily large cockroaches.

But he stopped short, by fractions of an inch, of claiming first spot and instead had to settle for a top-four place at the championships in Miami.

US pest controllers who have spent their lives among cockroaches say they were stunned by the size of the Riddell's Bay monster, who blitzed the 1,015 international entrants to earn his place among the finalists.

"Now I consider myself something of a cockroachologist," said Combat field director Mr. Michael Bohdan, "but I've never seen anything like it."

Mr. Bohdan, of Texas, said Pied Piper Pest Control had sent off Bermudian entries in the past, but this year they were tantalisingly close to a major victory.

He was in Miami yesterday when the four roaches were officially measured at a ceremony lit by the glare of the US media, which apparently followed the story with great enthusiasm.

Mr. Bohdan said Combat was overwhelmed by the response to the competition, which attracted entrants from Australia, Japan, South Africa, Uruguay and Hawaii.

While some roaches arrived at Combat's offices dressed as Batman or lying in wooden coffins, no gimmicks were needed for the big fellow from Bermuda, whose sheer physical presence left even hardened pest controllers gazing in silent awe.

"Grossly obese," was how Mr. Lawrence described his prize entrant: "And not surprising either. He lived the good life in Riddell's Bay for far too long - right by the water with the golf course across the road."

"When we found him drowned in that pool there were a couple of empty liquor bottles lying around him," he added.

Defeat came as a disappointment but Mr. Lawrence said he was pleased Bermuda was finally being recognised as a breeder of quality cockroaches.

He now has plans to take the island to number one, even if it involves bending a few rules.

"I've got a vet friend whose looking at putting a couple of roaches on a steroid programme for next year's championships.

"You've got to put some effort into things if you want to stay number one."

Mr. Lawrence would have won $1,000 cash if his cockroach, which measured nearly two inches, had gone the distance. Mr.

Bohdan said the winner, one of Japan's biggest exports, measured up at exactly two inches.

DOG LANDS ITS OWNER IN COURT

A barking dog landed its owner in Magistrates Court on Friday because of complaints from neighbours about noise.

Darren Woods, 32, of Admiral's Walk, Southampton, pleaded guilty to allowing his dog to bark unreasonably.

Insp. Peter Duffy, prosecuting, said police were called by Woods' neighbours and arrived at the Southampton estate at 6 a.m. on August 5.

Lawyer Mr. Michael Smith said Woods had tried many ways to keep his dog quiet, including using a muzzle. When he failed he got rid of the animal.

Woods said: "I even took the dog to the vet and he told me it was normal for him to bark. I tend to concur."

But Senior Magistrate the Wor. Will Francis said it did not seem normal for the dog to "bark and bark and bark."

Woods said he got rid of the dog after receiving complaints.

Mr. Francis released Woods on conditional discharge.

Woods said: "I have a burglar alarm system now."

Mr. Francis said: "Well make sure that doesn't bark. Sometimes alarms make more noise than dogs."

RESIDENTS ANGERED BY STRAY DOG ANTICS

A stray dog is making the lives of some Cedar Park Apartment residents in Devonshire a misery.

And they have appealed to the Society for the Prevention of Cruelty to Animals (SPCA) to come and collect it.

The dog has sparked anger by taking clothes off residents' lines and dragging them to other people's yards.

Some have also complained about her running off with their shoes and ripping them up, and digging in the trash.

One resident told *The Royal Gazette* the dog had been roaming the area for the last six months.

She said fed-up residents had turned to the SPCA for help.

"But all they tell us is to try and catch the dog and tie her up—that, however, is not for us to do," said the resident, who did not want to be named.

She added: "If we were calling from Tucker's Town [a rich residential area on the island] they would be there in a hurry.

"The dog has taken people's clothes off their clothes line and dragged them to others' yards. That happened to me last week.

"The dog has also taken people's shoes and torn them up and she digs in the trash."

The resident said the dog also gave birth to 10 puppies last week in a hole she dug outside her mother's house.

"Someone called the dog warden to inform him of the puppies and he came to pick them up, but he left the dog that we had been complaining about. This is very aggravating and something needs to be done about it.

"This is not the first dog that we have had roaming around this area. It's almost like people think of the area as a drop-off spot for unwanted dogs."

The frustrated resident pleaded to the SPCA to "come and get this dog."

However, Government dog warden Mr. Leonard (Shinah) Simons explained: "I went to pick up the dog's puppies last week hoping to entice the mother. But since there was a crowd developing, the dog just stayed in the background and watched."

The puppies, which were three days old, were later put to sleep.

"The only thing left to do now is set a trap," added Mr. SImons. "However, sometimes a dog is too smart for a trap. A dog will sometimes just walk around the trap a few times then walk away."

BAG HAS 'EM HOPPING!

Four toads that made a home out of a trash bag probably didn't expect a visit from Police yesterday - and the group of amphibians was the last thing officers expected to see when they investigated the suspiciously moving bag.

The episode began as a potentially serious call to police yesterday afternoon.

"A member of the public called police to say he'd found a large trash bag at Shelly Bay that might contain a body that was still moving," said police spokesman Insp. Roger Sherratt.

Six officers in three cars were dispatched to the scene at the railway right-of-way near Bethel AME Church.

"They approached the bag cautiously and there was a large object inside and it was still moving. They carefully opened it and out popped four very large toads. Apparently they were living inside."

The toad family, said Insp. Sherratt, "were allowed to return to their new-found home."

FED UP WITH THEIR FOOD, PARROTS FLEE THEIR HOME

Bermudians are advised to be on the lookout for two escaped parrots.

The parrots, apparently fed up with their food, flew off at dinner time recently from the home of their owner, Mr. Tom Gibbons.

Mr. Gibbons, who owns more than 60 of the birds, says, "they escaped through an open door while being fed. The parrot is not as domestic an animal as a cat or a dog and every once in a while, they will try to leave."

The African Grey Parrot speaks, often saying, "What fun to be a baby bird." It also imitates other birds and can pick up any sounds it might hear.

The pets escaped from "Palm Grove" in Devonshire. Anyone who has seen the birds is asked to call Mr. Gibbons at tel. 295-0022

BLACKIE IS DEAD

Exactly one month after celebrating his 110th birthday (in dog years), Blackie Edmead has died.

According to owner Lee Edmead, the dog was put down yesterday following a long fight against cancer.

On July 16, Blackie was guest of honour at a large birthday party whose guest list included the Mayor of Hamilton, the Wor. Cecil Dismont, Government officials, veterinarians and visitors from the United States.

Guests brought over 300 cans of dog food to the party, which were donated to the Society for the Prevention of Cruelty to Animals.

NEW DEAL FOR 'LETHARGIC DOLPHINS'

Soaring summer temperatures mean more time to cool out for Bermuda's dancing dolphins.

Blue Hole Dancing Dolphins spokesman Ms. June Caisey said the number of shows have been cut in half because the dolphins are too lazy and tired to perform.

"They have been so lethargic," she said.

"They can't perform in heat over 85 degrees and its been in the near 90s almost every day."

Shows are now scheduled at noon and 3 p.m. Monday through Friday and on Sunday, instead of the usual four shows per day.

FRECKLES THE FELINE FALLS FOUL AFTER FUR-RAISER

When it came to hitching a fur-tive ride, there was no doubt Freckles the kitten could knock spots off others.

But the mite's spirit of adventure also caused her—and others—a fair spot of bother.

And, sadly, there was to be no happy ending to her latest escapade.

It began last Friday when Freckles' wild nature took her from Somerset to Hamilton - courtesy of Ms. Paula Carlington and her car.

Ms. Carlington had no idea she had an extra passenger when she drove to the law firm where she worked.

Her passenger's flight of feline fancy, however, was discovered when Ms. Carlington pulled in at the Richmond Road Esso station on her way home.

When the service attendant opened the car hood, Freckles was spotted in a corner of the engine compartment.

Ms. Carlington instantly recognized the Kitty as the stray she had seen occasionally in her yard.

Sporting a few oily spots, Freckles, looking very much as if she had lost her bearings, was then plucked from her hideaway.

"We all thought it was amazing this kitten had gone on such a journey," said Esso gas attendant Ms. Roberta Lovell.

"I knew of someone who wanted a cat so I took her home with me."

Ms. Lovell said Freckles - red, black and white and no more than six weeks old - gave her a sharp nip on the finger as she reached into the engine compartment.

"She was in good health and looked well fed, although maybe a little traumatised from the journey."

After returning to her home in Mount Road, St. David's, Ms. Lovell handed the kitty to her neighbour, Miss Debbie Burgess.

A thrilled Miss Burgess immediately called her new charge Freckles.

Joy was to turn to sorrow, however, when Freckles had another bout of wanderlust and slipped out the sliding glass door of her new home.

It was the last time Miss Burgess saw the tiny kitty alive.

Freckles' body was discovered yesterday in the neighbourhood. It is believed she had been attacked by a dog.

"It's really tragic that her adventure should end this way," said a distressed Miss Burgess.

BULL'S WALKABOUT IN VAIN

A love sick bull who went looking for a night of romance with Mr. Harry Kromer's dairy cows spent a contemplative day yesterday tied to an avocado tree, cooling his passions with buckets of water.

The bull's search for love began on Sunday night when he left his home at Town Hill in Flatts in search of the Kromer harem, which is about one mile down Middle Road.

He took a wrong turn and ended up in the grounds of Mr. Robert Lee's property, Somerville, where he found only a bird bath and a wooden letter box to keep him amused.

"He's destroyed the letter box and the bird bath. I think he was trying to scratch himself," Mr. Lee said.

Mr. Lee said the bull must have wandered about his property for some time during the night: "Apart from the letter box and bird bath there's some hard evidence he went near our pool," Mr. Lee said.

Mr. Lee said his wife thought they had been vandalised when she saw the damage. "But then I saw the bull eyeing me."

Mr. Lee called Mr. Kromer, who sent two men over to confirm the bull wasn't one of their herd.

They then tied the subdued animal to an avocado tree, with just a fence and a few short feet separating him from his beloved dairy cows.

"I've fed him four buckets of water today. He was a bit aggressive in the morning, but this afternoon he just seems to have sacked out," Mr. Lee said.

"It's a long way to come for the girls and not get them."

Mr. Franklin Charles, the bull's owner, said the animal had wandered off before, but never that far.

Mr. Charles said he had no doubt what the bull was after: "He just took a wrong turn. If he'd got another eighth of a mile further he would have been home free."

The bull was resting comfortably last night after his ordeal.

WOMAN ATTACKED BY DOGS, LOCKS HERSELF IN COFFIN ROOM

A New York woman here for her uncle's funeral fought back tears as she told how she was forced to lock herself in the coffin room of a Sandys Parish funeral home after being set upon by two wild dogs.

Mrs. Laverne Davis, 41, of the Bronx, said she was leaving Pearman's Funeral Home at Ely's Harbour just before 10 a.m. on Wednesday when the dogs attacked her, knocked her to the ground and attempted to drag her off.

Mrs. Davis said she hit the larger of the two dogs, believed to be a rottweiler, repeatedly in the mouth with her handbag but she said the dog wasn't deterred.

"It jumped me and pushed me down," she said from her mother's home in Southampton. "I was hitting him in the mouth because I thought it would lessen the chance of it biting me - and as I hit it, I tried to crawl back into the funeral home's door.

"I was kicking and hitting the dog, but it grabbed me by the pant leg and tried to drag me away from the door."

Mrs. Davis was able to push the swinging door open and crawl inside the building.

"But the dog wouldn't go away," she said. "It tried jumping up against the door to push it open. I was on one side of the door struggling to keep it shut, and the dog was on the other side trying to force the door open."

After a struggle of "a few minutes," Mrs. Davis said she heard the dog run around to the other side of the building, presumably to find another point of entry.

At that stage, Mrs. Davis said she ran into the coffin room and locked herself in.

"I stayed there until the owner of the funeral home found me almost an hour later."

Mrs. Davis went to the hospital and was found to have a fractured coccyx - the triangular bone ending the spinal column - and contusions to her hip.

Speaking some eight hours after the incident, she was still shaken.

"I cried all the way through - it was the most frightening experience of my life," she said. "It was a difficult thing to visit the funeral home, and then this happens. It was the most devastating experience of my life."

Funeral home owner Mr. Colin Pearman said he was familiar with the two dogs linked to the attack.

The smaller of the two dogs belongs to a neighbour, he said, while the larger, more aggressive dog belongs to someone in the neighbourhood.

"I saw the two dogs earlier in the morning on the lawn of our property—it was only the second time I'd seen the larger of the two dogs," he said.

But Mr. Pearman wasn't convinced it was a vicious animal.

"I don't know if it's vicious or just a big, playful pup," Mr. Pearman said. "I've never had any real contact with the dog, but it's a well-kept, well-groomed dog. I don't know why it was loose—it's usually kept in its kennel."

TERRIBLE TROTTERS

A pair of porky pigs proved terrible trotters in a weekend race to find Bermuda's fastest bovines.

A group called "Pigs R Us" were "less than disappointed" when the two had to be chased to the finish line as close to 40 spectators looked on at the Bernard Park try-outs.

The group advertised in *The Royal Gazette* for "two fast pigs" they could enter in next year's Agricultural Exhibition pig races.

But one minute after they were given the go-ahead, the trotting twosome had still not made it the full distance.

"We've gotta have faster pigs than this," Pigs R Us spokesman Mr. Kent Holden said. "It took those two one minute and eight seconds to be chased 40 yards to the finish line.

"We're very disappointed. We don't want a Bermudian pig to lose to an import. We have to have the home team advantage."

Mr. Holden said he and his syndicate agreed they will readvertise the try-out so owners can have time to whip their pigs into shape.

"It's a question of educating the pig population," he said. "It's our lifelong dream to have a champion pig."

ELEPHANTS TURNED HIM INTO WILD BULL

A couple living in the old nurses residence were chased from their house by a man who insisted he wanted a tetanus shot, a court heard yesterday.

Gilbert C. Woolridge, 32, of Smith's, admitted breaking into the home of Antonio Bruno and his girlfriend Sharon Johnson, and damaging $1,642 worth of property there.

Insp. Peter Duffy, prosecuting, told the court Woolridge - diagnosed as a chronic alcoholic - went on a rampage in the Smith's home, destroyed furniture and threatened to kill the occupants.

The court heard that the couple awoke at 7 a.m. last Wednesday when they heard someone banging on the door.

"The man, Woolridge, said he wanted to borrow a block and tackle," Insp. Duffy said.

"The couple did not understand what he was talking about when he insisted the woman was a nurse and he wanted a tetanus shot.

"Bruno told Woolridge to go away but he would not, and said if he wasn't given a tetanus shot he would kill them," Insp. Duffy said.

Woolridge then began to smash things in the house, including four mugs, doors and ornamental glass.

Woolridge, who kept insisting the home was the nurses residence, then chased the couple from the house and down Middle Road, scaring a jogger and several motorists who tried to help the couple by telling them he would kill them too.

Insp. Duffy said the home had been the nurses residence some years ago. And he said Woolridge was uncooperative, violent and irrational after his arrest.

Woolridge was taken to St. Brendan's hospital where a psychiatrist said he was a chronic alcoholic and had experienced blackouts because he drank too much.

And yesterday he showed the court a burn on his arm, saying he thought he needed a shot and went to the house to get one.

"I was under the impression the house was the nurses residence and went there because I had a burn on my arm," Woolridge said. "I don't know how I got there because I don't remember the whole weekend before that happened."

Woolridge admitted he had been drinking Elephant beers before his blackout.

Duty counsel Mr. Henry Prasad suggested a psychiatric report be ordered, but the Wor. Granville Cox said that wasn't necessary.

"The report will only say that the beers he had turned him into a wild bull," Mr. Cox said before he ordered the social inquiry report.

REPORTER'S NOTEBOOK

The Royal Gazette's *Let's Fix It* column has been going for about six years now and is carried along by tips from concerned citizens about the look of the Island.

We have shown all sorts of dangers and eyesores from over-grown foliage to garbage piled high and uncollected.

But a call we received this week beats them all.

A man, who every day travels down Stowe Hill on his way to Hamilton, finally couldn't take it anymore. He called *Let's Fix It* to "clear up something that's been left too long."

Just after the first bend on Stowe Hill, he said, there's a black and white spot on the road. It's a cat. Dead flat in the pavement. Been there for years.

Not really believing him, *Let's Fix It* went to the spot out of, er, curiosity. Sure enough, there flat in the road, arms outstretched in its last desperate reach for safety, lay the black and white cat. Unfixable.

FOUR APPEAR ON DOGS CHARGES

Dogs landed four people before a magistrate yesterday - and enriched Government coffers by $1,200.

Mr. Cox levied $300 fines for all the offenses:

Anthony Thomas, 26, of Loyal Hill Road, Devonshire, pleaded guilty to letting his dog stray and to having an unlicensed dog. He was fined $300 on each account.

Crown counsel, Mrs. Cheryl-Ann Mapp said his dog worried a cow and when captured was found to have the licence tag of a bitch.

Thomas showed Mr. Cox pictures of his dog. "They are very beautiful, but what are they meant to show?" asked the magistrate.

"That he doesn't attack animals," replied Thomas.

Valerie Butterfield, of Cambridge Court, Sandys Parish admitted having an unlicensed dog but pleaded not guilty to allowing a bitch in heat to be approached by a male dog. The second charge was dropped.

LETTERS TO THE EDITOR

TOO CLOSE

Dear Sir,

My wife and I recently returned from a "local" wedding and holiday in Bermuda. The wedding was wonderful and the balance of our holiday was terrific.

We always leave your island looking forward to the day we can return. Keep up the good work!

One situation we encountered disturbed me and has prompted this letter.

While shopping on Front Street, I paused at the window of one of your finer jewellery shops. Their display windows are usually very attractive and conducive to "window shopping," if nothing else.

At first glance their Christmas creche display was very attractive and very traditional. Closer examination revealed that a Rolex wristwatch was placed immediately adjacent to the crib of Jesus, closer than his mother or any other of the first Christmas night visitors. I find this very distasteful and insensitive to the Christian tradition. Perhaps it mirrors our overly materialistic society.

I am not overly religious, but this borders on extreme bad taste.

I attempted to communicate my concerns to the owner of the store but unfortunately he was not available that morning.

Tom Coyle
Ringwood, New Jersey

FORECAST: SUNNY SKIES & SNOW

Dear Sir,

My wife and I are frequent visitors, staying with friends in Paget. I also was a resident from 1980 until our marriage in 1989.

During all those years, I never experienced wintry weather on the island, but according to the weather page from the Providence Sunday Journal, (September 2), you had very unusual conditions—a high of 86 degrees, a low of 79 degrees and SNOW on Saturday the 1st.

Should we bring our skis on our next visit?

Stuart G. Galloway

Rhode Island

WHO NEEDS EXERCISE

Dear Sir,

Who needs a physical fitness programme?

Most of us get enough exercise jumping to conclusions, flying off the handle, knifing friends in the back, dodging responsibility, bending the rules, running down everything, circulating rumours, passing the buck, stirring up trouble, sawing logs, shooting the bull, polishing the apple, digging up dirt, slinging mud, throwing our weight around, beating the system and pushing our luck.

Parts Pups

Warwick

THE BAND WENT WRONG

Dear Sir,

I find it very hard to believe how your reporter in the Gazette dated 24/5/86 failed to mention anything about the Ex-Artillery majorettes and band. This group got so much applause from the parade watchers that along the route they were stopped by crowds to perform. The parade was not a success:

- The route was too short.
- The front of the parade clashed with the tail of the parade on Church Street.
- One horse was frightened by the loud music coming off the floats at Court/Church Street.
- The parade was stopped every so often to allow traffic through.
- Floats were tangled in overhead wires.
- Participants were subjected to sweet fumes in Princess Street.

If the Department of Youth had listened to some of the more experienced participants to change the route this wouldn't have occurred.

Disappointed Participant
Warwick

FOR THE RECORD

A photograph in Friday's edition purported to show a house involved in a dispute between the National Trust & Gerald Woolridge. In fact the photograph showed the house next door. *The Royal Gazette* apologises for the error.

'THAT MAKES FOUR REPETITIONS. ONE MORE AND ART
COMES INTO FORCE — AND THE HONOURABLE MEMBE
WHAT ARTICLE FIVE IS, DOESN'T HE?'

RULES
COMMITTEE

MPs AND SENATORS AGREE THAT THE RULES COMMITTEE
ONE MEMBER DESCRIBED SPEECHES AS: GARRULOUS, RE

'...HANGE THE FORMAT OF FUTURE BUDGET DEBATES.
...OUS, UNINSPIRING AND UNRESEARCHED...'

The banning of
Bermuda shorts

CHAPTER EIGHT

AH, GOVERNMENT. You can't live with it, and you can't live without it.

Bermuda, like America, is a democracy.

A moment will now be taken for all Bermudian residents to collect themselves.

Finished? Good.

As I was saying, Bermuda is a democracy.

Oh come on now, I have a book to write. I shall now explain how this particular democracy works.

Many prominent businessmen and the greatest linguists are called to office. The Hon. Sir John Swan, a prominent businessman himself and director of several corporations, is the current elected leader of the country. The Queen of England recently knighted him making him Sir John and his wife Lady Swan. But the

Premier himself does not—and he has said this publicly—does not benefit financially from his position one bit. In fact, he says he takes a loss by being Premier.

You have to sympathize with the statesman. In the early nineties, poor Sir John was paid a $2-million cancellation fee on a construction project he was spearheading in Hamilton. Such noble sacrifices are rarely seen in the world of politics.

Cabinet ministers usually include doctors, lawyers, hoteliers, rich entrepreneurs, heirs to the island's biggest department store chains, bankers, bakers, huge profit makers. Salaries are reasonably low so as not to make the ruse, I mean local gentry, appear overly avaricious.

But the perks! Well, first-class air travel wherever you desire, you know, to further the goals of one's ministry; passage through customs without making a declaration (they'll send you a bill later —just think of all the goodies you can bring in); you get to appear on the news whenever your ego needs a boost; you can even try out some of those new words you learned from Masterpiece Theater, but be careful, they are awfully big words and you must practice your pronunciation over and over; and, most nobly of all, you have the opportunity to take a personal hand in "shaping the future of your island."

Hhhmmm . . . shaping the future of your island. In Canada and the U.S., they have another term for it: influence peddling. Conveniently, no such laws exist here so imagine how advantageous this is to your family business. No official government policies on corporate behavior, no tedious and time consuming rules forcing declaration of assets or investments or tax returns for all and sundry to inspect. Why, it's like legalized insider trading.

There is no such thing as impartial conduct at any level of the Bermudian government or bureaucracy, from the planning department to immigration. If someone likes you or needs you or feels that you might one day do something in return for them, then your request will be granted. If not, bugger off! Government has been known to literally seize (through the courts) private land that it wants when the rightful owner has demanded too much money.

In reality, becoming involved in politics in Bermuda is sometimes a licence to print your own stack of million-dollar bills. Most of the family-run businesses that line affluent Front Street today were begun by a group known as "the Forty Thieves," with money earned from rum running. Attitudes have changed very little. A blind eye is turned now as it was then, and sage businessmen find a parliamentary seat for their sons at the first opportunity.

The country is more like a mini-fiefdom than a democracy. You have the lords with their inherited parcels of land who issue edicts to their minions living in smaller quarters at the edge of estates. Like Singapore, Bermuda operates under the guise of democracy but is in reality one of the world's cleverest and most civilized police states. Don't forget, it is considered indecent to go out in public without wearing underwear.

The old Ayatollah would be impressed.

Anybody can become an MP if they desire, as long as they possess enough pseudo-profundity and self-importance for one of the two main parties to nominate them as a candidate. It really is only coincidence that most candidates demonstrate a willingness to fall in line with party politics if elected. Criticize the hierarchy before you are prominent enough, and you are out at the next available opportunity. Upset too many people—MP or important private citizen—and you may find your bank loans being called in, though you've never missed a payment, or your application for a building permit or mortgage declined. Any number of unforeseen "complications" may arise if you incur the anger of the wrong person.

That said, what is good for the MP or cabinet minister generally *is* good for the people here because what is good for the cabinet minister—i.e. greater cash flow for his or her respective family business—means more jobs for the common man which translates into more money to spend on the local economy. As inconvenient as a rejected bank loan is, it is infinitely preferable to the rape and pillage carried out by some tyrannical governments, many of which, incidentally, are former British colonies, once civilized and safe until they sought independence from Great Britain, much like Bermuda is seeking it now. One wonders if Sir John has ever heard the old adage "If it 'ain't broke, don't fix it."

Lamentably, once the budget is balanced or unbalanced as the case may be, a politician's job is basically done. Then begins a parliamentary struggle lasting nearly twelve months for something to do. There's not a lot, so MPs really have to do some digging to come up with useful projects. Recent examples: Should Parliament give themselves a hefty salary increase? Do departing travellers really need bathroom facilities in the airport? How do you spell Bermuda? What color BMW should the Premier buy? Who will Senator Woolridge beat up next? Oh, the enormity of it all.

WE'RE STILL RICHER THAN THE CAYMANS

Finance Minister the Hon. David Saul last night refuted claims from the Cayman Islands that it has the biggest income per head in the region.

The Caymans, a flourishing offshore banking centre, said yesterday that its per capita income had reached $25,300 topping that of the United States, Canada and the other nations in the Western Hemisphere—including Bermuda.

But Dr. Saul pointed out the announcement was using out of date figures. Bermuda had a per capita income of about $27,000 [in 1992], he said.

The island's figure is still believed to be the highest in the hemisphere.

"I would not make too many great comparisons between Bermuda and the Cayman Islands," said Dr. Saul. "Our area is international business and theirs is offshore-banking.

"We're not looking over our shoulder."

DEFENCE FOR THE DECOR

Christmas cheer got left behind in the House when the Hon. Sidney Stallard demanded an apology from a fellow MP who had criticised the seasonal decorations at the Bank of Butterfield.

Mr. Austin Thomas (National Liberal Party) had slammed the bank and some other Front Street merchants east of Burnaby Street whose decorations were poor.

He had urged them to join their colleagues to the west and decorate the City.

Transport Minister Mr. Stallard leapt to defend his employer, saying (the Bank of) Butterfield had been complimented on its decorations by a number of people.

Mr. Stallard said the bank had abandoned its traditional Christmas tree on the roof of its Front Street Headquarters because the site was dangerous.

Trees had been blown around and electrical wiring disturbed in the past, he said during the adjournment debate.

The tree flagpoles had been decorated with lights and, some said, the effect from Harbour Road was of a giant Christmas tree or even a cruise ship tied at the dock.

Other decorations had been put up in windows and on the walls of all Butterfield branches.

"The bank does the best it can. A great deal of time and money has been spent on decorating the bank as well as we can.

"Mr. Thomas owes the House and the people an apology," he said.

Unfortunately for Mr. Stallard, Mr. Thomas had already left the Chamber and no apology ever came.

CLARIFICATION

A Government spokesman yesterday clarified his comments concerning a specialist who had worked on the development of the Transport Control Department's computer system.

"He was let go at the end of his contract, but that's not the same as being fired," Information Services Director Mr. Bryan Darby said.

MP'S WIFE SLAPPED TWICE IN FACE DURING GROCERY FRACAS

Police were called after a bust-up involving an MP's wife and another shopper erupted at White's Supermarket on Thursday night after a third woman was allowed to jump a long queue of panicked buyers.

Police say that Mrs. Angela Hayward, wife of Pembroke West Central MP Mr. Stuart Hayward, complained she had been slapped twice by a 28 year old Southampton woman after the woman had offered to let another shopper jump the queue in front of herself and Mrs. Hayward.

Police were called to the Middle Road, Warwick store just after 5 p.m. by a White's employee who was responding to a complaint by Mrs. Hayward.

Police say a verbal exchange between the two women preceded a dispute in which Mrs. Hayward claims she was slapped in the face twice.

Police say Mrs. Hayward did not want to press charges, and was apparently satisfied that the other woman—whose name police refused to disclose—had paid a visit to Hamilton police station where she was warned about her behavior.

Mrs. Hayward yesterday declined comment on the bust-up, but the other woman in the dispute—Mrs. Devore Brangman of Industrial Park Road, a senior accounting assistant with a Hamilton financial firm—was more than willing to tell her side of the story.

Mrs. Brangman, who works at James Bermuda Limited in Hamilton, said she was standing in a check-out line at White's just after 5 p.m.—and was in front of Mrs. Hayward, who had a full trolley of goods.

Mrs. Brangman claims that a third woman carrying a small number of items, apparently not realising that Mrs. Hayward was in the line, stepped in behind Mrs. Brangman.

"Mrs. Hayward said: 'Excuse me, but I am before you in this line'," Mrs. Brangman said yesterday. "The woman said, 'I'm sorry, I didn't realise you were in line'—and then stepped behind Mrs. Hayward in the line.

"But when I looked and saw the girl had just four or five items—and Mrs. Hayward had a whole trolley—I figured I'd let her go in front of me."

And that's when the fireworks started, Mrs. Brangman said.

"The woman thanked me—but this angered Mrs. Hayward, who flew into a rage at me and said: 'Would you like to let everybody go before you?' I told her that one person with only a few items wouldn't make much difference, but she started shouting and carrying on at me, and I started shouting and carrying on at her."

Mrs. Brangman said she pointed her finger in Mrs. Hayward's face as she talked.

"I was pointing in her face and saying 'forget about the situation, we'll all get served' and she slapped my hand away from her face.

"So I slapped her face. She screamed that I had assaulted her, and grabbed my wallet away from me—so she could get my name, I guess.

"She had no right to take my wallet, so I slapped her again."

White's officials declined to comment on the fracas.

ASSAULT CHARGE

The woman who slapped MP Mr. Stuart Hayward's wife, Angela, in the face during a grocery line melee in April has been charged with assault.

In Magistrates Court yesterday, Devore Brangman, 30, of Southampton denied assaulting Mrs. Hayward.

Senior Magistrate the Wor. Granville Cox ordered Brangman back to court on February 2 to stand trial.

MPS CAN AVOID LINE AT CUSTOMS

MPs can avoid standing in line to have their bags searched at the Airport, Finance Minister the Hon. David Saul told the House of Assembly on Friday.

They can normally hand in their Customs declarations forms, he said, and a bill for the duty will be sent to them. The MPs are expected to pay these bills promptly, he said.

But Dr. Saul said this privilege is a courtesy and not an automatic right of office.

Dr. Saul spoke after several MPs criticised this newspaper for printing a brief story and two letters to the Editor after Opposition MP and BIU President Mr. Ottiwell Simmons was spotted bypassing the normal Customs line-up on February 2.

Mrs. Browne Evans (PLP), speaking in defence of Mr. Simmons, said the union president had brought in $1,200 in goods. She said he filled out his Customs declaration form and subsequently paid the $291.09 duty he owed.

Mr. Simmons himself said he always fills in the proper forms and pays his bills. On this occasion, he said, the forms were filled out and the bill paid before *The Royal Gazette* ran the story.

GOV'T TO 'PAY MORE ATTENTION' TO YOUTH NEEDS, SAYS PREMIER

Government has heard the message from young people "loud and clear" and will commit itself to "paying more attention" to their needs, Premier the Hon. Sir John Swan told close to 500 youngsters at Camden House yesterday.

Sir John, surrounded by children on the lawn at his official residence in the Botanical Gardens, said: "This is your moment. You must carve your place in history. You must give to your country something that your Country is supposed to give to you—a better future."

GOV'T DROPS PLANS FOR YOUTH COUNCIL

Government has dropped plans to establish a youth council as part of its programme to keep in touch with Bermuda's young people.

TEACHERS GET THEIR LESSON

The Island's new teachers got a lesson in priorities Bermuda-style at their orientation meeting yesterday. After sitting through speeches on tourism and offshore business, a talk on the education system was dropped for lack of time.

Chief Education Officer Mr. Sinclair Richards was to have detailed the system the new teachers are headed into. Unfortunately he was slated to speak late in the programme.

Preceding him were Tourism Director Mr. Gary Phillips, who told the teachers how important tourism was to Bermuda—complete with statistics—and Finance Secretary Mr. Mansfield Brock, who spoke on the history of captive insurance.

Between Messrs. Brock and Phillips was Miss Ruth Thomas, of Community and Cultural Affairs, speaking at some length on Bermudian culture.

Unionist Mr. Glen Fubler jokingly called the afternoon—held in a non- airconditioned room at Bermuda College—a "rite of initiation" for the approximately 30 new teachers who attended.

This year 47 teachers will join the education community, more than twice the number of new ones last year. Of those, 28 are Bermudian.

Miss Thomas warned the new arrivals that Bermudians were very friendly and not to ignore a good-morning greeting.

"But don't be lulled into thinking we are pushovers," she added.

"We are extremely materialistic, and we often criticize ourselves for that," said Miss Thomas. "And we are also politically alert, generous, courteous, sensitive and curious."

She said some students will seem spoiled, having too much money. But she speculated some working parents compensate for their absence by giving their children money.

US POST OFFICE BELIEVES SANTA'S HOME IS BERMUDA

A letter addressed to Santa's North Pole Headquarters has found its way to his local hangout via the US postal system.

The fact the letter reads simply: "Santa Claus, North Pole" has made our own Santa jolly.

Its return address is in Brooklyn, New York, and although the Brooklyn Post Office could not be contacted to relate how the letter reached Bermuda, a call to a Brooklyn information service verified there is an "Albergo" family listed at the given address by six-year-old Allyson.

The letter reads: "Dear Santa, my name is Allyson Albergo and I am six years old. I would like to thank you for all the gifts you gave me last Christmas. I have played with them all year and I enjoyed them very much. This year I have been a very good girl. I eat all my vegetables and listen to my Mommy and Daddy.

"I know how busy you are, but if you have the time I hope you could bring me a gift."

Allyson then goes on to list six items she would like to find under the Christmas tree and four items she would like Santa to bring her 18-month-old sister.

A delighted Santa Claus has reported he will be writing a return letter to the youngster.

LETTERS GO TO BOLIVIA BY MISTAKE

Bermuda's mail problems continued this week, this time thanks to the US Postal service, which sent a large batch of letters to Bolivia by mistake.

More than 100 air mail letters, most dated December 3, were returned to the USA on January 15 and arrived in Bermuda on January 30.

The letters, which will be delivered immediately, were in two lots labelled Bermuda Package 23 and 24.

The one question still being investigated by the US and Bermuda post offices is: where are the other letters in packages one to 23?

POST OFFICE ACT IS FINALLY PASSED

The Post Office Amendment Act finally became law yesterday after a lengthy struggle through both Houses of Parliament.

The Senate approved the Bill's third reading in a special session yesterday morning. The five Government senators and senate vice president the Hon. Norma Astwood (Ind) supported the Bill while the three Opposition senators and Sen. Albert-Jackson (Ind) and Sen. Joe Johnson (Ind) opposed it.

The controversial Bill—which allows mail to be opened by Customs and Post Office officials without the presence of the addressee—was passed at the special Senate session yesterday after being passed in breach of Senate rules two weeks ago.

The Bill was narrowly passed by the House of Assembly earlier this year amid claims that it violated human rights.

CUSTOMS ANSWERS ADVERT OFFERING MAN'S LUGGAGE

Little escapes the notice of Bermuda's Customs service.

It was a message Mr. Maxwell Roberts learned the hard way recently when trying to sell an expensive set of luggage.

The 33-year-old Bermudian took out a newspaper advertisement a few weeks ago, extolling the virtues of a $4,000 set of Louis Vuitton luggage.

At his office the next day, Mr. Roberts received a call—not from a potential buyer, but from a Customs official who wanted to know if he had proof that the luggage was either bought in Bermuda or had had duty paid on it.

"I bought the luggage from Calypso several years ago and never used it," Mr. Roberts recalled yesterday. "So I decided it was time to sell it."

But Mr. Roberts had neglected to keep his receipt over the years. Thankfully, a Calypso sales clerk managed to dig out some old records of the purchase and Mr. Roberts presented them to Customs.

"They apologised for the inconvenience," Mr. Roberts said, "after I asked for an apology."

While Mr. Roberts says he is satisfied with the apology, he questions whether "there were not more discreet ways" of Customs checking into the matter. He regrets being called at work.

Mr. Jerry Ardis, the acting Collector of Customs, said yesterday that it was all in a day's work for his men.

"The Customs officers are carrying out their duties under the law," he maintained. "It is our responsibility under the Revenue Act to investigate all matters that may involve smuggling.

"Our investigators read your newspaper and they are particularly interested in the classified pages," Mr. Ardis said. "We've had numerous cases of people buying jewellery and other merchandise overseas and then smuggling them into Bermuda to sell. These aren't isolated instances, they happen everyday."

Mr. Ardis disagrees with any suggestion that the Customs service operates on the presumption of guilt.

"We're telephoning people up to make sure that no laws have been broken," he said. "Customs doesn't assume anything."

Citizens do not have to keep stacks of receipts to prove their innocence, Mr. Ardis added.

"We're very amenable to any reasonable explanation."

CLAIM FAMILY'S PRIVACY INVADED

Bringing back a video camera from the United States can be a risky business, a Southampton family is learning.

Three weeks ago, Mr. Charles O'Neil brought back a Zenith video camera from a business trip in New York. He has not been able to shake Customs officials since.

"He paid duty on the camera and other bits and pieces," his wife Mrs. Jody O'Neil said yesterday.

Nevertheless, Customs agents have paid two unannounced visits to the O'Neil home in the past week. They seemed determined to prove that Mr. O'Neil spent more than the $495 he claimed he paid for the video camera in New York.

"Last Thursday, three gentlemen from Customs came to my home," Mrs. O'Neil recalled, "at about 6 p.m., just as my husband was dishing out the supper. They asked to see the camera."

Two days ago, three Customs agents returned to the O'Neil home at 7.30 a.m. and produced a search warrant.

"They said they had a warrant to search my home," Mrs. O'Neil said. "They picked mainly through my husband's drawers and looked through all our papers in the living room. They didn't take anything.

"They said they were hoping to find my husband at home, but he leaves for work at 5.30. My children were subjected to it—they are five and six years old—they didn't know what was going on."

Mrs. O'Neil says her family does not know what to expect next but she feels her privacy has been violated. She says her family has never been in any trouble before.

"I wonder when they're going to be at the door next," she said. "I think it is all a bit unnecessary. Why didn't they do something about it at the airport. Usually they seize things down there, don't they?

"Two weeks after his bags were searched, his duty paid...Why are they coming back?"

Repeated messages left for Customs director Mr. Richard Kellaway, designate director Mr. Jerry Ardis, and deputy director Mrs. Norma Smith all went unanswered yesterday.

DRUGS DOGS LET IN

Three new drug-sniffing police dogs were finally let into the country Friday after being sent away with their tails between their legs last Saturday.

The dogs were imported to beef up the Bermuda Police's canine drug detection squad, but when they got off the plane, Customs officials found their papers were not in order.

Although the dogs had been vaccinated against rabies, police spokesman Sgt. John Instone confirmed they didn't have certificates to prove it.

SIGN VIOLATION

A Front Street merchant was yesterday ordered to remove an illuminated sign from his shop window.

Mr. Douglas Patterson, the owner/manager of beachwear store Makin' Waves, was visited by Planning's chief enforcement officer Mr. Larry Dixon after a complaint was made about a sign two feet in diameter which was seen in the store's window.

The sign, which advertised a French clothing company, has been moved to another spot in the store—making it impossible to be seen from the street, Mr. Patterson said.

"That satisfies us," said Mr. Martin Lightfoot, assistant director of Planning. "As long as the sign is in a location where the public can't see it from the street, then it's perfectly okay."

Mr. Patterson said he wasn't aware of the law prohibiting illuminated window displays.

"I saw them in the windows of some of the major department stores last Christmas, and figured it was okay," he said. "But I had a visit from someone from Planning today, and the sign has now been moved."

A CRITICAL LOOK AT BERMUDA'S MEMBERS OF PARLIAMENT

MR. NELSON BASCOME—SHADOW MINISTER OF HEALTH, SOCIAL SERVICES AND HOUSING: A civil servant-turned politician can be dangerous and it gives him an advantage which he uses well. But he tends to shoot from the hip and miss the target. Needs to brush up his oratory skills as he tends to get lost in the middle of his speeches.

THE HON. HASKINS DAVIS: One of the most regular attenders (in the House) but his complete silence makes one wonder why he bothers. At 71, he is the oldest member of the House and gives an unfortunate impression he is only staving off complete retirement. As former Environment Minister he could bolster Mrs. Cartwright DeCouto—if only he would say something.

MR. DENNIS LISTER—SHADOW MINISTER OF YOUTH, SPORTS AND RECREATION: A major disappointment, the youngest MP appears not to know his subject—he once asked whether cricket watchers would be comfortable at the National Stadium, where there is no [cricket] pitch. A dull speaker, he has to improve greatly.

MR. WALTER ROBERTS—SHADOW MINISTER OF TRANSPORTA-TION, DEPUTY OPPOSITION LEADER: One of the Gang of Four who have survived 27 years in the House. His fascination with computers has allowed the PLP to update its internal operation. But a very dull speaker who is guaranteed to empty the Chamber when he gets up.

MR. ERNEST DECOUTO—DEPUTY SPEAKER: Earnest Ernest can appear to be a dull but worthy member, but occasionally proves that wrong. Is an effective chairman of the House in committee, one of the main functions of his role, although he can rouse the ire of the PLP which feels he is being unfair to them.

THE HON. QUINTON EDNESS, MINISTER OF HEALTH, SOCIAL SERVICES AND HOUSING: Lovable QE has all the PR skills to carry him through, but always manages to attract controversy. Has become the butt of (MP) Mr. Julian Hall's barbs—which rile him. Can annoy Cabinet colleagues by speaking on their subjects, which has earned him the nickname of The Minister of Everything.

BERMUDIANA 'NEEDS AN ARSONIST'

Finance Minister the Hon. David Saul last night called for a pro-gramme of development and destruction to bring in tourist dollars and revive Bermuda's economy.

Dr. Saul told a public forum that the tourism industry should embrace the Ritz Carlton proposals. But he said the Bermudiana [hotel] "needs an arsonist" and Club Med "needs a bulldozer" to get them out of the way.

REVEREND TAXI DRIVER UNDER FIRE

The son of St. George's Mayor the Wor. Henry Hayward says Opposition Senator (Reverend) Trevor Woolridge threatened to beat him up over a cab fare dispute.

In a letter to the Editor, Mr. John Henry Hayward claims Sen. [Rev.] Woolridge got angry over being asked to change a $100 bill for a $5 fare and demanded Mr. Hayward get change himself.

Mr. Hayward claims Sen. [Rev.] Woolridge drove him to the Hamilton Princess [hotel] with the meter running to get change. After he changed the $100 bill, Mr. Hayward wrote, Sen. [Rev.] Woolridge demanded he pay the $5 plus the extra $2 the meter ran up getting the change.

"I gave Mr. Woolridge the original amount only whereupon the Christian Mr. Woolridge (who is by no means a small man) threatened me in the parking lot with his '15' and a few other choice words if I did not give him the full amount," wrote Mr. Hayward.

The term '15' means fists.

"So I gave him the $2 in dispute and made a fast exit," said Mr. Hayward.

Last night Sen. [Rev.] Woolridge said: "From the moment I picked up the gentleman the whole fare was suspicious and he did nothing during the fare to relieve my suspicions."

"If he has a complaint I refer him to the Public Service Vehicles Licensing Board where I'm certainly prepared to meet him. Beyond that I have zero comment," said Sen. [Rev.] Woolridge.

TAXI PERMIT UP FOR GRABS

The auction of a taxi permit today may set the going price for getting into the business in the wake of Government's decision to sell 36 new permits for $50,000 each.

A public auction of a taxi and permit held by Mr. Samuel Brangman will be held at 12.30 p.m. at the Old Fire Station on Court Street. Although taxi permits have sold for tens of thousands more, Government's decision to sell the new permits for $50,000 might affect the going rate.

Transport Minister the Hon. Sidney Stallard hasn't said if the new licences will be released all at once or gradually during a set period.

Another factor which may affect the price is whether there are sufficient people with the interest—and access to enough money—to buy the new permits.

TAXI DRIVERS HAVE TOO MUCH MONEY

Government is considering increasing taxi fares as a way to improve service, Transport Minister the Hon. Sidney Stallard revealed last night. But the Minister hinted an increase would not be the answer to Bermuda's taxi problems which have stranded tourists at the Airport and hotels this year.

"Our problem is that there appears to be too much affluence in the community," he said. "We have good drivers who work hard but many drivers are not on the road to give service. It appears they don't want to make money because things are going well."

Mr. Stallard said drivers told him they would improve Airport, late-night and public holiday service "if you make it worth our while. We want to go where the money is."

IT'S 'TOUGH' BUT MPS TAKE CASH

Calling it a "difficult, painful, but necessary" move, Finance Minister the Hon. Clarence James yesterday gave himself a 74 percent pay raise.

Under his new salary plan, passed yesterday by the Lower House, Dr. James' salary will jump to $58,000 from its present $32,000.

Other members'—and Senators'—salaries will go up between 40 and 80 percent, depending on the position held.

Premier the Hon. John Swan defended the increase, saying the workload and responsibilities of MPs has increased in recent years. The increase will also encourage talented people to run for election, who otherwise couldn't afford to serve.

But he warned his cabinet: "I as the Premier will expect more of my Ministers, and I know they work very hard now, and I will expect more of myself, although I work 14 to 16 hours a day, even on weekends."

Both the Progressive Labour Party and the National Liberal Party opposed the pay increases, and Government backbencher Mr. Harry Soares spoke against it, but the increases passed on an unrecorded vote.

"There are two things you don't mess with—a person's wife and a person's money," said Mr. Soares. "I think we're messing around with people's money."

LUNCH HOUR HITS HOUSE ATTENDANCE

It seems not many MPs were listening very carefully to Premier the Hon. John Swan's pep talk a week ago—when the House resumed after its lunch break yesterday 34 of the 40 seats were empty.

During debate of Parliamentarians' pay raises last Friday, Mr. Swan promised he would "expect more" from his cabinet.

By 2.20 p.m., 21 seats were still vacant. Finance Minister the Hon. Clarence James arrived just before 3 p.m. At 3 p.m., 25 MPs had taken their places.

The House began a four month recess at the end of yesterday's session.

PLANS FOR CRACK HOUSE

Government's Housing Corporation has its sights set on buying and redeveloping the drug-infested Anglican Church property on St. Monica's Road.

Preliminary plans exist to build new housing in the crime-stricken area for low income families, Housing Corp. director Mr. John Gardner confirmed last night.

The St. Monica's Mission area is infamous for its ties to the Island's trade in cocaine, crack and cannabis. Church officials are particularly anxious to rid themselves of a highly fortified crack house—surrounded by a six-foot high fence and guarded by pit bulls—that they own next to St. Monica's Church.

The major stumbling block appears to revolve around what to do with the existing tenants. The Housing Corp. says it is prepared to find "suitable alternate accommodation" for the tenants but only after the Church has cleared the way—either by getting approval from tenants or by forcing the issue through evictions. A number of tenants are known to be opposed to any redevelopment plans.

But the Anglican Church is desperately looking for help. It is reluctant to take any action for fear of reprisal.

Lingering in the back of everyone's mind is the night of November 10, 1987, when St. Monica's Church was torched. The fire, which caused more than $17,000 in damages, was believed to have been set by local drug dealers bent on revenge for a recent police crackdown on their narcotics trade.

MAGISTRATE SAYS DON'T TAKE THOUGHTS SERIOUSLY

The island's top magistrate yesterday told lawyers they should not take anything he says seriously.

Instead, said the Wor. Granville Cox, when he speaks to them he is merely thinking aloud.

"You shouldn't take anything the court says seriously," he told Crown Counsel Mrs. Cheryl-Ann Mapp. "It is just talking to itself and letting you know what it thinks."

Minutes earlier Mr. Cox had scolded Mrs. Mapp for making an application he said she had no power to make.

HEALTH INSPECTOR 'CHASED FROM RESTAURANT PREMISES'

Police are investigating allegations a Smith's Parish cafe restaurateur chased a health inspector from the premises and damaged his car.

Community Relations Officer Insp. Roger Sherratt revealed last night the alleged assault and malicious damage to the inspector's car is said to have occurred on May 17.

"We have the matter under investigation," Insp. Sherratt said.

The health inspector, Mr. Roger Mello, declined to comment when he was contacted last night, saying the matter would be coming before the courts: "I am not allowed to say anything about it at the moment."

The Royal Gazette has learned the eatery is the Mid-Star Cafe—on Harrington Sound Road near Sommersall Road—which was being examined after reports of health regulation violations.

LOBSTER PROBABLY EATEN

The fate of a laboratory-infected spiny lobster, which disappeared last month from a tank on Coney Island, is likely to remain a mystery.

That is the verdict of Assistant Director of Fisheries Mr. John Barnes, who first sent out the warning that the five pound missing lobster was carrying potentially lethal chemical compounds as part of an ongoing experiment at the Department of Fisheries.

"What it boils down to," Mr. Barnes said, "is that we will probably never hear from it again."

Mr. Barnes fears that someone may have stolen the lobster for dinner despite warning signs.

"Anyone who thinks they can go to Coney Island for a free lobster dinner had better think twice," Mr. Barnes warned.

The lobster was one of a small number which are being analyzed, sometimes using chemical compounds, to try and establish the genetic composition of the Bermuda lobster.

PREMIER MEETS PRESS

The Premier is today due to give details of what Cabinet learned in its three-day brainstorming get-together which ended late last night.

The Hon. John Swan refused to comment on the meeting—which was partly to discuss better communications.

PREMIER'S 'JUNK' CAR STILL RUNNING

Government officials were yesterday still driving around in an eight-year-old car almost 12 months after it was described as junk.

The elderly blue Morris Marina was said to be on its last legs when used as official vehicle for Premier the Hon. John Swan. He was initially given Parliamentary approval to spend $31,640 on a luxury new BMW after complaining the elderly car was unreliable and too cramped for formal occasions.

The decision sparked a political row with [the opposition] MPs complaining the Premier was merely seeking an expensive status symbol.

Government Information director Mr. Bryan Darby yesterday said: "The car that was formally used by the Premier for his official engagements was taken over by the Public Works Department."

Mechanics worked on the eight-year-old vehicle and it was regarded as an addition to Government's car pool, although he added it was still far from reliable.

"The car is used from time to time by senior civil servants on Government business and for taking visiting officials to developments through the island.

"The Secretary of the Cabinet, Mr. Kenneth Richardson on occasions uses the car to get home when he has been working late at the Cabinet Office, a practice which does enable the battery to be recharged for the next day."

SENATORS BAN NATIONAL DRESS

Senators yesterday rejected a call to change a 350-year-old tradition and banned Bermuda shorts from the Upper House of Parliament.

Worried Government senators warned standards would slip and the Senate would suffer a loss of dignity if senators wore Bermuda's unofficial national costume in the ornate chamber.

Independent Senator Albert Jackson even complained senators would be distracted from important business if women senators turned up wearing Bermuda shorts.

He added it would give the Opposition an extra weapon in their debates as the only woman senator is the [Opposition party's] Sen. Jennifer Smith.

But [Opposition] senators argued it was time for Bermuda to shrug off its Colonial hangovers and to take pride in the Island's heritage.

Independent Senator James Williams called for a relaxation of strict dress codes after mistakenly wearing Bermuda shorts to a meeting of the Senate two weeks ago.

Last year the Senate voted to allow senators to wear Bermuda shorts but Parliament was dissolved before senators had a chance to don their shorts.

Opposition Senate Leader Sen. David Allen said Bermuda shorts had been introduced to the island by British Naval officers at Dockyard but had now been adopted as part of the national heritage.

"This is an expression of our awakening national identity," he said. "It is in tune with these times and the talk of Independence."

Sen. Albert Jackson (Ind.) said: "I hope we are not approaching this from a male chauvinist-point of view. I wouldn't want to have male members voicing disquiet if a female senator wore this attire."

But Sen. Jennifer Smith (PLP) insisted Bermuda shorts were traditionally only worn by men and the motion would not allow women to turn up in Bermuda shorts.

Sen. Llewellyn Peniston (UBP) warned: "If we start allowing our sartorial standards to slip, we could end up with open shirts and ample gold chains around our necks. I'm in support of preserving our traditions."

Senate President the Hon. Hugh Richardson, who recently attempted to demand a referendum on Independence, said he opposed changing the dress code.

"To wear a pair of shorts in the Senate chamber is certainly not going to prepare us for Independence," he said.

The proposal was defeated by seven votes to four.

BIU WANTS AN APOLOGY

A manager's offhand comment that "assassinating" Bermuda Industrial Union boss Mr. Ottiwell Simmons MP would be one way to boost a hotel's bar profits has the union demanding a big apology.

Marriott's Castle Harbour chief shop steward, Mr. George Scott, said workers want food, beverage and room service manager Mr. Michael Lima to say he's sorry to the entire hotel staff, and to Mr. Simmons.

And he wouldn't rule out the possibility of a strike, if the apology isn't made.

"That's what I'm saying—they have to clear the air," he said, when asked about the possibility of a strike.

Last night, a contrite Mr. Lima said he regretted the comment the moment it stumbled off his tongue.

"We were having a little brainstorming session and it just popped out of my mouth," he said. "There was no harm intended," he said, adding he was just joking.

'RETHINK BOOZE BID'

A [Opposition] Parliamentarian yesterday urged the Bermuda Fire Services to reconsider and withdraw its application for a liquor licence.

Speaking on the Motion to Adjourn, Mr. Reginald Burrows said he was distressed to see the application for licence published in recent newspaper legal notices.

"I would appeal to their better judgement and hope they would rethink this application," he said. "We already have too many liquor establishments in Bermuda and in any case firemen only have to walk a few yards from their headquarters to find clubs and bars where they can get drinks.

"All of us have a lot of respect for the Fire Services and normally we give them a tremendous amount of praise in this House. I just hope they will not go ahead with this and remain without liquor facilities at their headquarters."

SMALL TALK GETS MP IN HOT WATER

To the Hon. Clarence Terceira it was just a case of making small talk at a VIP reception.

But his Portuguese listeners felt otherwise—and gave the Education Minister short shrift.

It was belittling for the Minister to jokingly call small Portuguese men "pocket manuals," they fumed.

Now Dr. Terceira—himself of Portuguese descent—has apologised for any offence. "I certainly did not mean to offend anyone. I'm sorry if I did."

Dr. Terceira made the remark during a reception at Stonington campus for the All Star Games—the schools' soccer tournament.

Yesterday he said the lighthearted comment had been made while he was being introduced to the teams. "I noticed how the players of Portuguese descent were much smaller than the others."

Dr. Terceira, himself just 5 ft 6 in, said he pointed out how Portugal's famous soccer player Eusebio had also been short.

One of those offended by his quip was Mr. Michael Madeiros, vice chairman of the Portuguese Bermudian Association.

He wrote a letter to Dr. Terceira later, taking him to task over the remark.

"As you are aware Bermudians are currently working very hard to erase the negative racial stereotypes of the past and we hope that we can count on you to be a part of this process," wrote Mr. Madeiros.

BAA FIELD CLOSED

The BAA field was closed until further notice yesterday following revelations that live wires surrounding the grounds have electrocuted soccer players, spectators and even children over the last few months.

The latest incident, which occurred on Wednesday night, saw two soccer players in the Commercial Cup receive electric shocks from a live floodlight wire when they accidentally struck it during the game.

One of the players, Mr. Michael Cook, a winger for Exiles fell to the ground, clutching his heart and writhing in agony due to the wire hitting him in the throat. The game was abandoned.

Complaints to the BAA officials about incidents involving both senior and junior players being shocked were made by at least two other soccer clubs before Wednesday night's incident.

A spokesman for the Vasco Da Gama football club said yesterday: "One of our junior players, a 14-year-old, got shocked so badly two months ago it nearly bounced him right out of the car park.

"If he hadn't been told by someone to lift his feet off the ground he could have been seriously hurt," she said.

Vasco Da Gama is one of a number of clubs that use BAA to play matches on.

She added: "Another young player ended up with a burn mark right down the length of his back as a result of touching the wire, but you know it's not just our young players, this includes some of our senior players as well.

"This isn't a recent problem, this goes back almost three months. We complained because we didn't want to see some little kid come along and put his hand on the wire 'cause that would've been it for him," she said.

Mr. Nick Jones, the coach of Hamilton International, said that players who were wet and touched the wires and then touched another player were subjected to large jolts of electricity.

"There was one time when Hammer Simmons got stuck on the wire. At first we thought he was joking around when he said he couldn't let go but then we realized he was serious," Mr. Jones said.

He added: "We had been told that the problem had been rectified."

BAA vice-president Mr. Frank Brewster said that an electrician had already been contacted to look into the matter.

Mr. Donald Dane, president of the Bermuda Football Association said: "It was a shock to me. I thought BAA had remedied the situation."

RED FACES OVER MEDAL

What do they think we are. A suburb of Rangoon?

Hundreds of hard-muscled marathoners were given mis-spelled keepsakes this week-end, in the shape of triangular medallions for the BURMUDA 10-Kilometre and BURMUDA Marathon running races.

Bermuda Track & Field Association president Mr. Phil Guishard received the crates of medals by air on Thursday, and took a peek at the contents on Friday.

"I just opened the box to have a look at the design, and there it was," he said. "For someone from Bermuda it will hit you right away."

With 600 people entered in the next day's 10K race—and a medallion promised to everyone who finished—it was too late to send them back.

"It was a question of whether or not you give people nothing or give them the medal and take redress later," he said.

Mr. Guishard wouldn't say how much the medals cost, but said they were expensive.

So race officials kept a straight face and handed out medals to the 524 runners who completed Saturday's 10K. And on Sunday they handed out larger versions of the same misspelled medal to the 107 runners who completed the 26.2 mile marathon run.

Well, almost everyone.

It was when about 100 people had crossed the finish line that BTFA officials realised they only had about 100 marathon medallions, even though they ordered 150.

Mr. Guishard pointed out that the medallions are especially significant to runners who complete the marathon.

But this week-end's runners were good sports, Mr. Guishard reported: "Most people didn't say anything. But from our point of view it's embarrassing, frustrating and annoying."

REPORTER'S NOTEBOOK

One of the stickiest problems facing organizers of the Queen's visit to Bermuda is what to do with the portrait of her hanging in the City Hall.

It takes only a few telephone calls to art patrons across the island to get to the nub of the problem.

"How could they possibly ask the Queen to look at that awful thing. Everybody loathes it," one said of the portrait which hangs near the bottom of the grand staircase.

"Quite honestly, I think it's a pretty awful thing," another said. "It's cadaverous."

When the portrait was unveiled in 1987, the Bermuda Society of Arts called it "an artistic disappointment."

Although nothing definite has been arranged, take it as truth that when the Queen visits City Hall, she will not see her portrait.

The painting by Canadian Mr. Curtis Hooper was commissioned in the mid-1980s by Bermudian Mr. W.F. (Chummy) Hayward, who presented it to the Corporation of Hamilton.

The dilemma for people involved in the Queen's upcoming visit is to avoid offending the generosity and spirit behind Mr. Hayward's gesture.

Yesterday, one person in the know said "something is in the works" to have the painting "temporarily disappear."

GOVERNORS SIDE WITH HEADMASTER

The Sandys Secondary School Board of Governors last night came out in support of the way school principal Dr. Joseph Christopher handled the controversial affair involving a rope being put around the neck of a student.

278 / Bermuda Shorts

In a short statement issued last night, board chairman Mr. Eugene Cox, M.P., said that the incident had been discussed fully by board members.

"The Governing Body strongly supports the action taken by the principal, Dr. Christopher, before this became a public issue and his handling of it subsequently," said Mr. Cox in a written statement.

DOMINICANS TO BE DEPORTED BY PRIVATE JET

A pair of illegal immigrants were due to be flown back to their Dominican Republic home early today—in a private jet.

The planned deportation is already raising questions about why such an expensive method was chosen.

The pair stowed away on board an oil tanker, jumping ship in St. George's believing they were in New York, earlier this year.

Flying to the Dominican Republic aboard the jet were Mr. Ramorez's lawyer Mr. Mark Pettingill, an interpreter and two Bermudian immigration officers. They were expected to return later today.

An anonymous source, who informed *The Royal Gazette* about the flight, said: "It's a very expensive way to deport them. I don't know of them ever doing it before."

Ramorez, 24, fled the Dominican Republic hoping to reach America. But he got off in Bermuda and was arrested in July, on suspicion of stealing from a clothesline and convicted on two immigration offences, for which he was given three weeks in prison. While in Casemates he made at least one apparent suicide attempt.

'EXILE' WANTS TO DIRECT HOSPITAL

Bermudian "exile" Dr. Ewart Brown—who failed his local medical exams and was unable to practice medicine in Bermuda 15 years ago—is said to be one of at least three applicants to become the King Edward VII Memorial Hospital's medical director.

The monthly *Bermuda Times* reported yesterday Dr. Brown, now living in Los Angeles, was interviewed for the post in March and is awaiting a reply.

Dr. Brown's application to practice medicine in Bermuda was turned down by the Bermuda Medical Board after he failed a written exam in 1973.

AMBULANCE PROBE CONTINUES

An ambulance's failure to respond to a call to pick up a dying woman must not be repeated.

That is the view of people involved in an investigation into the incident which happened in May.

The family of 84-year-old Mrs. Eva Stovell were forced to take her to hospital in a car after an ambulance failed to arrive at the home where she was staying.

She died 18 hours after being admitted to King Edward VII Memorial Hospital.

Some of Mrs. Stovell's family are calling for the dismissal of the attendant on duty who they claim refused to respond to the emergency.

Mrs. Stovell was suffering from shortness of breath, which proved to be pneumonia.

Her family claimed they were contacted by the Matilda Smith Williams Home, where Mrs. Stovell was living, after a nurse unsuccessfully tried to summon the ambulance.

They said they called the attendant but again he did not believe it was an emergency. The family then drove Mrs. Stovell to the hospital where they accused the attendant of "life-endangering behavior."

Hospital administrator Mr. Hume Martin has refused to take any action until a full investigation has been completed.

He has been involved in discussions with the family, the attendant and the home, including the supervisor from St. Paul's AME Church Pastor the Rev. Silvester Beaman.

Rev. Beaman said: "We do not want to make any statement because we are talking about individuals' lives—the family, the staff at the home and the attendant concerned.

"We have all agreed that our main concern must be that this never happens again."

BATHROOMS OMITTED IN TERMINAL

Bathrooms were left out of the new [airport] departure terminal in order to save money, Minister of Transport the Hon. Sidney Stallard said yesterday.

He made the revelations while on a tour of the Civil Air Terminal for senior members of the media led by Works Minister the Hon. Quinton Edness.

Editors of *The Royal Gazette*, the *Mid Ocean News* and the *Bermuda Sun* were taken right through the airport and saw the new departure terminal, on-going construction and the old terminal building.

Representatives from ZBM and VSB [TV] were also on hand for part of the tour.

Mr. Edness confirmed the installation of bathrooms had been put on hold. But now Government is thinking about putting in the facilities. "We are considering with architects and consultants whether to put them in," said Mr. Edness.

Construction of the bathrooms got as far as the installation of plumbing fixtures between the United States airline check-in desks and Air Canada and British Airways check-in desks, but the area became a store room when Government became concerned about costs.

If bathrooms were installed in the new departure terminal they would be permanent fixtures and not a temporary measure, said the Minister.

AIRPORT CLAIM TO BE PROBED

Transport Minister the Hon. Ralph Marshall yesterday promised a full investigation into claims made by the Shadow Tourism Minister, Mr. David Allen, that security at the Civil Air Terminal is "non-existent."

Mr. Marshall said he had obtained details of the incident reported by Mr. Allen in the House of Assembly on Friday. He added that he had been unable to check the information over the weekend but would begin his inquiries today.

Mr. Allen sparked a row in the House when he told how the x-ray unit in the departure area was left unsupervised for some five minutes while he and other passengers were waiting to pass through.

He said passengers co-operated by waiting until security staff arrived "in a dishevelled state" but he said it would have been easy for them to walk through without undergoing routine searches of clothing and hand luggage.

Mr. Allen said the incident had serious implications for the future of the safety reputation of Bermuda's airport and for the Island's tourism industry, but he was attacked as "irresponsible" by Mr. Marshall, who said Mr. Allen should have immediately contacted other security personnel or even Government Ministers to report the incident.

TWENTY-ONE WOMEN FAILED POLICE TESTS

Just one police woman was taken on last year after 24 applied, the Senate was told yesterday.

Two more are having their applications processed, added Sen. Charles Marshall.

"There were 98 Bermudian applicants, of which 24 were women," said Sen. Marshall. "Thirteen failed the entrance exam, five were unable to satisfy the physical and medical examinations and three failed for other reasons such as having a criminal record.

"There doesn't seem to be a great desire among Bermudian women to join the police force at this time," he added.

JOURNALIST'S MIDNIGHT CAPER HAS COMMISSIONER SEEING RED

Bermuda's Commissioner of Police failed to see the funny side when a drunken journalist decided to cap a night out with a daring piece of mischief.

Mr. Clive Donald ordered his men to track down the culprit who stole his hat from last weekend's annual police boxing and booze night.

The search ended at the offices of *The Bermuda Sun* and was followed by the charging of reporter Tony McWilliam with theft.

Yesterday McWilliam, 25, took his place among the ranks of accused robbers and one accused killer at Court and admitted his crime.

McWilliam, an English journalist who joined the newspaper earlier this year, was one of a number of pressmen who came under suspicion at the end of Saturday's function, held at the Southampton Princess Hotel.

Mr. Donald noticed his official braided cap was missing from its position on the floor next to his seat.

A search was mounted, but despite the presence of so many of the island's top cops, McWilliam was able to slip away and take the cap with him.

As his fellow journalists, including staffmen from *The Royal Gazette* and *The Mid Ocean News* were eliminated from the investigation, the finger of suspicion pointed firmly at McWilliam.

Before yesterday's hearing he told how he came clean as soon as he was contacted at the newspaper's Victoria Street offices on Monday. He added that he took the officers to his Devonshire apartment and gave them the cap to return to the Commissioner.

Confusion resulted when Senior Magistrate the Wor. Will Francis read the charge, revealing that the cap was worth $97.50 and was the property of the Bermuda Government.

McWilliam, who misheard the magistrate, interrupted and said the cap belonged to the Police Commissioner, not the Governor.

Mr. Francis in turn misheard and explained that even if the cap was in the possession of the Police Commissioner, it was still the property of the Government.

After McWilliam pleaded, Insp. Peter Duffy, prosecuting, told the court the inquiry was launched after "a senior officer" reported the cap stolen. He added that McWilliam co-operated in returning the item.

Insp. Duffy said: "He said he stole it as a prank. He was drunk and he did not realise the full consequences of his actions.

"He also said he would like to apologise publicly to the Commissioner."

McWilliam told Mr. Francis: "I realise it's no excuse but this would not have happened if I had not been very drunk. I had every intention of returning the cap.

"I would like to apologise to the Commissioner and to the force and the court."

Afterwards he merely added that he was relieved with the outcome—Mr. Francis fined him $50 after hearing that the cap was recovered intact.

His editor, Mr. Adrian Drummond, said: "We cannot condone this sort of behavior but we regard it, and I must think the court regarded it, as a prank which got out of hand.

"Tony had apologised to the Commissioner and he has assured us that nothing like this will happen again. There is no question of him not continuing to be a valuable member of our staff."

Mr. Donald said: "I'd rather not comment on the incident."

TRYING LONDON ON

An opposition Senator tested the water to see just how far he could go with questions on the Bermuda Regiment following the visit of British junior minister, Mr. Timothy Eggar.

Sen. Alex Scott asked a tortuous 125 word, single question to see if he could find a way to get an answer on the force.

Just last week Mr. Eggar, a minister at the Foreign and Commonwealth Office made it clear no concessions would be made to further moves to give Bermuda more power over the Regiment until and unless the island goes Independent.

That means questions on the Regiment have to be directed to Governor Viscount Dunrossil, who has discretion on whether to answer.

Sen. Scott directed his question at Senate President Sen. Albert Jackson who promised to refer it to the Governor.

His full question read: "In acknowledgement of the March 18, 1988 statement presented to the Senate in response to questions submitted by PLP Senator W.A. Scott relating to matters that concern the Bermuda Regiment, would His Excellency the Governor, in the exercise of his discretion under 'The Reserved Powers,' relating to external affairs, defence, internal security be prepared to inquire of the Commanding Officer of The Bermuda Regiment if there currently exists a Family Liaison/Public Relations Officer who is authorized to provide immediate family members (next of kin) with information pertaining to the health and welfare of soldiers who are taken 'overseas' by the Regiment, and if not, in light of the unfortunate experience of at least two families, will consideration be given to establishing such a responsibility?"

HOUSE AGREES ON AIRPORT'S DULL, DIRTY GREEN PAINT

Complaints about "dull, dirty dark green" paint on a Civil Air Terminal wall were raised on Friday in the House of Assembly by NLP MP Mr. Austin Thomas—and he won agreement from UBP MPs.

Speaking during the motion to adjourn, Mr. Thomas first congratulated the Transport Minister for Airport renovations, especially in the baggage area.

He then went on to express amazement over a wall, that sports a "beautiful specimen of fish" on a most "filthy green background."

He could not for the life of him understand who could have painted the wall a "dull, dirty dark green."

"Who could have thought of that?" he said, adding that a more suitable blue paint could not cost any more than green.

When a UBP MP responded that the Airport renovation had not been completed, Mr. Thomas replied: "If it is not finished, God help us what it will look like when it is finished."

Mr. Thomas also said the Airport could use piped-in music.

Said UBP MP Mr. Anthony Correira: "I could not help but support the honourable member. Even the Minister for Tourism agrees it's terrible."

He agreed that paint cost the same no matter the color "unless the paint was on sale somewhere and was cheap."

Dr. John Stubbs (UBP) said that the Airport renovation was characterised by a lack in direction—"aesthetic and humanistic direction."

"The ambience could be vastly improved," he said, adding that the Airport could benefit from not only music but potted plants.

"We're not talking about financial extravagance," he said.

Premier the Hon. John Swan said he endorsed the sentiment concerning the Airport and would take the matter up with the Minister of Finance.

ZBM 10 OFF THE AIR

ZBM Channel 10 went off the air for several hours last night just as the station was about to announce its new programmes for the autumn.

The station went dead just three minutes into the 7 p.m. news last night when general manager Mr. Malcolm Fletcher was going to announce what will be on the screens over the next few months.

Last night he said: "Engineers are working on it. We are not sure yet exactly what the problem is."

Among the missing programmes was the 48 *Hours* special Return to Crack Street, which Mr. Fletcher said was especially important for Bermuda. He said the programme was being taped for possible later transmission.

Channel 7 remained on the air.

ZBM TV HAS SOUND AGAIN

Sound difficulties at ZBM TV which resulted in a lack of audio during the climax to a movie Saturday night and at other times in the past two weeks have been cleared up, a ZBM spokesman said last night.

Mr. Malcolm Fletcher said that the problem with the transmitter had been troubling station engineers since the beginning of the year because they couldn't pinpoint it.

Finally on Friday night, during a lengthy loss of audio, the engineers located the problem and fixed it. Saturday's difficulties proved not so hard to locate, Mr. Fletcher said, and were speedily addressed.

"As far as I know we're back in good shape again," said Mr. Fletcher. "We regret any inconvenience to the public this has caused. It's been aggravating for us as well because it was so hard to find what the problem was."

LETTERS TO THE EDITOR

CRITICISING GOVERNMENT

Dear Sir,

Tsk,tsk. My, my. Where do you get the nerve to write an Editorial like the one in today's Royal Gazette? Going on about the arrogance of the United Bermuda Party [the governing party], and then actually mentioning the Environmental Minister by name! And the way you criticised the Premier...I just hope your house is paid for, my boy, or you'll be finding your mortgage called in double quick time. And I just hope you drive very carefully and keep to the speed limit, or you'll be finding yourself in traffic court and catching cabs.

I don't see how you or anyone can have the gall to criticize Government or the UBP in such like.

Maegit Montcada
Smith's Parish

FEW TRUMPS IN HIS HAND

Dear Sir,

The Premier doesn't do a very slick shuffle—in fact he can't even count his cards. One thing is for sure he has a solid deck of jokers. Take a look at his new hand. He has:

A doctor in charge of finance.

A disc jockey in charge of health and housing.

A dentist in charge of public works and engineering.

A soft drinks merchant in charge of culture and transport.

A wholesaler in charge of foreign affairs.

A lawyer in charge of telecommunications.

A mechanic in charge of labour and immigration.

An accountant in charge of tourism.

A banker in charge of the environment.

A life insurance salesman in charge of education.

A nothing in charge of youth and sport.

The card that fell out of the stacked deck wasn't exactly a trump and we do have a lawyer in charge of legislative affairs. At least the mechanic should be able to communicate with his new permanent secretary, who is an engineer, better than his predecessor, who taught French.

Alice
Wonderland

RUSH HOUR

Dear Sir,

Having just spent one hour between 4.45 and 5.45 p.m. crawling bumper to bumper most of the way between Hamilton and Somerset, I am left wondering what twit named it the rushhour?

Moya Boyd
Somerset

SITTING ON WALLS

Dear Sir,

Maybe it's because I'm not Bermudian; maybe I've just led a deprived life. But can someone explain to me what the fascination is in this country with sitting on walls?

Who knows? maybe it's a mistake for all the travel brochures to show pictures of the beaches when the walls of Bermuda are such a natural attraction.

I can see it now, tourists from around the world will be heard saying, "look dear!, this place is beautiful and check out these walls. Wow!"

Can promotions such as free seat cushions be far behind?

Maybe the National Stadium should be built with concentric walls instead of seats, then tourists could take pictures of large crowds of Bermudians in their native habitat.

I plan to make my personal fortune by selling motor cycles with concrete seats to combine the thrill of seeing the island while sitting on your very own personal, portable wall. Or maybe I'll specialise in building private walls in Tucker's Town that can be sold to non-residents at triple the price. The opportunities are virtually endless.

Blisters

P.S. A high-tech variation would be to give everyone on the wall their own horn so they can communicate with passing traffic and each other, but that's another issue altogether.

FOR THE RECORD

A story in yesterday's newspaper said this year's fish pot ban was supported by environmentalists concerned about declining fish pots. The story should have said "declining fish stocks."

QUOTE OF THE DAY

"All the Opposition is trying to do is put a five-letter word— equity—into the budget statement."

The Hon. Clarence James proving you don't have to be able to count to be Finance Minister.

Native tongue

ALTHOUGH ENGLISH is the spoken language, there is a distinct native patois that is unique. The nearest I can come to accurately describing it is a cross between the Duke of Westminster and a Jamaican dope dealer, as if the poor Duke fell most inopportunely backwards onto a broomstick handle. The accent has a rather uncomfortable sound as though the speaker is in a small measure of pain.

It isn't quite British yet neither is it Caribbean. The word "boy" is pronounced "bye." The word "going" is "gahn." "Down" is "dahn," and "town" is "tawn." Got it? Hence, Mark Twain might have been asked whilst walking in the dunes behind Chaplin Bay, "Hey bye . . . you wan a piece of dis up yer lily white Connecticut ass or you gahn dahn de road into tawn for a few Dark 'n Stormies?"

Aside from dialect, locals have some unusual terminology. "I want to have his baby" means "I think I like him." "I'm on the tack" means someone who is no longer consuming alcoholic beverages, usually only a temporary condition. If you hear someone described as a "parish bull," it means he has several outside chil-dren (Bermuda is divided into several parishes). Twenty miles per hour to a Bermudian means sixty miles per hour. "Bermuda time" always means late. "Cribbing" from another author's book on Bermuda slang is what Canadian writers sometimes do when they are desperate for material to fill out their narrative.

Of course, all the international profanities exist as well, which leads me to our next set of shorts on that most disturbing element of modern Bermudian society, the urge to blaspheme. You will be comforted to hear that government is trying to contain this insid-ious problem, but as you will read, it is an uphill battle. There could be *b-i-i-i-g-g-g trouble* if the wrong person overhears you.

JUST TOO MUCH STUPID FOOL

The ears of a Bermuda police officer were offended when a man stopped for his driving called him a "stupid fool."

And when Sheridan Talbot protested by telling him: "I only called you a stupid fool, you stupid fool," it all got to be too much.

Friday Talbot, 38, was charged with using offensive language to the officer, whose identity was not revealed in court.

Talbot initially pleaded not guilty, and Insp. Peter Duffy said he would press for a trial. "I would say it is offensive to call some-one a stupid fool," said the officer.

Talbot, of Sommersall Road, Smith's Parish, then changed his plea. "I don't want to come back. I will plead guilty," he told Senior Magistrate the Wor. Will Francis.

Talbot also admitted driving without due care and attention. Insp. Duffy said he had caused another car to brake heavily to avoid a head-on collision on King Street, Hamilton last Saturday.

ST. GEORGE'S MAN OPTS FOR CASEMATES

A 47-year-old St. George's man was fined $250 in Magistrates Court when he admitted disrupting a public dance, swearing in public and swinging at police.

But Alvin (Alabama) Anderson said he would pass on the fine and take a "holiday" at Casemates Prison instead.

"I'm not going to pay any money," he told the court. "I'm going to take a holiday. I can make more money inside these days than I can outside."

'Alabama' cried as he told Senior Magistrate the Wor. Granville Cox how he was enjoying a dance at Kings Square in St. George's at about 8.30 p.m. when officers snatched him and pulled him from the dance.

Sgt. Earl Kirby, prosecuting, said 'Alabama' was disrupting the event as close to 200 visitors looked on. He was stepping in the way of the dancers and waving his arms.

Sgt. Kirby said when officers tried to stop him, he swore at them in front of the crowds. He was not drunk, but his breath smelled of alcohol, Sgt. Kirby said.

Mr. Cox fined 'Alabama' $100 or sentenced him to 10 days in prison for offensive words and $150 or 15 days for violently resisting arrest.

SWEARING COSTS A MAN $200

Swearing at a woman and police netted a Pembroke man a $200 fine when he appeared in Magistrates Court yesterday.

Elroy Harvey, 29, of Parson's Road was charged with the offence after an altercation with the woman last month at Wellington Slip Road.

It began when the woman approached Harvey about the illegality of removing a parking ticket from a car.

Harvey ignored warnings about his language from on-duty policemen.

Harvey told the judge that he did not use all the words police said he did.

"I didn't mean them in a bad way," he said.

"You meant to say them in a nice way?" Mr. Cox asked, before ordering the $200 fine.

MAN THREW UP ON HIS SHOES

A young Paget man who swore at a man for throwing up on his shoes in a local night spot was fined $50 when he appeared in Magistrates Court yesterday.

Nicholas Dyson admitted using offensive words in the wee hours of Saturday.

Sgt. Alan Cleave, prosecuting, said Dyson, of Bostock Hill, was heard by police swearing at another man while being restrained by a friend outside GQ Boutique on Front Street.

Miss Charles-Etta Simmons, defending, told the court Dyson, 20, swore at the other man after leaving the night-spot because he had thrown up on Dyson's shoes.

STILL LOVES HIS HONEY

A 24-year-old Loyal Hill man, who declared continuing love for his "honey" was fined $200 for swearing at her. Mr. Cox imposed two $100 fines against Anthony Thomas after he pleaded guilty to the charges.

Sgt. Barker told the court that police twice saw Thomas swear at a woman as she motorcycled by him at the North Shore Loyal Hill Road intersection last June.

"I was just exchanging words at the time," Thomas told the judge about the two incidents. "She was my honey," he later admitted.

"One must not speak to your honey like that," Mr. Cox said. "You have to find nice words. Do you still love her?"

"Yes," Thomas said.

"I suspected that. Not that it's any of my business."

'ALABAMA' PICKS JAIL

Alvin (Alabama) Anderson of Old Wells Lane, St. George's, yesterday opted for 20 days in jail instead of paying a $200 fine in Magistrates Court for using offensive words.

Anderson admitted he swore at a liquor store owner who, Anderson said, would not take his money.

Sgt. Peter Duffy said Anderson had wandered into a St. George's store and swore at the owner and tourists.

"If this is going to appear in the paper," said Anderson, "I want it clear that I never swear at tourists."

MAGISTRATES COURT

The Wor. Granville Cox yesterday fined a man $250 for using offensive language to police.

Llewellyn P. Simmons, a 42-year-old Southampton construction worker, was arrested last Saturday after police responded to a complaint of noise coming from Victoria Park.

Several men were there drinking, and left when police ordered them away. Simmons stayed, however, and swore at the police.

He told Mr. Cox he is a construction worker and was on strike at the time of the incident.

"Construction workers don't wear gold earrings," Mr. Cox said. (Simmons has several gold studs on his left ear.)

Simmons explained: "Some guys have their own style."

"And your style is earrings?" Mr. Cox asked.

"They're studs, not earrings," Simmons pointed out.

"But do you have to wear so many?" the judge queried. "They make you very conspicuous."

NO SWIMMING ON PARLIAMENT STREET

A woman who told police she wanted to go swimming at 11 p.m. was fined $200 in Magistrates Court yesterday.

Police were called to the corner of Parliament and Reid Streets on Thursday where Maxine Smith, 40, of Parson's Road in Pembroke was swearing to passersby.

Police prosecutor, Insp. Peter Duffy, told the court Smith was warned by officers, but she continued using offensive language.

Smith then walked up to the police station "cursing and complaining" that she wanted to go for a swim. She was warned again to stop swearing and when she refused to listen, officers arrested her and took her into custody.

The judge pointed out to Smith that he could not think of anywhere on Parliament Street to go swimming.

"The police probably thought I wanted to go and drown myself," Smith said. "But the humidity was high and I felt the heat so I wanted to go swimming. I was on my way to Albouy's Point."

Mr. Francis fined Smith $200 for using offensive language and told her that if she kept swearing he would have to take a "different course of action."

CITY SWEARING

A Pembroke man was fined $100 for swearing on Angle Street on March 15 this year.

Malcolm Dears, of Tills Hill, admitted that he had sworn mightily that afternoon. But he was not cursing the police who happened to be driving by at the time, he said. He did not say at whom he was swearing.

BARRACKED FOR SWEARING

Barrack room language at a Bermuda Regiment parade sent one reader running for the Action Line phone.

"I was watching the Regiment rehearse for the opening of Parliament and there was one sergeant or sergeant major—a senior NCO, anyway—who was swearing at them all the time. He used particularly foul language, loud and clear," he said.

The caller accepted that soldiers traditionally swore a lot but he did not see why they had to do so in a public place, particularly when it was only one NCO out of a number who were on parade.

Women and children were present, watching the rehearsal, all of them able to hear what the NCO was saying, he said.

Commanding Officer Lt. Col. Gavin Shorto agreed with our caller saying the Regiment was always concerned about swearing in public.

"We take the view that parades can be conducted perfectly well without the necessity of swearing and I have said so a number of times before.

"The person concerned has been reminded forcibly about this," Col. Shorto said.

SANDYS MAN'S COSTLY CURSE

A curse, which should have been a congratulation, has cost a Sandys man $250.

David Anthony Sousa, 40, of Huntley Lane, admitted using offensive words to a police officer on Reid Street, on January 4.

Prosecuting, Sgt. Rex Osborne, said the defendant was sitting on the side of an open-sided van at 1 p.m. "A police officer was passing and the defendant said: 'Eff you.' He arrested him."

Sousa told the officer that he did not mean it. "It just slipped out," he said. Sgt. Osborne said Sousa had five familiar convictions over the last four years.

Sousa told Magistrates Court: "I had a friend back from the United States, after he had a bad case of diabetes and almost lost a leg.

"I was delivering bananas. The policeman walked by. It just slipped out. I did not say it loudly. I was not abusive. It was an accident.

"When he arrested me I shook his hand. I congratulated him on his promotion. I know the gentleman."

Senior Magistrate the Wor. Will Francis said: "It seems, as far as you are concerned, that these words do just slip out. You should practice holding on to them, especially that word." He fined Sousa $250.

Responding to laughter from the back of the court, Sousa said: "It's not funny. One word for $250. That is very expensive."

'VICIOUS TONGUE' COST $500

A young woman with a "vicious tongue and bad temper" was fined $500 when she admitted swearing and slapping a police officer about the head. Janine Oatley, of Coot Pond Road, St. George's, confessed to using offensive words and assault.

Mr. Georges told the 24-year-old her behaviour was "disgraceful for a young lady" and warned her to control herself.

P.c. Earl Kirby, prosecuting, said police responded to a complaint on Water Street in St. George's shortly before 6 p.m. on November 4. When they arrived Oatley was shouting and swearing at her husband. Both were sitting in a parked car.

The officers warned her about her language and she told them to mind their business. Oatley then got out of the car and began slapping one of the officers about the head. She was arrested and taken to St. George's Police Station. Mr. Georges fined her $300 for assaulting the officer.

WOMAN IS JAILED

A 28-year-old woman with a long criminal record was yesterday sent to jail for three months, just two days after she was given a conditional discharge for the same offence.

Janet DeSilva, of Cone Valley, St. David's, was escorted out of a bar by police Tuesday, a day after she was conditionally discharged for causing a scene outside the Shelly Bay MarketPlace last Friday.

Sgt. Peter Giles, prosecuting, said DeSilva threatened police officers called to remove her from the Sparrow's Nest bar. She then hit a police car with the contents of her purse and shouted obscenities at passing motorists. At the Salvation Army she emptied two bags of garbage and threw them into the street.

"You'll never win," DeSilva told the police when she was arrested. "I've got the Lord on my side."

WINSTON CHURCHILL GETS BLAME

A 50-year-old man who swore about the Queen and blamed everything on Sir Winston Churchill was fined $100 in Magistrates Court after pleading guilty to offensive behaviour.

Brendan Bancroft of no fixed address was given the choice by Senior Magistrate the Wor. Granville Cox of a $100 fine or 10 days in jail, to which he replied:

"You won't get a dollar out of me. I'll take the ten days anytime."

Sgt. John Eve, prosecuting, said Bancroft was spotted by police on May 10 standing on a Queen Street corner swinging a stick and a metal rod yelling: "Damn the Queen. It's all Winston Churchill's fault."

LETTERS TO THE EDITOR

HONKING

Dear Sir,

Honking is so rude and unnecessary. So if you don't have a honking law you should. This island is as bad as New York City. I could have stayed home and I will next time. It's more peaceful there.

Mrs. B. Syms
New York

UNWANTED VISITORS

Dear Sir,

Since becoming Devonshire residents, we have received numerous unwanted visits from trespassers. These include a pair of youths making love in our garden shed, numerous young men abusing drugs and a drunk wielding a bottle of sherry at 9 a.m.

Our garden is used as a picnic area, a fishing port, a dumping ground and most recently a human toilet for all manner of excrement.

Our efforts to remove these characters have been unsuccessful. Several phone calls to the police have been ignored. Does anyone else have a similar problem?

Waiting for Godot

CROSSWORD COMPETITION

Dear Sirs,

To the organizers of the ZBM (TV) Crossword Contest:

Your contest is an insult to the intelligence of Bermudians—surely this was meant to be a contest for up to 10 year olds!

The opposite of 'up'? Um-um, let me see, is it don (like don de road, bye?) Or how about this one—the abbreviation for 'Cash On Delivery' or 'Missing in Action'?

Come on, ZBM, give your viewers/listeners a little more credit and next time produce a contest worthy of adult participation!

Beverly Scarcliffe

Smith's Parish

UNPROFESSIONAL

Dear Sir,

Please tell the ZBM TV reporters that when they interview Alt Oughton, or anybody else for that matter, they should hold up the microphone closer to the subject's mouth so that the sound recorded is audible and can be understood. ZBM should get some professionals.

Better Viewing
Smith's Parish

FOR THE RECORD

A letter this week on the Anglican Bishop's appointment of The Rev. Ewen Ratteray as Archdeacon should have stated the Bishop "shall" appoint the Archdeacon, not "should" as appeared in our story.

EL AGENT
OURSE,
1UDA
STRIKE PLAN
IF GADAFFI THREATENED TO BLOW UP NEW YORK CITY ON MAY 18, 19 & 20 — WOULD YOU GO THERE?

Moving forward

WHAT BETTER way to end than another glimpse at Bermudians enjoying their national pastime, drinking. Because I didn't have quite enough articles on drinking to round out this chapter, I have included a few stories about that associated vice, driving. All manner of driving. Bicycles, motorbikes, taxis, cars, horses. There are some excellent and some not-so-excellent excuses for driving when people shouldn't be.

Oh, and I also located a heartwarming story about a homeless man who won two tickets on British Airways to Paris. Additionally, I found some useful material on fish seasonings, postal workers, and a scandalous tidbit about a devoted reader of *The Royal Gazette*.

Truthfully, there are enough articles from this newspaper to fill ten books, but I have to end somewhere and this seems like a good place. I may need glasses after spending three years in the

Hamilton Library working with idiosyncratic microfilm machines, and I shall shortly be visiting my chiropractor after months of sitting hunched over my computer. (Please, hold your sympathy. I feel it from afar.) However, as Gloria Gaynor once so aptly put it: I will survive.

I am hopeful that by the next time we meet I will have an OBE after my name in gratitude from the Bermudian government. Add that to the peerage I am expecting any day now from Her Majesty due to my previous book on her devoted staff, and I might be grand enough to purchase one of those coveted Bermudian taxi licences I've heard so much about.

As for you, my legions of readers (Hi Percy!), if you are already a habitual visitor to these enthralling shores, I hope you have learned something new about your home away from home. If you've never experienced Bermudian hospitality but always yearned to do so, I can highly recommend the rum, not that I have ever sampled it personally, of course, for as you will have gathered from my chaste comments throughout this book, I am entirely too pure for such wanton human indulgence.

Two pieces of advice if you do decide to hop on a plane or ship to call on us: bring *lots* of cash. And don't forget to mention my name when you arrive at the airport. Immigration and Customs will wave you right through. Works like a charm at Buckingham Palace.

POLICE DIDN'T BELIEVE HIM

I've often driven home in a worse state than this, waiter Roger Bogine told police after staggering out of a Hamilton disco and onto his motorbike.

But they didn't accept his word that he was safe to drive to his quarters at the Southampton Princess and arrested him.

Yesterday, Bogine, 28, appeared in Magistrates Court just hours after his early-morning brush with the law. He was fined $400 and disqualified for 12 months after admitting having care and control of a vehicle while over the limit.

P.c. Earl Kirby, prosecuting, said Bogine was seen coming out of the Oasis [nightclub]. "He staggered backwards and had to lean against a wall before regaining his balance and walking across the road. He put on his helmet and staggered again."

The officers approached him after he switched on his engine. "He said he had had a few drinks," said P.c. Kirby. "He was subsequently arrested and told police: 'I can ride home. I have been in a worse condition than this many times before'."

Bogine told Acting Senior Magistrate the Wor. Ephraim Georges: "I didn't know what was going on. I have never been in this predicament before."

SEASONINGS NEEDED FOR HIS FISH

A 37-year-old Hamilton Parish man admitted it was "stupid" of him to drive when he was off the road but he said he needed to buy seasonings to finish cooking his fish.

David Trott of Crawl Hill was stopped by police at 5 p.m. on May 23, when he told the officers he was already off the road [meaning disqualified from driving a motor vehicle].

Trott was disqualified for 18 months on March 19 for speeding at 61 kph.

Senior Magistrate the Wor. Granville Cox fined Trott $350 and took him off the road for an additional 18 months.

Trott told the court: "It was very stupid of me. I was just going to the shop. I was cooking up some fish and I needed some seasonings, so I drove to the shop."

BANNED DRIVER SEEKS A HORSE

A 29-year-old St. George's man left Magistrates Court yesterday vowing to buy a horse after he was disqualified from driving all vehicles until June, 1990.

Oluf Ingemann of Ferry Reach pleaded guilty to riding while disqualified. He also admitted riding without a helmet. He was taken off the road for two more years.

Ingemann told Acting Senior Magistrate the Wor. Ephraim Georges: "I have to buy a horse."

JOHN HARVEY IS FINED AND BANNED

Former Road Safety Council chairman Mr. John Harvey was yesterday fined $350 and banned from the road for six months after admitting drink-driving.

Magistrates Court heard a breathalyser test showed Mr. Harvey had 167 mgs of alcohol in a milliliter of blood. The legal limit is 100.

One of the council's major successes under Mr. Harvey was the introduction of the alco-analyser to dissuade people from drink-driving.

Mr. Harvey, 40, the chief-executive of the Hotel Association, resigned from the council soon after police stopped him early one morning in March.

WHY MAN'S CAR WENT OVERBOARD

A night out drinking ended with a splash for John Henry O'Connor.

Police found him walking along the North Shore soaking wet, with his Nissan station wagon under 12 feet of ocean.

When approached by officers he confessed: "I'm drunk," Magistrates Court heard yesterday.

O'Connor, 55, of Sofar Lane, St. George's, admitted driving with excess alcohol on May 30 and was disqualified for a year, with a $350 fine.

Insp. Peter Duffy, prosecuting, said police were called to where a car had plunged into the sea off Penhurst Park, Smith's, at around 3 a.m. Police divers searched the car and found it was empty with the driver's door open. Minutes later O'Connor was seen walking nearby.

"You can imagine how embarrassed and remorseful he is," Miss Keren Lomas, defending, told the court.

CELEBRATION ENDS IN DRIVING BAN

Drink driver John Rocha, who asked if he could ride a Mobylette after getting a year-long ban, was told he could not use even a pair of roller skates.

Rocha, 34, of Chain Gate Hill, Devonshire, admitted impaired driving and was fined $350 on top of the ban after Magistrates Court was told he had a previous conviction for speeding.

P.c. Cyril Plant, prosecuting, said police saw Rocha staggering along Front Street before getting into his car at 10.20 p.m. on February 7.

They stopped him. His eyes were glazed and his breath smelt strongly of liquor.

They arrested him and a breath test at Hamilton Police Station showed he had 148 milligrams of alcohol per 100 milliliters of blood.

Self-employed Rocha told the court he had just won a good contract and had a couple of drinks to celebrate.

"It is going to cost my business. Is there any way I can have a Mobylette?" he asked.

Magistrate the Wor. Ephraim Georges said: "I am not even giving you a pair of roller skates."

NAKED FOR DARE, CYCLIST IS FINED

An 18 year-old Bermudian college student who was seen by police riding his cycle stark naked was fined $250 in Magistrates Court yesterday.

Sean Moran, of The Lane, Paget, pleaded guilty to openly exposing his person after police noticed him riding his cycle wearing nothing but a crash helmet and a smile at 2.45 a.m. yesterday morning near Corkscrew Hill.

Insp. Peter Duffy, prosecuting, said that Moran told police he had done it for a dare and that his clothes were in the basket on the front of the bike.

Magistrate the Wor. John Judge called the behaviour "absolutely disgraceful" and said young men with a promising education should know better.

POSTAL WORKER ADMITS DRINK-DRIVE CHARGE

A 34-year-old postal worker who admitted drink driving was taken off the road for a year and fined $350 when she appeared in Magistrates Court.

The court heard how Coreen Ford of Curving Avenue Pembroke was arrested by police on the emergency ward of [the hospital] where she was being treated for minor injuries following a road accident.

P.c. Earl Kirby, prosecuting, said police attended the scene of an accident at the junction of Dundonald and Union Streets involving a cyclist and a truck.

Defence lawyer, Ms. Charlene Scott, said Ford had finished her morning delivery route by about 11 a.m. and then went home, had a few drinks and was on her way back to do her afternoon route when the accident happened.

P.c. Kirby said police arrested Ford in the hospital when they noticed her eyes were glazed and her speech was slurred.

TEEN PINCHED CYCLIST'S BOTTOM

A social inquiry report was yesterday ordered for a 17-year-old youth who sexually assaulted a woman while she was riding a pedal bike.

Allan K. Hypolite of St. John's Hill, Pembroke, pleaded guilty to the charge in Magistrates Court.

Police prosecutor Sgt. Rex Osborne told the court that on March 29 at 10.15 a.m. a woman was riding her pedal bike along North Shore Road.

"When she reached Black Watch Pass, Hypolite rode up behind her, reached out, squeezed her bottom, and rode off," Sgt. Osborne said.

"The woman took note of the licence and reported the incident to police."

Sgt. Osborne added that when asked by police why he did what he did, Hypolite gave no reason.

He told the court that Hypolite had two previous charges for similar assaults.

Senior Magistrate the Wor. Will Francis bailed Hypolite in the sum of $500 with a like surety until the reading of a social inquiry report on May 10.

MAGISTRATE FINES SPEEDER WHO 'FELT' NOT GUILTY

A Hamilton Parish man discovered this week that 'feeling' not guilty doesn't necessarily sway the magistrate.

Eugene Gibbons, 42, of North Church Lane, told the Wor. Will Francis that he was pleading not guilty to speeding at 62 kph, because he didn't feel that he was going that fast.

"I don't feel that I was travelling at that speed. I was on an upgrade and I just don't feel that my car was going that fast."

Mr. Francis replied: "What do you mean you don't feel you were going that fast? Are you pleading guilty or not guilty? A well-tuned car can creep up very easily."

"I'm pleading not guilty," Gibbons said. "Do you think that the police radar could have been defective?"

"No," Mr. Francis replied. "There are four or five checks that an officer must do before and after he uses that radar gun. But the machine is a lot more reliable than your 'feelings'."

Gibbons replied: "I still feel that I wasn't travelling at that speed. Can I be extended grace by not paying a fine? I don't want to come back to court."

Mr. Francis fined Gibbons $180.

REPORTER'S NOTEBOOK

Bermuda's taxi drivers have long been seen as unofficial ambassadors for the island.

But a recent experience by a local journalist sheds a different light, at least on one taxi driver.

About 9 o'clock one morning this week, the journalist's bike broke down forcing him to flag a cab in Southampton.

Within moments of getting in one, the driver said: "You want a beer?"

"No," the passenger replied. "I'm going to work."

"Well I had a rough night last night," the driver responded, pulling into a mini-mart just past PHC Stadium in Warwick. He got out of the car, paused, then looked back in: "Do you have 30 cents?"

The passenger did and handed it to his driver, who returned a few minutes later with a "greenie" wrapped in a paper bag.

"Do you have an opener?" he asked. Sure enough, the passenger had one on his key chain. Opening the bottle, the cabbie then stood by his car and downed the beer in three or four gulps.

"That's a lot better," he said getting back into the car. "Hair of the dog."

POLICE WARN DRIVERS WHO BLOCK TRAFFIC BY CHATTING

Complaints about rush-hour drivers who stop to chat when they drop off passengers have led police to warn motorists they will be ticketed if they park or stop illegally.

Specially assigned officers are being dispatched this morning to a particularly bad area on Reid Street east of Burnaby Hill and will ticket vehicles which block traffic, police spokesman Insp. Roger Sherratt warned.

Some drivers, he said, stop for several minutes to chat to departing passengers blocking traffic. In some cases people have reported drivers becoming abusive when other motorists use their horns to try to move them.

Another bad spot is outside the Government Administration Building, especially at 5 p.m., he said, but officers will patrol all rush-hour routes.

The Police Community Relations Office has mentioned the problem in public service announcements on television but said some people haven't heeded that warning.

RED OR BLACK— YOU BET ON BLACK OR WHITE.'
'S
ONALISED
NO
ISN'T THAT CARRYING THINGS A BIT FAR?
LIKE EVERYTHING ELSE— YES

MAN FINED DOUBLE

A 21-year-old Warwick man had to pay more than double the normal fine for riding his bicycle without a light, after he tried to excuse his action by saying he was riding on the sidewalk at the time.

Charles Leroy Simmons, of Khyber Pass, admitted the charge and was being warned by Acting Senior Magistrate the Wor. John Judge on the dangers of riding without a light when he said he was only riding on the sidewalk.

"Sidewalk!" exclaimed Mr. Judge. "I'll fine you $50." Normally the fine for Simmons' charge, if paid on time, is $20.

Mr. Judge said riding on the sidewalk was even more dangerous as Simmons might have hit a pedestrian.

TOMMY TUCKER GETS HOPE FOR HIS PARIS TRIP

Another woman has volunteered to accompany Mr. Tommy Tucker [a homeless man] on his long-awaited European jaunt, weeks after he had given up hope of ever realising his raffle-won award.

Mrs. Claire Burgess said she was willing to accompany Mr. Tucker on the London/Paris vacation.

Mrs. Burgess, who has yet to apply for a visa, said everything else has been settled.

"I talked to Tommy Monday night and he was quite keen about it," she said.

"He's like everybody else so I decided to take a chance and accompany him."

Mrs. Burgess said she was flexible about the travelling dates since she does not work, but she would prefer to leave on the weekend of September 22.

"I think the trip will work out fine," she said. "The sooner we leave the better."

Last Month, Mr. Tucker had given up hope of finding a travel companion, and was determined to sell the $2,800 airline ticket to London and Paris.

But he insisted that he would not settle for anything less than its full value.

"It's been almost a year now," Mr. Tucker said. "They told me I'd won in November, and if I live 'til this November, it'll be a year. I would sell the tickets, but not for $1,000. It has to be the full price."

Since winning the King Edward VII Memorial Hospital extended care unit's annual raffle almost a year ago, Mr. Tucker decided he should make use of the opportunity and somewhat reluctantly began to search for a companion.

After advertising in *The Royal Gazette* classifieds, he received several offers. But Mr. Tucker did not seem confident about any of the people who approached him.

First he said it could be a male or female companion, but at Christmas time ruled out the possibility of any woman taking him on the European jaunt.

A month later, Mr. Tucker changed his mind when a married woman said she would take care of him and provide spending money for the six-day vacation.

The woman, who has asked not to be named, arranged for him to have a bath at the hospital, and left a change of clothes for him. But in June, she backed out of the deal, saying she couldn't handle the responsibility of taking Mr. Tucker on the trip.

Mr. Tucker has apparently tired of the preparations that go hand in hand with international travel.

He elected not to talk to the press about the latest development, but used a spokesman.

"He is willing to go on the tour with this lady, but only if she makes all the arrangements and picks him up when she is ready to go to the airport," the spokesman said.

PHOTOCOPY COSTS IRATE DRIVER $8

The Transport Control Department director has defended the price of photocopying a vehicle registration form.

Mr. Donald Dane said $8 was a standard fee, and included the cost of labour.

He was answering criticism from a man who tried to clear up a traffic ticket by obtaining a copy of the form from TCD.

"Eight dollars is far too much for a photocopy of a registration form," Mr. Andrew Correia, 30, told *The Royal Gazette* yesterday.

He added: "I could see if it was a dollar. It took the woman no longer to do it than if I had done it myself."

Mr. Dane, however, said: "The person who has to make the photocopy has to stop what they are doing and look for the registration form. They then have to copy it and stamp it.

"Part of the payment is for labour."

FINE AND BAN FOR MAN WHO PUSHED CAR WHEN IMPAIRED

A Warwick man was convicted yesterday of impaired driving for pushing his car on Front Street after drinking alcohol.

Manuel Cabral, 41, a Middle Road gardener, was fined $350 and disqualified from driving for one year by Senior Magistrate the Wor. Granville Cox.

Police Prosecutor Sgt. Peter Giles told the court that Police saw Cabral and another man pushing the defendant's car along

Front Street and Parliament Street on February 11. Cabral was pushing the driver's side and was holding the steering wheel, the court heard.

When the officers stopped and offered to help, they noticed that Cabral was unsteady on his feet and slurring his speech, said Sgt. Giles. At that point, the defendant jumped in the car and appeared ready to take off before an officer grabbed the keys.

Later, Cabral registered 209 mg. of alcohol per 100 ml. of blood, the court was told and he was charged with impaired driving and having care and control of a car while impaired.

DRINK-DRIVE MAN 'FELL INTO BUSHES'

A man who was found by police lying in the road was fined $350 in Magistrates Court yesterday after he admitted driving while impaired.

Francis La Fontaine, 35, who lives in the Southampton Princess staff quarters, pleaded guilty to the offence before the Wor. Granville Cox.

Sgt. Peter Giles, prosecuting, said police found La Fontaine on South Shore, Paget, with his motorcycle on top of him. They stopped and asked him if he was alright.

He told them yes and that he was just trying to get home.

La Fontaine fell into the bushes after attempting to stand and collect his motorcycle.

Mr. Cox also took La Fontaine off the road for 12 months.

DRIVER 'PRE-OCCUPIED'

A St. George's man, who said through his lawyer that he was so pre-occupied with radio reports of the doomed space shuttle

Challenger that he didn't realize how fast he was travelling, was fined $70.

Earlington Basden of York Street was stopped by police on January 28 after he was clocked at 55 kph. After he pleaded guilty yesterday, counsel Mr. Peter Farge offered the defence in mitigation.

"Do you believe it?" asked Senior Magistrate the Wor. Granville Cox before fining the man.

LETTERS TO THE EDITOR

JOB HUNTER

Dear Sur,

Frum readin' today's paper Um see dat de job of Adituh to de Royal Gazette is available, an' so Um ritin' rite na to axe for de job. I am a um Barmoojian so I rackon Um shood get it.

Um wood like $200,000, please to start

Bo-Bommy

TOPLESS WIFE

Dear Sir,

Phew! I sure am glad there wasn't one of your photographers in my bathroom last week. I stumbled in there by mistake, the door was un-locked, Mr. Editor, and do you know what I saw? My wife was in there TOPLESS!

Well, I ask you, sir, in the name of decency, where will it all end? I must find out from the Senator who to turn to.

Bo-Bommy

Smith's Parish

WARNING TO VAN DRIVER

Dear Sir,

This letter is addressed to the "so called" driver of a van who almost ran me over this morning at approximately 8.50 a.m. at the traffic lights outside the Buckaroo restaurant.

Please take note of the following as next time I will see you in court:

A red light means STOP!

No this is not a threat but a promise.

A Pedestrian who is tired of playing dodge the traffic.

Paget

NOTHING TO SAY

Dear Sir,

Oh, this is such a lovely island. Everyone is just so friendly and nice. The scenery is beautiful, the people are so friendly. Your newspaper is the greatest.

This letter really doesn't have anything to say. I just noticed that you print whatever anybody writes in to tell you about. I have a $10 bet with a friend that you will print this, even though all I have had to say is that the island is beautiful, and everyone is friendly and nice.

Hedonist The Third

Smith's Parish

FOR THE RECORD

In yesterday's Food and Family section, the ingredients for the bread recipe should have read two packets of yeast and not two pints of yeast.

AND FINALLY, THIS STORY:

IT'S EVEN WORTH STEALING

Stealing a copy of *The Royal Gazette* from outside a Front Street liquor store on his way to work cost a Spanish Point man $15, a court heard yesterday.

Craig Staff, 27, of Spanish Point, pleaded guilty to stealing the $0.40 newspaper from a stack of papers outside Dismont Robinson & Co. Ltd.

Police Insp. Peter Duffy told Acting Senior Magistrate the Wor. John Judge that when Staff stole the paper yesterday at 7.00 a.m. he was seen by a witness who reported the theft to a nearby police officer.

Staff said: "I'm very sorry the incident had to happen but I didn't have very much money on me.

"I picked up the newspaper because it keeps me occupied as I walk to work," he said.

When Mr. Judge ordered Staff to pay a $15 fine he said: "Being that I didn't have any money to pay for the newspaper this morning can I have time to pay?"

"No!" said Mr. Judge. "You have one hour to come up with the money or two days in default."

Quite honestly, your honour, with stories like these who could blame him?

UPDATE

Just prior to going to print with this book, Sir John Swan resigned as Premier of Bermuda after the island voted overwhelmingly to reject his call for independence from Great Britain. For the next ten years, at least, expatriate English housewives can continue to swan around Miles Supermarket pretending to be British aristocrats.

The Minister of tourism, C.V. (Jim) Woolridge, is also available for employment having been fired—again—from his post by the newly appointed Premier, Dr. David Saul. Although Jim's political career looks doomed, don't be surprised if he bounces back into a tourism position one day. The man is harder to knock off than Rasputin.

Union leader Ottiwell Simmons once again demonstrated his own special brand of logic when he announced following the referendum that the issue of independence for Bermuda is "far from over." The vote was 25 percent in favour of separating and 75 percent against.

T.C. Sobey
Amsterdam, 1995

SOURCE NOTES (SELECTED)

The Royal Gazette Newspaper

CHAPTER ONE

Woman is bound over: April 19, 1989
Chronic Window Breaker: June 6, 1989
Carpenter struck colleague on head: August 18, 1989
Discharge for man who beat wife: July 21, 1990
He was driven to despair: April 13, 1989
Fight erupts as women go for same movie seat: January 15, 1991
Smacked with wet sheets: April 18, 1988
Feud between shop women erupted into brawl: February 7, 1985
Woman breaks leg in freak accident: January 18, 1990
Woman: I should have slapped him: June 7, 1989
Felt he 'needed a woman that night': August 18, 1989
Juror is admonished for oversleeping: September 14, 1989
Lawyer: Punching women is normal: March 19, 1988
Pick on someone your own size: September 10, 1987
Golfball was an unwelcome mourner: June 17, 1989
Dishwasher wanted to be a star: September 5, 1987
Incest Case: September 21, 1989

CHAPTER TWO

Tales of a monster: August 27, 1988
Impaired: August 3, 1988
Bizarre case in court: November 18, 1986
Time to zip up: June 3, 1988
Costly history lesson: November 27, 1987
Going up . . . one naked man: November 10, 1987

Man jailed for indecency: November 10, 1987
Flashers target cruise ship visitors: June 17, 1992
Remanded: July 13, 1988
Wrong bed: September 4, 1987
Discharge for wearing naughty T: August 29, 1994
Obscene caller waits for reports: July 14, 1990
Dance school ogler caught in stake-out: April 2, 1985

CHAPTER THREE

Party-goer ends up on a roof: June 7, 1989
Teen grew cannabis: April 10, 1989
Guilty, just guilty: July 1, 1989
Living it up: July 12, 1989
Woman warned against drink: November 7, 1987
Expected his son to smoke: January 12, 1989
The cocaine road: September 6, 1989
No more beer: April 11, 1989
Morning after: September 16, 1989
Man found asleep on Front Street: August 20, 1988
Arm lock was good for his shoulder: October 29, 1989
One too little: January 25, 1989
Resting with night train: November 26, 1987
Going home to hide: March 3, 1990

CHAPTER FOUR

Carts row at airport: July 22, 1988
Abrupt halt to Bermuda holiday: April 5, 1988
Unexpected swim in harbour: October 5, 1990
Starting off on wrong foot: October 7, 1989

Cruise officials embarrassed over mistake: October 24, 1989
The Tribulations of local beauty contest: September 24, 1992
Desperate boyfriend forced plane back: March 25, 1988
Reporter's notebook—Ooops!: April 28, 1995
Bermudians be cautious: November 17, 1989
He wanted a good view: October 4, 1987
All aboard for swell food: October 30, 1987

CHAPTER FIVE

Man stole vodka: July 24, 1989
Trying to overcome his behavioral problems: September 4, 1987
Sweet-toothed: December 22, 1987
Accused changes his plea: August 30, 1989
Request for Casemates: September 6, 1989
Psychiatric report for a fruit thief: September 4, 1987
Chocolate milk taken from school: September 29, 1987
Teenager 'felt nice' and decided to steal: August 11, 1988
Burglar claimed to be policeman, court told: March 1, 1988
Thief is jailed: September 19, 1989
Who took the call?: October 30, 1987
Please return the bingo machine: March 26, 1988
Thief gets some unusual items: August 17, 1990
Sharp shock: September 27, 1988
Man stole $55 watch: March 18, 1994

CHAPTER SIX

Cook not to blame in oven cleaner case: November 6, 1989
No dinner man is fined: February 6, 1989
Steak thief is jailed: December 4, 1987
Take-out cost man year in jail: October 29, 1988

Julie Fong's busy last night: September 11, 1987
Reporter's notebook: March 10, 1995

CHAPTER SEVEN

Shakin' the Ag show bacon: April 6, 1989
Tomfoolery: September 1, 1987
Fed up with food: June 9, 1989
Bull's walkabout in vain: July 24, 1990
Terrible trotters: December 19, 1988
Lobster warning for amateurs: January 13, 1990
Four appear on dogs charges: July 13, 1988

CHAPTER EIGHT

We're still richer than the Caymans: June 16, 1992
Clarification: November 27, 1987
Assault charge: September 1, 1989
Teachers get their lesson: September 2, 1987
US post office believes: December 11, 1987
Post office act is finally passed: July 25, 1991
Customs answers advert offering man's luggage: April 6, 1990
Bermudiana needs an arsonist: April 20, 1990
Taxi drivers have too much money: July 6, 1988
It's tough but MPs take the cash: June 27, 1987
Plans for crack house: September 16, 1989
Health inspector chased from restaurant: June 6, 1989
Premier meets press: October 10, 1989
BIU wants an apology: October 6, 1989
Rethink booze bid: June 4, 1988
Governors side with headmaster: July 1, 1982
Dominicans to be deported by private jet: September 11, 1993

Exile wants to direct hospital: June 3, 1988
Bathrooms omitted in terminal: August 4, 1988
Airport claim to be probed: November 27, 1989
Twenty-one women failed police tests: March 3, 1988
Lunch hour hits house attendance: July 4, 1987

CHAPTER NINE

Just too much stupid fool: February 12, 1990
Man threw up on his shoes: December 8, 1987
City swearing: March 19, 1988
Barracked for swearing: November 6, 1987
Woman is jailed: December 17, 1982

CHAPTER TEN

Seasonings needed for his fish: September 4, 1987
Photocopy costs irate driver $8: August 31, 1993
Drink-drive man fell into bushes: January 17, 1987

Bermuda's Crime & Punishment 17th Century Style, Terry Tucker, Island Press Limited

Insight Pocket Guides Bermuda, David F. Raine, APA Publications (HK) Ltd.

Bermewjan Vurds, A Dictionary of Conversational Bermudian, Peter A. Smith & Fred M. Barritt, Lizard Press

Bermuda's Story, Terry Tucker, Island Press Limited

Who's Who: Bermuda's Top Business People, Professionals & Politicians, Bermuda Marketing Limited

The Story of Bermuda and her People, W.S. Zuill, Macmillan Publishers Ltd.

Tea with Tracey, Tracey Caswell, Print Link Ltd.